Sexual Identities in English Language Education

"Cynthia Nelson's powerful book is not only timely and important, but a great pleasure to read. ... What is clear from her research is that struggles for legitimacy have a marked impact on both teachers and students, and that addressing sexual identity in the language classroom requires insight, integrity, and creativity. These are the very qualities that characterize Nelson's work. This book makes an outstanding contribution to the field."
Bonny Norton, University of British Columbia

"Nelson eloquently navigates a web of theory, classroom discourse, and pedagogical opportunities. ... This groundbreaking scholarly inquiry into an oft-avoided yet significant topic in second language teaching and learning is highly recommended for teachers from all sexual backgrounds."
Ryuko Kubota, The University of North Carolina at Chapel Hill

"Clearly written and richly detailed, this exceptional book ... is certain to become a key resource for an international readership."
Brian Morgan, York University

What pedagogic challenges and opportunities are arising as gay, lesbian, and queer themes and perspectives become an increasingly visible part of English language classes? How are language learners and teachers experiencing gay-themed discussions in class, and what are the implications for teaching practices? How can language learning be enhanced through teaching approaches that do not presume an exclusively heterosexual world?

This cutting-edge book skillfully interweaves the experiences of over 100 language teachers and learners (from over 25 countries) with theoretical analysis. It provides a practical framework for engaging with issues of sexual identity in the classroom, whether these arise in planned or spontaneous ways. An invaluable resource for second- and foreign-language teachers and teacher educators, this book will also appeal to anyone interested in the complexities of social diversity within education contexts worldwide.

Cynthia D. Nelson is a Senior Lecturer at the Institute for Teaching and Learning, University of Sydney. Her innovative research on issues of language, identity, and pedagogy has been widely presented and published in the fields of applied linguistics and education.

Sexual Identities in English Language Education

Classroom Conversations

Cynthia D. Nelson

Routledge
Taylor & Francis Group

NEW YORK AND LONDON

First published 2009
by Routledge
270 Madison Ave, New York, NY 10016

Simultaneously published in the UK
by Routledge
2 Park Square, Milton Park, Abingdon, Oxon OX14 4RN

Routledge is an imprint of the Taylor & Francis Group, an informa business

© 2009 Taylor and Francis

Typeset in Minion by
Book Now Ltd, London
Printed and bound in the United States of America on
acid-free paper by Edwards Brothers, Inc.

Library of Congress Cataloging in Publication Data
Nelson, Cynthia D.
Sexual Identities in English Language Education: Classroom Conversations/
Cynthia D. Nelson.
    p. cm.
Includes bibliographical references and index.
1. Homosexuality and education. 2. English language—Study and
teaching—Social aspects. 3. Sexual orientation—Study and teaching.
4. Queer theory. I. Title.
LC192.6.N45 2008
428.0071—dc22   2008009714

ISBN10: 0–8058–6367–2 (hbk)
ISBN10: 0–8058–6368–0 (pbk)
ISBN10: 0–203–89154–6 (ebk)

ISBN13: 978–0–8058–6367–3 (hbk)
ISBN13: 978–0–8058–6368–0 (pbk)
ISBN13: 978–0–203–89154–4 (ebk)

December 22, 2008

Dedication

For all the marvelous people in my classrooms over the years, especially two young lesbians—Chen, full of fear and trepidation about her future, and Aya, full of joy and aspirations.

Contents

Preface

This is the first book-length investigation of the pedagogic challenges and opportunities that are arising as gay, lesbian, and queer themes and perspectives become an increasingly visible part of English language classes. It asks how sexual diversity and sexual identities are being talked about within language learning contexts and what sorts of teaching practices are needed in order to productively explore the sociosexual aspects of language, identity, culture, and communication.

Drawing on the experiences of over 100 language teachers and learners, the unique empirical investigation presented in this book analyzes the findings of focus groups, interviews, and classroom observations using a wide range of research and theory, especially queer education research. By interweaving classroom voices and theoretical analysis, this book provides educators with informed guidance in thinking through the challenges and complexities of teaching English in ways that take into account sexual diversity.

The research participants, who are quoted extensively throughout the book, represent a distinctly international group. The language teachers taking part in my study were based mostly in the United States, where I conducted the research, with some based in Australia, Canada, Germany, Hong Kong, Italy, Japan, and the United Kingdom (and attending an international conference in the United States). The language learners were immigrants, refugees, and international students from numerous countries—including China, El Salvador, Ethiopia, Gambia, Japan, Korea, Laos, Mexico, Morocco, Taiwan, Thailand, and Vietnam—who were living in the United States and studying English.

Sexual Identities in English Language Education: Classroom Conversations will interest novice and experienced teachers who are working in a second- or a foreign-language environment, in varied geographic locations and educational institutions, and with students at any language-proficiency level. The book should prove useful to teachers of English or other languages, as well as to educators working in related areas such as teacher education, academic literacy, intercultural communication, international or bilingual education, writing/composition, or adult basic education. It may also appeal to anyone with an interest in sexual, linguistic, or cultural diversity in relation to teaching or learning, including education researchers, international student advisors, curriculum developers and material writers, program administrators, learning support staff, and second or foreign language learners themselves.

Chapter 1 sets out the research approach and design and then contextualizes this investigation in relation to existing work on social identities in general, and sexual identities in particular, from language and other subject areas of education.

Chapters 2–5 examine teachers' reported experiences of sexual diversity issues in their classrooms, with each chapter addressing a key issue that the teachers considered significant.

- Chapter 2 looks at teachers' efforts to meet the needs of gay, lesbian, and transgender students in their classes and programs and also looks at transnational, transcultural understandings of sexual identity.
- Chapter 3 provides an overview of general issues to do with the inclusion and exclusion of lesbian/gay subject matter in language curricula and classroom conversations.
- Chapter 4 examines the challenges teachers faced in responding to homophobic comments or innuendo and critically analyzes the different approaches that teachers in this study took.
- Chapter 5 considers the complexities for teachers of negotiating their own (hetero- or homo-) sexual identities in the classroom.

Chapters 6–8 take a look at how the issues discussed in the first half of the book play out in actual classroom moments and interactions. These chapters analyze some queer-themed conversations that I observed (and audiotaped) in three different English language classrooms in the United States. The analyses take into account not only the teachers' perspectives but also those of their students, with an emphasis on points of divergence or misunderstanding.

- Chapter 6 investigates an intensive English as a Second Language (ESL) class that elected to study 'lesbian/gay culture.'
- Chapter 7 examines class discussions of gay people and online communities, within a university-based academic English class.
- Chapter 8 analyzes a grammar lesson in which lesbian/gay themes arose, as part of a community college ESL class.

Chapter 9 consolidates the main insights from the book by articulating a framework of macrostrategies that can guide teachers (of any sexual identification) in engaging with lesbian/gay themes in the classroom and teaching multisexual cohorts.

By presenting innovative, cutting-edge research on an identity domain that has, until now, been largely neglected in language education research, this book will help to keep language educators informed and up-to-date with regard to current practice and theory about sexual identity issues in the language classroom. In so doing, this book illuminates broader questions about how to address social diversity, social inequity, and social inquiry in a classroom context.

Acknowledgments

I could not have written this book without the help of an amazing team of people. First and foremost, I thank the teachers and students who generously agreed to take part in my research. I am also grateful to legions of my own students, whose openness and zest for learning have enriched my life immeasurably over the years. My deep gratitude goes as well to the many colleagues and loved ones (too many to name here!) whose stimulating conversation, home cooking, and general good cheer sustained me while I was undertaking this research and writing this book. For detailed feedback on early versions of this book, I thank Chris Candlin and Fran Byrnes. For encouragement and long-standing interest in my work, I thank Alastair Pennycook and Ping Ho. My gratitude also goes to Naomi Silverman of Routledge and her production team.

Special thanks to two people in particular: Russell L. Nelson, my father, who has been reciting poetry to me since I was an infant and to whom I owe my love of language and of simple pleasures, and Tricia Dearborn, my companion in life's mysteries, who adds a bit of bliss to each and every day.

Invaluable material support was provided by my former workplace, the ELSSA Centre at the University of Technology, Sydney, and by an Australian Postgraduate Award from Macquarie University. I also thank colleagues who have invited me to present this research internationally—especially Judy Sharkey (University of New Hampshire), Kenneth G. Schaefer (Temple University Japan), and Richard F. Young (on behalf of AILA, the International Association of Applied Linguistics). Last, I gratefully acknowledge TESOL for permission to reprint short excerpts from my 1999 article entitled 'Sexual identities in ESL: Queer theory and classroom inquiry,' which was published in *TESOL Quarterly, 33*, 371–391, and Haworth Press for permission to reprint short excerpts from my 2004 article entitled 'A queer chaos of meanings: Coming out conundrums in globalised classrooms,' published in the *Journal of Gay & Lesbian Issues in Education, 2*(1), 27–46 (for copies of the original article, contact The Haworth Document Delivery Service at 1-800-HAWORTH or docdelivery@haworthpress.com).

Prologue

In one of the first English as a Second Language (ESL) lessons that I observed as a student teacher in the late 1980s, the class was going through a grammar exercise on adverb clauses. One student gave his answer: "When I love someone, I tell him." Amid muted laughter, the teacher said "Try it again." With far less certainty the student ventured "When I love someone, I tell he?" Eventually, he provided an answer that satisfied the teacher: "When I love someone, I tell her."

As I gained experience teaching ESL to adults in the United States in the early to mid 1990s, I found that whether their level of proficiency in English was beginning, intermediate, or advanced and whether their place of study was a university, a community college, or the workplace, it was not unusual for matters pertaining to (homo)sexual identities to come up in one way or another. Such moments could be at once poignant, paradoxical, humorous, and frustrating. Two more stories:

Once after a listening class, a student was telling me how thrilled she was that all her teachers that term were superb. As we chatted, she asked what I'd done earlier that day, and I replied that I'd taken my conversation class on a field trip to such and such neighborhood. She told me that was a gay neighborhood. I said that perhaps that was why the students had asked to go there. She then hissed with sudden vehemence "I hate gays!" As it happened, the three teachers she had just been praising were two lesbians, myself included, and one gay man.

In a writing class, a student asked if she could do her research paper on gay people in her home country. Her research interest was inspired by the experiences of a close friend who had immigrated to the United States after being disowned by his family because they disapproved of his being gay. Her successive drafts were read and commented on by her classmates, one of whom would be overcome by giggling whenever he read her work. One day when he and I were alone in the classroom, he said he wanted to ask me something. Without speaking, he wrote in his notebook "Gays = AIDS?" and then looked at me with a solemn face.

Though incidents like these were occurring regularly in my own classes, at that time lesbian, bisexual, or gay matters were not even mentioned within professional forums on language teaching—not in my master's program in teaching ESL, nor at staff meetings, at language teaching conferences, in language-education research, or in commercially produced teaching materials. Alongside a handful of like-minded colleagues, I began presenting and publishing reflections of my own teaching experiences (see Nelson 1993, 2005). Going public made it possible to make contact with colleagues nationally and internationally who, like me, were attempting to create curricula and teaching practices that acknowledged and engaged with sexual diversity. However, knowing that similar efforts were being made in other institutions and countries did little to assuage the predominant feeling when facing my own classes that I was 'making it up' as I went along, for there were few, if any, resources offering guidance in dealing with the intriguing teaching dilemmas that arose with regard to sexual identities.

My own experiments with using lesbian/gay subject matter in class were consistently positive and thought provoking—for me and, it seemed, for the vast majority of my students. Yet there was an underlying sense that this was dangerous territory. While I was speaking at conferences in colloquia with titles like 'We are your colleagues: Lesbians and gays in ESL' (Carscadden, Nelson, & Ward, 1992), one of the teachers with whom I shared an office was publishing virulently anti-gay editorials in the local newspaper—a paper and a neighborhood that were overwhelmingly conservative. In that context I felt that I had to be prepared to justify every pedagogical choice I made—which, I reasoned, was not entirely negative since such scrutiny was bound to benefit my teaching. Yet there was little in the literature of my profession that I could point to as rationale for what I was trying to do.

My interest in finding out how other teachers were handling lesbian/gay content and any dilemmas it engendered led me to undertake the empirical investigation described in this book.

PART I
Introduction

CHAPTER 1

Queering Language Education

> Whether in advertising, film … the Internet, or the political discourses of human rights …, images of queer sexualities and cultures now circulate around the globe.
>
> **Cruz-Malavé & Manalansan, 2002a, p. 1**

> I'm here because I really think it's really an important topic … Most of us haven't thought out well enough how issues of sexual identity affect our teaching … and we ought to be working on it.
>
> **'Clay', a teacher-educator who took part in my study**

By investigating issues of sexual identity in English language education, I seek to contribute to the broad project of keeping education socially relevant and up-to-date in these times of 'postmodern globalization' (see Canagarajah, 2006). Understanding classrooms to be "social spaces where cultures meet, clash, and grapple with each other" (Pratt, 1999, p. 584) has brought to the fore pedagogic questions about how to address important but potentially contentious issues of social identity and inequity and what exactly a teacher's role, and goal, ought to be in such endeavors (see Pennycook, 2001).

The central question of this book is how language teaching practices are changing—and should be changing—given the worldwide proliferation of increasingly visible lesbian, gay, bisexual, transgender, and queer identities and communities and the widespread circulation of discourses, images, and information pertaining to sexual diversity. This book presents an empirical investigation into teachers' and students' experiences of talking in class about sexual diversity and of negotiating their own (and others') sexual identities in the classroom context. Participating in this research were over 40 English language teachers, most of them based in North America but some in Asia, Australasia, and Europe, as well as over 60 adult English language learners, from Africa, Asia, Central and South America, and Europe, who were living and studying in the United States.

The first half of the book draws on focus groups and teacher interviews in order to analyze the teachers' perspectives on what sexual identities have to do with learning or teaching English and their reported classroom experiences. The emphasis is on identifying those teaching practices—and the theoretical frameworks that underpin them—that serve to open up rather than close down learning opportunities. The second half of the book draws on class observations and follow-up interviews with the participating teachers and students in order to take a close look at classroom interactions in which gay or lesbian themes arose. Here the emphasis is on how participants experienced these interactions and what their often divergent accounts imply for pedagogy.

This introductory chapter outlines the research approach and book structure and then situates the study theoretically. It shows that research on social identities in language education has usefully engaged with poststructuralist theories of identity and, similarly, that research on sexual identities within the broad field of education has usefully engaged with queer theory. It then traces a similar trajectory in relation to the (largely grassroots) body of work on sexual identities and language education, which emerged in the 1990s and is starting to become a new area of research informed by queer and poststructuralist theoretical frameworks.

Interweaving practice and theory throughout, this book makes a case for queer inquiry as a valuable tool in language study, and it maps out what this looks like, or could look like, in language classes.

About This Study

Since the early 1990s, there has been growing interest in sexual identities in language education, particularly within the field of English language teaching (ELT). Through conference presentations and newsletter articles, teachers have been sharing classroom experiences and offering advice on such things as framing sexual diversity as a class topic (Kappra, 1998/1999; Snelbecker & Meyer, 1996), teaching literature that includes gay or lesbian characters (Jones & Jack, 1994), responding to homophobia in the classroom and in teaching materials (Brems & Strauss, 1995; Neff, 1992), and incorporating lesbian, gay, and bisexual perspectives when discussing cultural practices associated with romance and marriage (Hanson, 1998). Some teachers have recounted their own experiences of, or dilemmas about, coming out as a lesbian to students (Destandau, Nelson, & Snelbecker, 1995; see also Mittler & Blumenthal, 1994). In addition, commercially produced teaching materials began to incorporate references to lesbian or gay characters or concerns (e.g., Clarke, Dobson, & Silberstein, 1996; Folse, 1996; Thewlis, 1997).

Taken together, these initiatives have created valuable opportunities within professional forums for discussing sexual identity issues, thereby paving the way for a nascent body of research (see Nelson, 2006). In this newly emerging literature, a handful of publications explore the practical and theoretical factors that teachers are taking into account as lesbian and gay discourses infuse their classes (Benesch, 1999; Curran, 2006; De Vincenti, Giovanangeli, & Ward, 2007; Nelson, 1999, 2004a; Ó'Móchain, 2006). Another main focus of recent research is participants' own sexual identity negotiations in and out of class and how these shape their experiences of language learning and/or teaching (King, 2008; Nelson, 2004b, 2005; Simon-Maeda, 2004; see also Ellwood, 2006). Also of interest is how students are positioning themselves as they discuss topics such as gay rights and homosexuality (Nguyen & Kellogg, 2005) and as they grapple with 'discourses of heteronormativity' in educational institutions (Dalley & Campbell, 2006).

The empirical investigation presented in this book builds on and significantly extends this existing literature by asking the following questions:

- What initiatives are being taken to move beyond monosexual language pedagogies, and what teaching challenges and opportunities are arising as a result?
- How are language learners and teachers experiencing class discussions with lesbian or gay themes, and what are the implications for language teaching practices?
- How might poststructuralist identity theories (especially queer theory) be of practical use when engaging with gay/queer themes in language classes?

By addressing these questions, this book aims to provide rigorous empirical research and theory that can usefully inform collegial discussions—among language teachers, teacher-educators, researchers, materials developers, learning advisors, and interested others—about matters of sexual diversity within contemporary language classes. It may also interest educators working in other subject areas, perhaps especially those with a language or literacy focus, or with multilingual, international student cohorts.

Eliciting Teachers' Experiences and Perspectives

To investigate the research questions outlined above, it seemed important to hear from a number of teachers about their experiences of gay, lesbian, bisexual, queer, straight, or transgender themes in the classroom. Freeman (1996) argues that teachers' narratives should be taken seriously because they convey "the vital substance of what teachers know and how they think" (p. 101). In this study, I sought to identify key issues of concern to teachers across diverse programs, educational institutions and, insofar as possible, geographic regions.

Through focus groups and interviews, all of which were audiotaped, I elicited the experiences and viewpoints of a total of 44 teachers. The focus groups were advertised as discussion sessions for those interested in 'sexual identities in ESL,' and attendance was voluntary. I facilitated one focus group at an international conference for language teachers held in the United States (which drew focus-group participants who were teaching in that country as well as in Australia, Canada, Germany, Hong Kong, Italy, Japan, and the United Kingdom) and another two focus groups at two campuses of a U.S. university. Attending the focus groups were teachers, student teachers, and teacher-educators, some of whom were also material writers or program administrators. I refer to them collectively as 'teachers' because each of them was actively involved in teaching (see Silverman, 1993).

In each focus group I put forward just one question:

What, if anything, do sexual identities (straight, gay, bisexual, lesbian, trans-gender, queer, etc.) have to do with teaching or learning English?

My minimal facilitation was mostly limited to questions of clarification or inviting those who had not spoken to speak; in other words, "the style of questioning and interaction … [was] minimally interventionist" (McLeod & Yates,

1997, p. 27). I wanted to find out what issues and questions were pertinent for teachers, rather than impose those of interest to me.

In addition, I conducted individual interviews with six teachers who had already participated in a focus group and with five teachers who had been unable to attend one.

Once I had transcribed the tapes and undergone the iterative processes of analyzing and coding the transcripts, I identified recurring themes, and these have determined the focus and structure of this book.

Introduction (Part I) and Teachers' Perspectives (Part II)

After setting out the research design, Chapter 1 draws on a variety of studies and theories to sketch out a broadly interdisciplinary, poststructuralist/queer framework that informs the rest of the book. This general framework is introduced in this chapter because it emerged from, and is applied to, the analyses of classroom practices that feature in the subsequent chapters.

The Introduction to Part II provides more detailed information about the data collection and analysis processes pertaining to Chapters 2 to 5.

Chapter 2 explores teachers' experiences of, concerns about, and strategies for teaching gay and lesbian students; in so doing, it considers understandings of sexual identities internationally.

Chapter 3 provides an overview of why and how lesbian/gay subject matter is incorporated into some language classes yet prohibited in others, and it explores the teaching opportunities and challenges that are associated with this subject matter.

Chapter 4 examines one aspect of engaging lesbian/gay themes that teachers in my study found especially challenging—responding to homophobic comments or innuendo. The chapter critically examines teachers' experiences of homophobic talk in class, and their attempts to respond to, or preclude, such comments.

Another main challenge for teachers was negotiating their own sexual identities in the classroom, and this is the focus of Chapter 5. While some teachers worried that their knowledge of lesbian/gay subject matter was inadequate, others felt this subject matter was a bit 'too close for comfort.' The chapter also looks at the advantages and the disadvantages of coming out in the classroom as a teaching tool.

Observing Classes and Interviewing the Participants

The teachers' accounts help to paint a broad picture of the issues important to teachers across diverse education contexts, but these accounts are necessarily limited because they cannot convey the specific details of teaching practices (see Gore, 1993; Lather, 1991) nor how these are accomplished discursively (Lee, 1996). Neither can teachers' accounts convey their students' experiences or perspectives.

Given the relative dearth of research on this topic, I wanted to gain an understanding of the nitty-gritty of gay-themed classroom interactions— including who said what to whom and also how the participants experienced these interactions (following Luhmann, 1998; Schegloff, 1997). To find out how the issues identified through the focus groups and teacher interviews were playing out in actual classrooms, I observed classes and interviewed the participating teachers and students.

Like Allwright and Bailey (1991), I was not as concerned with "what *would* be the best way to teach" as with "what *actually happens*—not just what happens to the plans we make, but what happens anyway, independently of our designs" (p. xvii). Therefore, I did not set up any form of experimental classroom research but simply observed 'naturally occurring' classes (Nunan, 1992), and I made no attempt to influence the teachers or learners in the direction of my research topic. Thus, my investigation was 'naturalistic,' or noninterventionist (Watson-Gegeo, 1988).

I contacted teachers whom I had met through professional forums, seeking volunteers to take part in my study who, for one reason or another, considered it likely—or at least not unlikely—that lesbian/gay themes might emerge during their class. I was able to make arrangements with three teachers to observe ESL classes at three educational institutions in two different cities in the United States: a speaking/listening class, an academic English class, and a grammar-based ESL class.

I conducted numerous interviews with the three teachers, before, during, and after my 2-week observation period in each of the classes; I also interviewed 28 students, which amounted to nearly half of the students in the three classes. The interviews made it possible for me to find out what teachers and students considered significant or noteworthy about specific classroom interactions in which gay, lesbian, bisexual, or transgender themes had arisen.

Given the inevitably subjective nature of conducting research, I have taken what Clarke, Davis, Rhodes, and Baker (1998) call "a relentlessly empirical stance" (p. 597). I have tried to ensure that my approach to collecting, coding, and analyzing the data has been as consistent, systematic, and detail-oriented as possible—given the organic nature of naturalistic inquiry, the unpredictability of classroom research, and the necessary selectivity of data transcription and analysis.

I should also mention that, throughout the book, I have made a point of including participants' voices, not merely paraphrased versions of them. In this I have been guided by the following questions: "How do we frame meaning possibilities rather than close them in working with empirical data? How do we create multi-voiced, multi-centred texts from such data?" (Lather, 1991, p. 113).

Inside Three Classrooms (Part III) and Conclusion (Part IV)

The Introduction to Part III elaborates on how the data presented in Chapters 6–8 were collected and analyzed.

Chapter 6 examines an intensive English class whose international students, all of whom were from Asia, decided to study a unit of work on 'lesbian/gay culture.' It explores issues to do with eliciting personal experiences of lesbian/gay people and framing gay/lesbian people as 'other' and as controversial.

Chapter 7 examines discussions of the gay community within a university-based academic English class comprising refugees and immigrants, mostly from Asia and Central America. Among the issues it explores are responding when students insinuate a classmate is gay and the technique of asking students to adopt a gay vantage point.

Chapter 8 analyzes a gay-themed grammar lesson in a community college ESL class comprising immigrants and refugees from Africa, Asia, and the Americas. It discusses engaging students whose levels of familiarity with gay/lesbian themes vary greatly and approaching these themes with a focus on intercultural inquiry.

The concluding Chapter 9 synthesizes the pedagogic implications drawn from the classroom experiences (and theoretical frameworks) discussed in the book. It outlines some key macrostrategies of a queer inquiry approach, which can help teachers of any sexual identification to incorporate lesbian/gay themes (whether these arise in planned or spontaneous ways), to pose queer questions, and to engage multisexual cohorts.

Interweaving Practice and Theory

This book is concerned with teaching practices, which is meant in a very broad sense to encompass pedagogies and curricula, classroom interactions and discourses, teaching approaches and learning experiences, and the participants' perspectives and positionings, as well as the concepts, values, and politics underpinning and shaping all of these aspects. Pedagogy, as Lusted (1986) explains it,

> draws attention to the *process* through which knowledge is produced. Pedagogy addresses the 'how' questions involved not only in the transmission or reproduction of knowledge but also in its production … How one teaches … becomes inseparable from what is being taught and, crucially, how one learns.
>
> (pp. 2–3)

(I should mention that, throughout this book, any italics that appear in quotations are from the original sources unless noted otherwise.) As Gore (1993) puts it, "pedagogy implies both instructional practices and social visions" (p. 15). In this book, teaching practices are understood to be social practices (e.g., Lave & Wenger, 1991; Mercer, 1995) and sociopolitical practices (e.g., Bernstein, 1996; Bourdieu, 1991). By 'teaching practices,' then, I mean what and how one teaches, what and how one learns, how knowledge is not simply passed on but produced, how learners and teachers interact, and what social visions permeate all of these processes.

Though teaching practices are the main focus of the book, I take the view that there is no practice without theory (Belsey, 1980). As Stern (1983) explains it,

> No language teacher—however strenuously he *[sic]* may deny his interest in theory—can teach a language without a theory of language teaching, even if it is only implicit in value judgments, decisions, and actions, or in the organizational pattern within which he operates.
>
> (p. 27)

This means that "[t]he choice is always between one theory and another, even if the theories involved are never clearly spelled out" (Mercer, 1995, p. 65). This book attempts to spell out some of the key theoretical frameworks that seem to be underpinning particular teaching practices in order to identify useful ways of thinking about sexual identities as an aspect of classroom practice.

In this endeavor, theory is considered "a tool in social activity" (Lemke, 1995, p. 156). In this sense, theory is used not to find 'truth' but to understand the meanings people are making of their experiences. As Lemke (1995) puts it,

> [C]laims about truth or reality are meanings made by people according to patterns that they have learned, and … trying to understand how and why people make the meanings they do is more useful than fighting over the truths of their claims.
>
> (p. 156)

In this book, theory is used not only in analyzing teaching practices but also in rethinking them, since research can be simultaneously "a knowledge-gathering … [and] a problem-solving activity" (van Lier, 1988, p. 21).

Thus, my aim is to provide a deeper understanding of a range of current teaching practices with regard to sexual identities by presenting, critically analyzing, and theorizing these practices (all the while foregrounding participant voices)—and in so doing, to point out ways in which language pedagogies might be further enhanced or improved. (On that note, while this book is informed, in a general sense, by critical as well as poststucturalist theorizations of pedagogy [e.g., Auerbach, 1995; Giroux, 1993a; Gore, 1993; hooks, 1994; Pennycook, 2001; Simon, 1992; Usher & Edwards, 1994], it does not attempt to outline the distinctions and debates of those literatures or to take up a particular stance in relation to them.)

Taking an Interdisciplinary Approach

In analyzing reported and observed teaching practices and their theoretical underpinnings, this book takes an interdisciplinary approach. It draws not only on literature from second (and foreign) language education and applied linguistics but also from education and from socially oriented disciplinary areas such as critical social theory and queer theory (and, to a lesser extent, sociology and social psychology). There are a few reasons for this.

In a general sense, as the first book-length study of sexual identities and language education, it seems important to take an expansive approach rather than a constricting one—that is, to 'cast a wide net.' Given the complexity of the research questions addressed in this book, a 'problem-oriented' approach seemed preferable to a 'discipline-oriented' one (following van Dijk, 1993). Also, there is no single meta-theory that can account for or encompass the complexities of ESL learners and teachers engaging with lesbian or gay themes in classroom contexts.

With regard to specific disciplinary areas, as we shall see further on in this chapter, language education literature on social identities provides a useful starting point for this investigation, but its contribution is limited because it has largely overlooked the sociosexual dimensions of identity. Education literature on gay/queer issues proves very useful throughout this book, but its usefulness is also limited because it rarely takes a detailed look at classroom interactions or pedagogic discourses and rarely considers the perspectives of student (and teacher) cohorts that are multilingual, transcultural, or international (Nelson, 2005, 2006). Anecdotal and activist accounts of sexual diversity issues in language education are, of course, valuable to this study, but as a research area this work is still at an early stage, with only a handful of small-scale, mostly self-reflexive studies published to date.

For all of these reasons, in discussing the language teaching practices and perspectives that feature in my investigation, this book draws freely on a wide range of research and theory.

Key Terms

Participants in my study were asked to comment on the relevance (or irrelevance) of a range of sexual identities to language learning and teaching, but their responses were almost exclusively about 'lesbian and gay' identities and themes, so these became the main focus of this book. While in some arenas the terms 'lesbigay' (referring to 'lesbians, bisexuals, and gay men') and 'LGBT' (referring to 'lesbian, gay, bisexual, and transgender people') have been somewhat popularized, neither term is used here because they were not used by my research participants, who rarely mentioned bisexual or transgender identities. In this book, I sometimes use the term 'gay' as a concise (albeit sexist) way to sum up the rather lengthy phrase 'bisexual, gay, lesbian, transgender, and queer.' I also use the term 'queer' in some instances to sum up that same lengthy phrase but in other instances, following queer theory, to signal a more fluid, even skeptical way of thinking about sexual identities (a distinction that will be elaborated further on in this chapter).

Also, throughout the book, I tend to use the broad term 'language education' because the research presented here may have implications across a wide range of second-language, foreign-language, and (academic and school) literacy education. However, the specific site of empirical investigation here is ELT, and much (though not all) of the language-education research drawn on in this book is from that field. Within ELT, most of the teachers in this study were teaching English as a Second Language, but some were teaching English as a Foreign Language (EFL), with many having taught both over their careers.

In this book, I distinguish 'ESL' from 'EFL' teaching in order to distinguish the teaching of English in those regions in which it is a locally pervasive and dominant language from those regions in which it is not, a usage akin to Pennycook's (1995) distinction between ESL as "intranational" in scope versus EFL as "international" in scope (p. 36). While 'ESL' and 'EFL' are problematic terms, in both a political sense (Phillipson, 1992) and a pragmatic one (Canagarajah, 2006), I use them here because they are still more widely recognized than other terms, such as English as an Alternative (or Additional) Language, English as an International Language, or English as a Lingua Franca.

Social Identities, Language Education, and Poststructuralism

Since sexual identities can be considered an aspect of social identities, it is useful to situate this study in relation to existing work on social identities in language education.

In the 1980s and early 1990s, second language research was criticized for studying the classroom as "a site of mere linguistic transaction rather than trying to understand it as a complex locus of social interaction" (Pennycook, 1990, p. 16). However, as Breen (1985) described it,

> a language class … is an arena of subjective and intersubjective realities which are worked out, changed, and maintained. And these realities are not trivial background to the tasks of teaching and learning a language. *They locate and define the new language itself … and they continually specify and mould the activities of teaching and learning.*
>
> (p. 142)

According to Candlin (1989), the move toward making language education more 'learner-centered' led to a greater recognition among teachers that learners' social identities are an important aspect of their everyday interactions in the context of families, schools, communities, leisure activities, workplaces, and so on (see also van Lier, 1996).

McGroarty's (1998) call to examine "the subjective and the social dimensions of language learning and teaching along with the linguistic aspects" (p. 592) has coincided with the increasing prominence of a social theory of language, with discourse characterized as a social practice (Fairclough, 1992). This emphasis on the social also aligns with the view that knowledge is not discovered but socially constructed (Foucault, 1972); that teaching involves 'the guided construction of knowledge' (Mercer, 1995); and that learning is an intrinsically social practice, a 'situated activity' (Lave & Wenger, 1991). For all of these reasons, the social identities of learners have come to be considered integral to learning. As Norton (1997) puts it, "every time language learners speak, they are … constantly organizing and reorganizing a sense of who they are and how they relate to the social world. They are, in other words, engaged in identity construction and negotiation" (p. 410).

In language education, there has been much interest in considering poststucturalist conceptions of knowledge and identity and what these imply for language teaching and learning (e.g., Norton, 2000; Pennycook, 2001).

Poststructuralism

Postmodernism, as Usher and Edwards (1994) explain it, is difficult to define. It is simultaneously "an historical juncture, a cultural movement, a certain type of critique, an epistemological challenge, a turn to language" (p. 225). (For my purposes, it is not necessary to differentiate postmodernism from post-structuralism; for an explanation of the distinctions between these, see Usher & Edwards, 1994, pp. 17–18.) Some of the key aspects of poststructuralist thinking that are pertinent to this investigation are highlighted here:

- All knowledge-claims are partial, local and specific rather than universal and ahistorical, and … [are] imbued with power and normative interests […]

- There is ... a heightened awareness of the significance of language, discourse and socio-cultural locatedness in the making of any knowledge-claim [...]
- Postmodernity ... describes a world where people have to make their way without fixed referents and traditional anchoring points. It is a world of rapid change, of bewildering instability, where knowledge is constantly changing and meaning 'floats' [...]
- In postmodernity, it is complexity, a myriad of meanings, rather than profundity, the one deep meaning, which is the norm.

(Usher & Edwards, 1994, p. 10)

Learning a second or a foreign language can be understood to involve grappling with myriad meanings; making one's way without traditional anchoring points; and developing a heightened awareness of the centrality of language, the cultural specificity of knowledge, and the ways in which language and knowledge are infused with relations of power.

Because poststructuralist theories provide useful ways of conceptualizing learning and teaching (e.g., Lather, 1991; Usher & Edwards, 1994), perhaps especially when the focus is on matters of language, literacy, discourse, culture, and/or communication, it is worth turning to poststructuralist theories of identity.

Poststructuralist Theories of Identity

Social identities, according to poststructuralism, are "[not] self-contained, packaged, and ready to be unwrapped and named" (Giroux, 1993b, p. 31). In other words, identities are not autonomous properties or discovered attributes. Instead, they are relational; they are positionings; they are negotiated and renegotiated through social interactions (Hall, 1990). This means they are not discovered but constructed, not transcendent of time and place but specific to them, not static but changeable (Hall, 1990; Weeks, 1987). A person does not have just one identity but multiple identities, and one identity can be foregrounded while another is backgrounded. Moreover, multiple identities are not necessarily consistent but can be in contradiction with one another.

Poststructuralist theorists argue that, although identities may seem natural, this is because they are made to seem natural—in other words, they must be naturalized (Hall, 1990). Of course, some identities are made to seem 'unnatural' rather than natural since identities are sites of struggle and contestation (Weedon, 1987). These ideas will be elaborated on later in this chapter. The important point here is that poststructuralists see identities not as essences but as strategies, or social actions with particular purposes (Spivak, 1990).

Furthermore, identities are understood to be discursively produced (Gumperz & Cook-Gumperz, 1982)—not facts of life but acts of discourse (Le Page & Tabouret-Keller, 1985). This means that undertaking 'identity work'—that is, accomplishing, constructing, negotiating, and regulating social identities—involves language. This has two implications for language education. First, when attending to issues of identity, it can be helpful to attend to the language acts whereby identities are accomplished. Second, when attending to issues of language, it can be helpful to attend to how identities (one's own and others') are being constructed and interpreted through the acts of speaking, listening, reading, and writing. Thus, poststructuralist identity theories may be valuable in language education precisely because they foreground both identity work and language work, and more importantly, the interrelationships between the two.

Poststructuralist Theories of Identity in Language Education

Since the 1990s, language education research has increasingly drawn on poststructuralist and feminist theories in order to illuminate the interrelationships between language, learning/teaching, and identity. Though a comprehensive review of this work is not called for here, it is worth mentioning a few of these publications and the relevant issues they raise. Studies have examined how learners' identities shape their language use (Leung, Harris, & Rampton, 1997) and teachers' identities shape their teaching practices (Duff & Uchida, 1997). As to pedagogy, Morgan (1997) found that learners' understanding of intonation was enhanced through classroom work that highlighted intonation as a strategic aspect of identity work.

While focusing on identity work in class can be a means of assisting learners with their day-to-day interactions outside of class, it is also being recognized that language classes are themselves critical sites for the construction and negotiation of identities. In a study of 'Further Education' classes, Roberts and Sarangi (1995) analyzed how, in class, "allowable identities" for students were constructed through "allowable discourses," which were determined in large part by the teacher (p. 378). Given the newcomer status of many second-language students (as immigrants, refugees, international students, visiting workers, or tourists), it is especially important that teachers "recognize that classroom relationships and interactions both consciously and unconsciously define what is desirable and possible for newcomers" (Morgan, 1997, p. 433). Thus, there is a need to consider how classroom practices encourage or discourage certain aspects or domains of identity.

If questions of identity are overlooked or trivialized in the classroom, then historically inequitable patterns may be reinforced, even inadvertently. As Schenke (1991) has pointed out, because "personal and social histories ... in ESL teaching in particular, are traversed by legacies of colonialism, it matters fundamentally who speaks and who listens" (p. 48; see also Auerbach, 1995). Attending to the social dimensions of language learning necessarily means attending to social inequities since inequitable social structures are reproduced in daily interactions (Norton Peirce, 1995; van Dijk, 1993).

At the same time, as Schenke (1996) points out, teachers need to be wary of approaching 'social issues' in a simplistic way. The "infantilizing approach ... to high-interest topics" that is common in ESL resources and curricula may be of limited use in examining the complexities of how gender identities, for example, are constructed and understood (pp. 156–157; see also Pavlenko, 2004).

Taken together, such studies make a compelling case that social identities are integral to language education, and they raise important questions that serve as a kind of backdrop to my empirical investigation, namely:

- How do language learners and teachers construct their own and others' identities?
- How might examining the discursive processes through which identities are produced and interpreted be of use to learners as they go about their day-to-day interactions?
- How do teachers and curricula send messages, even inadvertently, about the sorts of identities that are valued or devalued, and how might these messages support or impede learning?

Exploring such questions in relation to sexual identities is the central concern of this book and the focus of the next section of this chapter.

But before focusing in on sexual identities in language education, it is important to note that 'acts of identity' are interconnected and mutually inflecting. In other words, sexual identities are constituted "in a particular class-, race-, or gender-mediated way, and only so" (Seidman, 1993, pp. 136–137), in the same way that cultural identities are constituted differently depending on whether one identifies as female or male, gay or straight, and so on (see Mac an Ghaill, 1994). Given the interconnectedness of identity domains, any research project that focuses primarily on sexual identities (or cultural identities or gender identities) is in some sense limited since each identity domains needs to be understood in relation to other identity domains. At the same time, narrowing the focus to just the one identity domain does make it possible, I think, to provide detailed, in-depth analysis— which in this case seems warranted, given how little research has been published to date on sexual identities in language education.

Sexual Identities, (Language) Education, and Queer Theory

The few research publications that do exist on this topic owe much to the groundswell of discussions that language teachers began to have in professional forums in the 1990s (see Cummings & Nelson, 1993), so here the main themes of those talks are, for the first time, mapped out. Mostly through newsletter articles and conference presentations, teachers began to advocate for, and exchange practical advice about, such things as considering the educational needs of learners who themselves identify as lesbian, bisexual, gay, or transgender; including gay themes in curricula and teaching resources; addressing heterosexist discrimination and homophobic attitudes among teachers, students, and administrators; and creating open working environments so that no teachers have to hide their sexual identities. Each of these points will be discussed in turn below.

Considering Lesbian, Bisexual, Gay, and Transgender Learners

Teachers have begun to draw attention to the importance of addressing the educational needs of learners who themselves identify as bisexual, gay, lesbian, or transgender. In a paper presented at the 1992 TESOL Convention, later published in *TESOL Quarterly* (Nelson, 1993), I recommended that teachers assume they have gay, bisexual, and lesbian students in each of their classes (even if they are not sure which individuals these are) and consider whether these students have opportunities to talk or write about their lives: For example, when teachers ask students to write about 'personal' information, do they always make it clear to students in advance which information will be shared with whom? The potentially detrimental effects on gay students of anti-gay comments in the classroom have also been raised. In the newsletter of a 'Lesbigay' special interest group within the Association of International Educators (NAFSA), Roseberry (1999) relays a classroom experience of a gay ESL student in the United States, who reported that, in class, another student had made anti-gay comments, which the teacher then challenged (in part by telling the class that he, the teacher, was gay himself); the gay student had found the classmate's remarks distressing and was pleased (if amazed) that the teacher had boldly intervened.

Another concern is whether gay and lesbian students take part in the full range of campus-based services intended to support learning. According to one Australian study, male international students from Asia who are "homosexually active" are "[o]verwhelmingly ... very reluctant" to approach international student advisors and other service providers on campus (Pallotta-Chiarolli, Van de Ven, Prestage, & Kippax, 1999, p. 33). A related concern is how the challenges that gay students are likely to face beyond the classroom may be affecting their studies. For example, Kato's (1999) survey of 59 lesbian, bisexual, and gay international students in the United States found their predominant concerns to be fear of political persecution or social discrimination after returning home to countries that were not 'gay-friendly' and the legal difficulties of remaining in the United States to be with a partner—which raises the question of how such concerns might affect these students' in-class experiences. Issues pertaining to gay and lesbian learners will be elaborated on in Chapters 2 and 8.

Including Gay Themes in Curricula and Learning Materials

Another key issue has been a desire for greater diversity within curricula and learning resources so that the characters, vocabulary, and issues that are represented are not overwhelmingly straight. In a TESOL colloquium (Carscadden et al., 1992) Carscadden pointed out how common it was for curricula to include vocabulary pertaining to straight relationships, such as 'wife,' 'spouse,' or 'father-in-law,' but questioned whether more gay-inclusive or gender-neutral vocabulary, such as 'partner,' was being taught. Jewell (1998) criticizes ESL textbooks for representing sex roles and sexualities in prescriptive ways that may be alienating to transgender students (among others), like the transgender Thai woman he interviewed who was studying in Australia. A TESOL presentation by Jones and Jack (1994) demonstrated how literature that includes gay or lesbian characters might be incorporated into ESL curricula. Snelbecker and Meyer (1996) noted that students might raise LGBT topics, in the form of jokes, opinions, or questions, and that teachers might use textbooks, readings, guest speakers, anecdotal experiences, movies, television, games, or role plays that focus on "lgbt culture/history" or include "lgbt perspectives in topics like dating, marriage, and family" (p. 19). Summerhawk (1998) offers similar tips about integrating gay themes into EFL curricula.

Some commercially produced learning materials have begun to include gay or lesbian themes. Perhaps especially in earlier work, gay themes tended to be introduced as controversial in some way. For example, *The non-stop discussion workbook* (Rooks, 1988)—a best seller in its time—includes a discussion task asking students to select which six characters (out of ten) will be saved after a nuclear war, the remaining four characters being left to die. One of the characters is described only as "a homosexual doctor (male, age 46)" (p. 146). (In Chapter 3, a teacher-educator describes observing a lesson based on this material.) At an International Association of Teachers of English as a Foreign Language conference workshop entitled 'Confronting heterosexism in the classroom' (Neff, 1992), teachers critiqued stereotypical representations of lesbians and gay men in EFL materials. A textbook published several years later, *Discussion starters: Speaking fluency activities for advanced ESL/EFL students*, includes a unit entitled 'Out of the closet: Gay and lesbian issues,' in which students are asked to discuss their opinions about gay rights and attitudes about gay people (Folse, 1996). Other textbooks do not aim to generate controversy but to integrate gay characters or concerns in less 'marked' ways by embedding them within another theme. For example, in *Choice readings*, a unit on families includes the story of a boy whose parents are two gay men (Clarke et al., 1996), and *Grammar dimensions (Book 3)* includes a grammar exercise about two male characters who live together as well as a mention of homophobia in a reading about types of social discrimination (Thewlis, 1997). While the integration of gay/lesbian themes in materials is not a primary focus of this book, the emergence of these themes in classroom interactions is discussed throughout, especially in Chapters 3 and 6–8.

Addressing Heterosexism and Homophobia in Class and on Campus

Another major concern that teachers have raised is how to respond when heterosexism (discriminatory actions against gay people) or homophobia (prejudicial attitudes) become evident among other teachers, students, or administrators. In 'Heterosexism in ESL: Examining our attitudes,' I identify seven attitudes about gay people that are common in the ESL profession and explain why each is problematic (Nelson, 1993). These attitudes include the view that sexual identity has nothing to do with teaching English or with learning it, that ESL students would find discussing gay people unfamiliar and too difficult, and that only gay people can address gay issues. In a TESOL convention workshop (Brems & Strauss, 1995), teachers examined negative or stereotypical portrayals of gay people in ESL textbooks (such as Reid, 1987, p. 137) and discussed how such materials could be used in class "as an opportunity to model a positive approach to sexual diversity" (handout from Brems & Strauss, 1995). In a *TESOL Matters* article, Kappra (1998/1999) recounts a gay ESL student's difficult "encounters with homophobia" in class and on campus, where all students were assumed to be straight (p. 19), and he advises teachers to "be careful of activities that ask students to talk about romantic relationships," to ensure that "negative comments about gays and lesbians are kept to a minimum," and to refrain from "ask[ing] students what they think about gays" (p. 19).

A lively in-print debate was sparked by Vandrick's (1997b) *TESOL Matters* article entitled 'Heterosexual teachers' part in fighting homophobia,' which argues that teachers, especially straight teachers, have an obligation to challenge homophobia because it is a form of social injustice (p. 23). One reader strongly objected to Vandrick's 'politically correct' article for "exhorting heterosexual teachers to campaign for understanding for homosexuals in their classroom," yet to be sure to do so "humbly" and not "tokenistically" or "inappropriately" (Lindstromberg, 1997, p. 21). In a counter-response, Anderson et al. (1997) (a letter with 26 signatories from Canada, Italy, Japan, the United Kingdom, and the United States) agree with Vandrick that teachers need to be willing to "stand against homophobic actions," for example, by not being passive when witnessing "a gay or lesbian student ridiculed and taunted in class" (p. 22). They argue that taking such a stance is a matter of "promoting diversity and tolerance," goals shared by many in ELT (p. 22). Yet another reader points out that, in some countries, it is dangerous to introduce the topic of homosexuality (Ford, 1997, p. 6). How participants in the current study experienced homophobia in the classroom context is the focus of Chapter 4 and also features in Chapters 7 and 8.

Supporting Openly Bisexual, Gay, and Lesbian Teachers

In addition to considering the needs of gay learners, representing gay people in curricula, and addressing anti-gay comments or actions, there has been interest in creating working environments in which any teachers—not just straight ones—can be open about their sexual identity without fear of reprisals. In a presentation I gave at a 1995 TESOL colloquium (Destandau et al., 1995), I noted several ironic contradictions between widely held beliefs about what constitutes good language teaching and what gay, lesbian, and bisexual language teachers often experience in the classroom: While classroom work should mirror 'real life,' gay teachers often feel they must ensure that their own 'real lives' never come up in the classroom; while classroom work should be respectful of 'minority' cultural identities, gay teachers often feel compelled to hide "those aspects of our cultural lives that could identify us as gay"; while classroom work should encourage critical thinking, gay teachers rarely feel able to encourage students to critically analyze and discuss the issue of gay rights; and finally, while classrooms should be supportive places free from intolerance, intimidation, or harassment, gay teachers rarely "feel free simply to be themselves in the classroom."

These contradictions can present dilemmas for gay-identified teachers in the classroom. In an edited collection entitled *Tilting the tower: Lesbians/teaching/queer subjects*, Mittler and Blumenthal (1994) present a dialogue where a lesbian ESL teacher and her administrator discuss dilemmas associated with the teacher's desire to come out as a lesbian to students. The administrator cautions that "coming out must be clearly tied to content" in case she needs to field complaints from students, while the teacher argues that "my role is not simply to give information to my students … [but also to] challenge all students to examine their attitudes and behaviors" (p. 6). The teacher also points out that, as a lesbian, she has "faced both overt and subtle discrimination," which has made her "especially sensitive to the need to encourage students faced with issues that involve race, sex, ethnicity, religion, politics, or sexual orientation, and at the same time to lead others to examine their own biases" (p. 7).

The question of whether or not to come out to students was the most pressing concern of lesbian, gay, and bisexual ESL teachers in the United States who were surveyed and interviewed for Snelbecker's (1994) master's thesis. Their trepidation had to do with "fear not only of losing one's job but also of losing the respect of one's students" (p. 54). Yet, of those respondents who had come out (the majority in the study), all but one reported positive responses from students (pp. 54–83). In an article in the grassroots *GLESOL Newsletter: The Newsletter of Gay and Lesbian Educators to Speakers of Other Languages*, Shore (1992) describes coming out as a lesbian in a writing class in the United States as a way of extending a main theme her students were writing about—namely, "trying to find an identity in America without losing one's own culture in the process" (p. 3). Destandau's 1995 TESOL talk recounted how coming out as a lesbian to students in her academic ESL classes has been useful pedagogically for fostering critical thinking and a greater awareness of audience (Destandau et al., 1995). For example, in one class discussion, a student was arguing that you could tell who was gay because "they held hands and besides they all dressed alike." In her (unpublished) talk, Destandau reports that she asked the student

> to look around her and tell me if she saw anybody who looked gay in the classroom. She said "Of course not!" To which I responded "Isn't that interesting? I'm sitting right here in front of you and I'm lesbian and you can't even tell." The class laughed, and she did too. What mattered here was the argument, not my sexual orientation.

Issues pertaining to teachers' sexual identity negotiations in the classroom are the focus of Chapter 5 and also feature in Chapters 6–8.

Gay and Lesbian Issues in Education

Such efforts, through the 1990s, to make ELT pedagogies more 'gay-friendly' in large part paralleled, and in some cases were directly inspired by, education literature of the 1980s and into the 1990s, which had already begun to engage quite substantially with issues of sexual diversity. In that education literature, major concerns (especially at secondary and tertiary levels) included making classrooms and campus environments 'safe' from the intimidation, harassment, social discrimination, and violence routinely directed at students who are, or are thought to be, lesbian or gay (Harbeck, 1992) and protecting the civil rights of lesbian or gay educators (Khayatt, 1992; Parmeter, 1988; Spraggs, 1994). Ensuring that gay and lesbian characters or issues were represented within curricula was also an objective, especially within certain secondary-level subject areas such as English (Harris, 1990), sexuality education (Sears, 1992), and social studies (see articles in Epstein, 1994, and Laskey & Beavis, 1996).

The close links between these studies and the grassroots efforts within ELT outlined above can be illustrated by an excerpt from an article entitled 'Peering into the well of loneliness: The responsibility of educators to gay and lesbian youth' (Sears, 1987), which appears in an edited volume entitled *Social issues and education: Challenge and responsibility*.

Educators have a social responsibility to promote human dignity and to further social justice for gays and lesbians. In simplest terms this means providing a learning environment that is free from physical or psychological abuse, that portrays honestly the richness and diversity of humanity ... that integrates homosexual themes and issues into the curriculum, that counsels young people who have or may have a different sexual orientation and that supports gay and lesbian teachers.

(Sears, 1987, p. 31)

What Sears advocates is echoed by claims made in the 1990s in *TESOL Matters*, which at that time was the bimonthly newsletter for the approximately 20,000 members of the international organization of Teachers of English to Speakers of Other Languages (TESOL):

- Lgbt students may face the terrifying prospect of dealing with their sexual orientation in a strange language and culture ... Moreover, there is a clear omission of lgbt people, culture, and issues in textbooks. This omission creates an environment in which lgbt students do not feel represented or safe, and therefore affects their ability to learn English effectively. (Snelbecker & Meyer, 1996, p. 19)
- I feel that everyone in ESL, and particularly those who are heterosexual, should be more proactive in fighting homophobia ... Heterosexual people have a particular obligation to deal with these issues because it is often safer for them than it is for LGBTs to do so. (Vandrick, 1997b, p. 23)
- We have seen a gay or lesbian student ridiculed and taunted in class ... Vandrick's [1997b] article served as a reminder that we, as teachers, can stand against homophobic actions in our classrooms, and that we can take action to make our classrooms safe places for all students, including those who are gay, lesbian, bisexual, or transgendered. (Anderson et al., 1997, p. 22)
- Inclusion of gay and lesbian characters in our ESL materials and textbooks also allows for other students to begin to notice that ... gays and lesbians are in fact a part of the multi-colored fabric of our lives. (Kappra, 1998/1999, p. 19)

As these quotations indicate, many efforts to develop gay-inclusive pedagogies (and policies) have been theoretically aligned with a humanist or modernist view. In this view, individuals are thought to be "endowed with a stable 'self' constituted by a set of static characteristics such as sex, class, race, sexual orientation" (Lather, 1991, p. 5). Gay-inclusive efforts are often framed within a general move to make education more inclusive, which is usually meant in a multicultural sense, with gay and lesbian people considered a minority cultural group. These efforts also tend to be emancipatory in that they call for social justice for all people, regardless of sexual identity.

However, when gay issues are approached from the vantage point of queer theory, the emphasis on a social-inclusion model is called into question (see, e.g., Britzman, Santiago-Valles, Jimenez-Muñoz, & Lamash, 1993). Before turning to studies in education and then in language education that are informed by queer theory, it is necessary to first introduce queer theory—what led to its emergence and how 'queer' and related terms are used in this book.

The Emergence of Queer Theory

Queer theory, which has had a wide-reaching influence on contemporary thinking—not just in sexuality studies but across many different fields of knowledge, including education—emerged as an academic field in the 1980s and 1990s, as a sort of counterpoint to lesbian/gay studies, which had emerged not long before. While lesbian/gay studies were developed largely by historians, social scientists, and independent scholars, queer theory has been developed largely by "professors of English who were deeply influenced by poststructuralism" (Seidman, 1994, p. 270). Thus, the concerns and approaches of queer theorists, as specialists in literary studies and critical theory, differ considerably from those of the earlier gay/lesbian theorists. The account that follows traces changes to the notion of 'gay identity.' It should be noted that queer theory/queer studies has emerged in the context of what Allatson and Pratt (2005) call the "liberal arts of the liberal west" (p. 3), a vantage point that informs much of the work cited below.

In response to the widespread invisibility and pathologizing of 'homosexuals,' the gay liberation movement of the 1960s and the subsequent creation of a lesbian and gay community and culture encouraged an 'out and proud' approach (see Seidman, 1995, writing about the United States). The term 'gay,' which is associated with legitimacy and participation in a community, came to be preferred over 'homosexual,' which is a medical/legal term that suggests pathology (see Goffman, 1963). 'Lesbian and gay' then came to be preferred over 'gay' as a description of this community or culture, due to criticisms of female invisibility (Phelan, 1994). What made it possible to form a cohesive social movement based on gayness and lesbianism was essentialism—that is, the notion that gay or lesbian identity expressed an inner, universal essence (Seidman, 1994; Weeks, 1991). In an essentialist view, sexuality was seen as "a natural force that exists prior to social life" (Rubin, 1984/1993, p. 9). Sexuality, as an individual's "property," was seen to have "no history and no significant social determinants" (Rubin, 1984/1993, p. 9, writing of 'Western cultures').

However, a transforming influence was Foucault's (1990) *The history of sexuality*, which argued that all sexualities, whether considered 'conventional' or 'deviant,' are historical/social/discursive constructions. According to Foucault (1990), new sexualities are constantly being produced; homosexuality, and for that matter heterosexuality, are relatively recent and predominantly Western constructions. He noted that, in the 1870s, the "psychological, psychiatric, medical category of homosexuality" was constituted, making "the homosexual" a (stigmatized) "species" (Foucault, 1990, pp. 43–44; for a linguistics perspective, see Murphy, 1997). Apparently, the term 'homosexual' preceded 'heterosexual' in entering Euro-American discourse (Sedgwick, 1990, citing Katz, 1983). Of course same-sex erotic activity existed before the emergence of "a distinctive homosexual identity" (Weeks, 1987, p. 40), just as different-sex erotic activity indubitably preceded the concept of 'heterosexuality.' However, the act of creating 'homosexual' and 'heterosexual' identities required that the "gender of object choice" be prioritized over many other possible taxonomizing criteria related to sexual activities (such as preferences for certain sensations, acts, relations of age, number of participants, spontaneous versus scripted, and so on) (Foucault, 1990, pp. 43, 105; see also Sedgwick, 1990). Over the past century it was heterosexual monogamy, and only heterosexual monogamy, that became normalized, at least in the Western world. All other expressions of sensuality or sexuality, including (but not limited to) same-sex relations, came to be viewed as "peripheral" and "unnatural" (Foucault, 1990, pp. 36–39).

Given the influential work of Foucault (1990), the theoretical dominance of essentialism gave way to social constructionism—in this case, the belief that gay or lesbian identity is not innate but socially constructed. Among gay theorists, a main proponent of social constructionism was Weeks, who pointed out that

> [w]e now know ... that [sexual] identities are historically and culturally specific, that they are selected from a host of possible social identities, that they are not necessary attributes of particular sexual drives or desires, and that they are not, in fact, essential—that is naturally pre-given—aspects of our personality (Weeks 1985) ... that what we so readily deem as 'sexual' is as much a product of language and culture as of 'nature'.
>
> (Weeks, 1987, p. 31)

But this theoretical shift to social constructionism did not significantly change the widespread belief that gayness was a 'fact' that could be either acknowledged and expressed (albeit in culturally determined ways) or denied and suppressed (for more detailed accounts of this period, see Seidman, 1993, 1994, 1995).

As the gay/lesbian movement and community gained in numbers, visibility, and political power, the focus began to shift from what its 'members' had in common to what they did not. Gathered together under the political/cultural umbrella of a gay and lesbian movement were not only people who identified as lesbian or gay but also those who identified as bisexual and transgender, as well as those who were 'in transition' from one sexual identity to another or who simply did not align with any of the culturally available identity categories (Seidman, 1995). Much debate ensued regarding who was being included and who excluded by sexual minority 'labels' (see Murphy, 1997). This community included individuals and subcultures whose sexual practices, sexual values, relationship styles, multiple identities, and political affiliations were not only diverse but also in some cases conflicting. It began to seem that the 'gender of object choice' did not necessarily provide sufficient grounds for constructing identities and communities (Seidman, 1993). Meanwhile, as discussed previously in this chapter, poststructuralist theorists and linguists were theorizing identities as cultural and discursive acts (see Gumperz & Cook-Gumperz, 1982; Le Page & Tabouret-Keller, 1985). In the mid-1980s, as a result of practical and theoretical challenges to identity-based social movements, queer theory and activism were developed.

Questions about how, or whether, queer travels internationally are beginning to be asked in recent investigations of sexual identity in the context of globalization, such as the edited collections *Postcolonial, queer* (Hawley, 2001) and *Queer globalizations* (Cruz-Malavé & Manalansan, 2002b). However, as Allatson and Pratt (2005) point out, the two volumes cited above include few contributors based outside the United States. Thus, there remains a need for queer studies to seriously engage with the possibilities and challenges offered by queer theorizations within international contexts.

Why 'Queer'?

Before the 1980s, the homosexual meaning of the word 'queer' had largely been (and in some contexts still is) a term of derision. As Jagose (1996) explains, "Once the term 'queer' was, at best, slang for homosexual, at worst, a term of homophobic abuse" (p. 1), but the word has been appropriated by activists and theorists. Interestingly, Cameron (1995) points out that understanding the meaning of 'queer' in a particular utterance may require knowing, or being able to work out, or at least having to consider, whether the speaker (or writer) hates gays—or is gay. Queer activists, according to Seidman (1995), rejected the notion of a unified 'homosexual' subject because that notion was linked to "white, middle-class, hetero-imitative values and liberal political interests" (p. 124). Meanwhile, queer theorists articulated this challenge to the identity politics of the gay/lesbian mainstream by drawing on (French) poststructuralism. Whereas sexual identity formed the basis of the lesbian/gay movement and community, queer theory follows poststructuralism and deconstruction in making sexual identity the subject of critique.

One meaning of 'queer' is not associated with critique. It is simply used to encompass 'lesbian, gay, bisexual, and transgender'; in other words, 'queer' serves as shorthand for what has become a rather lengthy phrase. In this sense, 'queer' is an identity (though, as Williams [1997], and others have noted, 'queer' can render lesbians invisible in the same way as the terms 'homosexuality' or 'gay'). But 'queer' is also used to challenge clear-cut notions of sexual identity and to purposely blur the boundaries between identity categories (Warner, 1993). In this second meaning, 'queer' "defin[es] itself against the normal rather than the heterosexual" (pp. xxvi–xxvii) and is therefore 'deconstructionist' for it describes people who are united in *not* taking up cultural norms of gender and sexuality (see Phelan, 1994). Thus, there is a fundamental tension between the two meanings of 'queer.' The term includes all 'minority' sexual identities, while, at the same time, it troubles the very notion of sexuality as a basis of identity. This paradox is central to queer theory.

Jagose (1996) explains that these different, even contradictory, uses of 'queer' do not indicate "that queer has yet to solidify and take on a more consistent profile, but rather that its definitional indeterminacy, its elasticity, is one of its constituent characteristics" (p. 1). She goes on to argue that "part of queer's semantic clout, part of its political efficacy, depends on its resistance to definition" (p. 1). In Seidman's (1995) analysis, "queer suggests a positioning as oppositional to both the heterosexual and homosexual mainstream" (pp. 117–118). In other words, queer "problematises normative consolidations of sex, gender and sexuality ... [and] consequently, is critical of all those versions of identity, community and politics that are believed to evolve 'naturally' from such consolidations" (Jagose, 1996, p. 99).

'Queer' is primarily used as an adjective (as in 'queer theory' or 'queer activism' or 'I'm queer'), but it is sometimes used as a verb: "[Because] the queer and the theory in Queer Theory signify act*ions*, not actors ['queer'] can be thought of as a verb" (Britzman, 1995, p. 153).

In this book, 'queer' is sometimes used to encompass any and all sexual identities—including 'bisexual' and 'transgender' as well as those who are questioning or those who embrace a more fluid notion of sexual identity. 'Queer' is also used to signal that sexual identities are being conceptualized in a poststructuralist sense—that is, as processes rather than properties. 'Sexual identity' is used in this book, primarily to align this study with work on identity in ELT but also to avoid the debates of causality associated with 'sexual orientation,' which implies innateness, or 'sexual preference,' which emphasizes choice. Though some theorists (e.g., Weedon, 1987) prefer the more fluid term 'sexual subjectivity' over the fixedness of 'sexual identity,' 'sexual subjectivity' is not used in this book because it is not in common usage either within language education or more broadly. In this book, 'sexual identity' is intended in a queer theory sense, that is, as suggesting that identities are not 'natural' or inherent but constructed and contingent.

Queering Education

Since the 1990s, education literature on sexual diversity has begun to grapple with the pedagogical implications of queer theory. The six publications included below seem to me particularly applicable to language education contexts and as such have significantly shaped the approach that I have taken to the empirical research presented in this book.

Fuss's (1989, 1991) arguments are grounded in the classrooms of identity-based tertiary courses in the United States, such as women's studies, African-American studies, and gay studies. Fuss's (1989) chapter titled 'Essentialism in the classroom' argues that, in the classroom, 'experience' tends to be equated with 'truth' and a person's 'identity' tends to be seen as 'knowledge' (p. 115). These tendencies, Fuss argues, are theoretically problematic because identities are treated as if they are fixed essences. They are also pedagogically problematic because a student, or a teacher, can thereby be "reduced" to their 'maleness,' their 'Asianness,' their 'lesbianness,' and so on, which can result in the 'authority' of some students or teachers being delegitimated (p. 116).

Textual orientations: Lesbian and gay students and the making of discourse communities (Malinowitz, 1995) presents a study of two tertiary level composition classes in which lesbian and gay experience was the central theme of the class readings and the writing assignments. These classes were open to all students, of any sexual identity. Malinowitz, the teacher/researcher, examined the writings and experiences of selected students who identified as gay, lesbian, bisexual, or questioning. She draws on this empirical research, along with queer theory and critical pedagogy, in proposing a pedagogy that goes beyond "mere 'inclusion'" and instead involves rigorous critique (p. 251). The gay-themed classes "didn't invite students to simply 'express' their feelings and opinions in an uninhibited 'natural flow' of ideas; on the contrary, anything that felt 'natural' was systematically subjected to scrutiny, probed to unearth its roots in culture and discourse" (p. 253).

Britzman's (1995) article in *Educational Theory* is entitled 'Is there a queer pedagogy? Or, stop reading straight.' Noting that "pedagogies of inclusion" are limited to either providing information about 'minorities' or attempting to change attitudes about 'them' (p. 158), Britzman makes the case that queer theory offers a viable alternative by attempting "to exceed such binary oppositions as the tolerant and the tolerated and the oppressed and the oppressor yet still hold onto an analysis of social difference" (p. 164). Drawing on Foucault and others, Britzman calls for educational practices that explore the limits of 'thinkability' and knowledge, of ignorance and innocence (see also Britzman, 1997, 2000).

Sumara and Davis's (1999) article in *Curriculum Inquiry* draws on their research with teachers, children, and parents in order to articulate "a queer curriculum theory" (p. 191). Following Foucault (1990), one of the main points is that queer theory "does not ask that pedagogy *become* sexualized, but that it excavate and interpret the way it already *is* sexualized ... [particularly] how it is explicitly heterosexualized" (Sumara & Davis, 1999, p. 192). Citing queer theorist Warner (1993), Sumara and Davis argue that it is important to challenge the common understanding that 'normal' and 'heterosexual' are synonymous. Attempting to challenge or 'interrupt' this view is one way "to broaden perception, to complexify cognition, and to amplify the imagination of learners" (p. 202). The authors' goal is not to develop curricula for and about queers but to show "how *all* educators ought to become interested in the complex relationships among the various ways in which sexualities are organized and identified and in the many ways in which knowledge is produced and represented" (p. 203).

In *Troubling education: Queer activism and antioppressive pedagogy*, Kumashiro (2002) rethinks "antioppressive education" through multiple readings of narratives by queer activists in the United States about the in-school and out-of-school experiences that fueled their activism. Kumashiro contests the tendency for educators with culturally diverse classrooms to consider it "culturally inappropriate" to discuss issues of heterosexism and sexuality (p. 81); he challenges the widespread notion that "queer sexuality is often racialized *as White*," while "heterosexuality is often racialized *as Asian*," for example (p. 83). Kumashiro advocates reading queer narratives in a way that foregrounds the "desires, resistances, and senses of self" that readers bring to the act of reading—that is, "putting our routes of reading themselves under analysis" (p. 117). What he calls 'reading paradoxically' means "learning from the stories, while troubling the very knowledge we produce and reproduce; affirming our differences, while troubling the very identities and cultures that offer affirmation" (p. 117).

Lastly, a recent publication that is distinguished from most other queer work in education by its international scope is Sears' (2005) two-volume international encyclopedia on *Youth, education, and sexualities*, with content and contributors spanning Africa, the Americas, Asia, Europe, the Middle East, and Oceania. In his introduction, Sears assesses different countries' educational policies in relation to lesbian, gay, transgender, and bisexual youth and to sexual diversity in education. Countries whose policies are described as "persecutorial" or "homophobic" include Bulgaria, Egypt, Mexico, Russia, and the United States, whereas those described as "supportive" or "proactive" include Australia, Canada, France, Israel, and the Netherlands (Sears, 2005, p. xxviii). Entries in the encyclopedia present research, policy, and activism on topics such as "LGBT issues in China," "Colonialism and homosexuality," "Lesbians and the internet," "Queer pedagogy," and hundreds more. The publication of this encyclopedia demonstrates the substantial amount of work that has been generated in recent years on sexual diversity issues in education contexts around the world.

Queering Language Education

In recent years, the worldwide proliferation of queer discourses is clearly beginning to infuse the fields of second- and foreign-language education, with a growing number of educators working to update and transform monosexual pedagogies and research agendas. Both the need for this work and possible ways forward are illustrated by several papers in a queer issue of the *Journal of Language, Identity, and Education* (Nelson, 2006).

Dalley and Campbell (2006), for example, examined heteronormative discourses—that is, "linguistic and/or cultural practices which construct and circulate heterosexual representations, practices, and identities as *the* natural or normal expression of humanity" (p. 13)—within peer interactions among bilingual youth at a multicultural Francophone high school in Canada. Their 3-year ethnographic study found that, despite the strong pro-diversity rhetoric permeating the school and the efforts of some students, "the subject of homosexuality was repeatedly silenced" both in and out of the classroom (p. 17).

Ó'Móchain (2006) recounts his efforts as an EFL teacher to integrate discussions of gender and sexuality issues into an institutional and cultural context that seemed to discourage open discussions of such issues—namely, a Christian women's college in Japan. Using the life-history narratives of Japanese lesbians and gays who lived locally, Ó'Móchain had his students analyze and critically discuss the narratives, focusing initially on issues of gender and sexuality and then on issues of language and communication.

I have argued elsewhere (Nelson, 1999) that a queer framework holds much promise for engaging lesbian and gay issues in language classes. With queer theory, sexual identities are conceptualized as performative and communicatively produced—"not facts but acts" (p. 375)—and sexual identity categories are considered useful yet problematic because they "can exclude as well as include, limit as well as liberate" (p. 376). Furthermore, the homo/hetero binary is recognized to be a broadly significant category of knowledge that "shapes ways of thinking and living," albeit in culturally specific ways (p. 375). Applying these concepts when lesbian or gay themes arise in the classroom turns the teaching emphasis away from gay inclusion per se and towards sexual-identity inquiry.

To provide a brief overview of additional research on queer issues, studies of language learners and/or teachers include the following: Nguyen and Kellogg's

(2005) analysis of how ESL students (from Asia, studying in the United States) positioned themselves in online discussions of gay rights and homosexuality; Ellwood's (2006) reflective exploration of the multiple conversational constraints faced by a gay Japanese student of English in Australia; an account from Clemente and Higgins (2005) of a man in Mexico who considered his English classes an invaluable sanctuary where he could be openly gay; King's (2008) study of Korean men who found being gay to be advantageous in learning English; Simon-Maeda's (2004) investigation of the 'professional disempowerment' experienced by lesbian (and other) EFL educators in Japan; and my examination of complexities and mismatched understandings associated with teachers' sexual-identity negotiations in the transcultural arena of ESL classrooms (Nelson, 2004b).

As to queer issues in curricula and pedagogy, recent studies include Shardakova and Pavlenko's (2004) critique of compulsory heterosexuality, among other things, within Russian language textbooks; my case study of how an ESL teacher in the United States used lesbian and gay themes to explore cultural meanings and meaning-making practices (Nelson, 2004a); Curran's (2006) reflections on his own attempts, as an openly gay teacher, to put queer theory into action in an Australian ESL class; and a discussion by De Vincenti et al. (2007) of queer issues in foreign language teaching, such as the sexuality-representation dilemmas that can arise for learners of French, Italian, and Japanese due to the linguistic imperative in these languages to index gender (in adjectives, vocabulary, or intonation). Points raised here will be elaborated in subsequent chapters.

Alongside the general interest in what social diversity means for education is a growing interest in how sexual identities and inequities are featuring within language classrooms. As I have shown in this chapter, language teachers are beginning to explore what queer pedagogies might look like—that is, how to create teaching practices and curricula that make spaces for sexual diversity as subject matter, that unpack heteronormative practices and discourses, and that recognize sexual diversity as a feature of classroom cohorts. However, as would be expected in a nascent area, most of the existing literature tends to be limited to anecdotal, self-reflexive accounts, which often present only the perspective of the sole teacher-researcher (not their students and not the varied practices of a range of teachers), only a brief example from one lesson (not a detailed analysis of that lesson or how it was followed up), and only a limited engagement with queer education research and queer theory, given the limited scope afforded by a journal article.

If our education programs are to adequately address the contemporary communication needs of second and foreign language learners, useful knowledge about how to frame sexual diversity issues in language classes is urgently needed. My aim with this book is to present a timely, rigorous, in-depth study of these issues, on a much larger scale than has been seen to date in language education literature and in a style that is practical and broadly accessible while still being theoretically sound. The move to queer language education has been introduced in this chapter and will be further consolidated, deepened, and extended in the remaining chapters, which present my investigation of queer conversations—both reported and observed—that have taken place within English language classes.

PART II
Teachers' Perspectives

Introduction to Part II

> What, if anything, do sexual identities (straight, gay, bisexual, lesbian, trans-gender, queer, etc.) have to do with teaching or learning English?

Teachers' responses to this question are the focus of the next four chapters, which analyze data collected from audiotaped focus groups and interviews involving a total of 44 teachers (31 women and 13 men). Before looking at what the teachers had to say, it is necessary to explain the contexts in which their comments were made and some key decisions and concepts underpinning the research design.

Conducting Focus Groups and Interviews

Each focus group was advertised as an open discussion of 'sexual identities in ESL,' and attendance was voluntary. At each focus group, I briefly introduced my research project, obtained written consent from participants, and then posed the question shown above to the group. That single question prompted ample discussion, with minimal facilitation required on my part. Each focus group lasted about 1 hour.

Focus Group ESL-1

This focus group was held at a university as part of an existing series of professional development sessions for ESL teachers. It was attended by 11 people, most of whom already knew at least some of the other participants through their work as teachers, teacher-educators, student teachers, international student advisors, material writers, and/or administrators at that university. The discussion focused mostly on the challenges of addressing homophobia and supporting gay and lesbian students.

Focus Group ESL-2

Participants of the focus group described above asked me to facilitate a follow-up session so that they could share with the group specific activities or approaches they had developed for teaching lesbian/gay themes. The session ran as an informal show-and-tell. Taking part in the session were nearly all of the participants from the first focus group, plus one additional teacher.

Focus Group IEP

Teachers in an intensive English program (IEP) located at a second campus of the same university heard about focus groups ESL-1 and -2 and requested a focus group to be held at their campus. This group comprised three teachers and the program administrator, all of whom had been working together closely for some time. Their discussion centered on teaching lesbian/gay issues as part of American culture.

Focus Group TESOL

This session took place at an international TESOL convention held in the United States. Advertised through the Lesbian, Gay, Bisexual, and Friends Caucus, this focus group was attended by 24 people who mostly did not know each other (or knew each other only from annual conferences). The participants were English-language teachers, including a few teacher-educators and student teachers. Some seemed nervous about being seen to be taking part in the session, so in order to maximize their anonymity, I deliberately did not ask participants to specify their geographic location; from the discussion it became clear that most were based in the United States or Canada, with others working in Australia, Germany, Hong Kong, Italy, Japan, and the United Kingdom. Main themes in this discussion were dilemmas about coming out as gay or lesbian to students and dealing with homophobia in the classroom.

Interviews

I also interviewed six teachers who had participated in a focus group and wanted to talk further about the issues, as well as five teachers who did not have the opportunity to attend a focus group. Each interview lasted between 1 and 3 hours.

About the Teachers

Appendix A provides some basic information about each of the teachers quoted in this book—their professional role(s), the source of their quotes (focus group[s], interview, or class observation [see Chapters 6–8]), and the chapter(s) in which they are quoted.

Designing the Research

My Positioning as Researcher

Several points must be noted about my own positioning vis-à-vis the teachers in my study. I already knew approximately half of the teachers through various professional affiliations, which meant that in some cases I had insider familiarity with the teachers or their programs. At the same time, I had a more distant, outsider status because I no longer lived in the United States. Thus, with many of the teachers, a certain degree of trust had already been established, yet at the same time I was not someone they would have dealings with professionally. I think this mixed status helped me to approach the research with "a judicious combination of involvement and estrangement" (Hammersley, 1993, p. 255), by providing me with 'emic' insights into those aspects that the teachers thought were obvious as well as 'etic' insights into those aspects that did not seem to be within their conscious awareness (Watson-Gegeo, 1988).

In the focus groups and interviews, I did not contribute my own views or experiences of the subject matter. Even so, many of the teachers either knew me or had seen my conference presentations or publications on gay/lesbian issues and so knew me to be a self-identified lesbian. It is not possible to know whether, or how, this knowledge may have affected what people said in my presence or what they thought I wanted to hear—though these questions would apply to any researcher, whatever their actual or perceived sexual identity.

Creating the Transcripts

Transcribing the focus groups and interviews was itself a complex process. Transcripts are necessarily limited; they do not include "those things that cannot be seen or heard, but only *felt*, such as sudden sensations of impatience, urgency, relaxation, frustration, and so on" (van Lier, 1988, p. 80). Transcribing involves deciding exactly what to include and how to represent the participants; these decision-making processes involve interpretation, analysis, and theory (Ochs, 1979) and have political and ethical dimensions (Roberts, 1997). Given the many decisions that transcribing involves, my guiding principles were to include only those features that were pertinent to my investigation (e.g., I did indicate when laughter occurred but I did not measure the length of pauses) and to balance accuracy with readability (Edwards & Westgate, 1994; van Lier, 1988). The transcribing key is presented in Appendix B.

Analyzing the Teachers' Accounts

In selecting data from the focus groups and teacher interviews to be included in this book, I have chosen quotes that reflect "both variation and central tendency or typicality in the data" (Watson-Gegeo, 1988, p. 585). My intentions are threefold. The first is to represent the range of teachers' reported experiences and perspectives. This seems important because this study is the first of its kind, so there is a need to map out the key issues that teachers identified as salient.

The second is to indicate the general frequency of the issues they raised so that readers have a sense of whether these were common or rare. On that point I should clarify that I do not track the precise number of teachers who described a similar experience or made a similar point; instead, I use impressionistic terms such as 'a number of' or 'a few.' In this I follow Hammersley (1990), who cautions that "overprecision" or "insisting on precise quantitative measures ... may produce figures that are more precise than we can justify given the nature of the data available, and which are therefore misleading" (p. 9).

My third aim is to highlight aspects that generated conflicting reports or perspectives. This is because examining points of divergence or contention can illuminate some of the underlying tensions, competing discourses, and changing practices that are at play.

While the teachers' first-hand accounts provide valuable insights, the limitations of relying on these accounts need to be acknowledged. As mentioned previously, the teachers in this study were not selected at random—each volunteered to participate because they had an interest in the research topic, which means their experiences and viewpoints are not representative of teachers in general.

A related point is that the teachers' reported experiences are understood to be shaped by the following dimensions: the broader societal context, in terms of social, political, and economic structures and values; the educational institution, including its programs, policies, and staff; and the social identities and unique 'psychobiographies' of the individual teachers themselves (Layder, 1993). These societal, institutional, and individual dimensions are understood to be "intermingling" (p. 70), yet any research project requires "selective focusing" (p. 74). In this book, it is the last category—the individual dimension—that receives the most explicit focus, for reasons that are largely pragmatic. In the focus groups and interviews, teachers recounted classroom experiences that had been significant to them, but without necessarily contextualizing these experiences in terms of specific programs, institutions, or geopolitical contexts.

Lastly, I take the view that data obtained through focus groups and interviews do not necessarily 'represent' teachers' views since these are fluid and changeable—and are more likely to be built through conversational exchange than discovered. Poststructuralists criticize the notion that it is possible to "know the world in a direct and unmediated way—'as it really is'" (Usher & Edwards, 1994, p. 18). While it is useful to consider teachers' perspectives, it must be acknowledged that "the confessional mode does not necessarily offer unmediated access to some core or central truth" (McLeod & Yates, 1997, p. 28).

Interrelated Chapter Themes

The next four chapters focus on acknowledging sexual diversity in terms of who is being taught (Chapter 2) as well as what is being taught (Chapter 3), addressing homophobia (Chapter 4), and teachers negotiating their own sexual identities in class (Chapter 5). However, owing to the high degree of interplay between these matters, there is not always a strict separation between chapter themes. Introducing lesbian/gay themes, for example, often raises issues about representing one's own sexual identity, and these dilemmas are inseparable from the social valuing of certain sexual identities and the devaluing of others. Each of the general areas, then, tends to spill into or infuse the others. Yet, for the purposes of cogent analysis, it is necessary to foreground a particular aspect, even though in some cases it is the interconnections that prevail.

CHAPTER 2
Teaching Multisexual Student Cohorts

Some teachers in this study were keen to support the lesbian, gay, and transgender students who were in their language classes and programs; a few teachers described their attempts to teach in ways that would take into account these students' needs and perspectives. Yet, for the most part, these efforts were limited to providing support or assistance only to specific students who were known by the teacher to be sexual minorities, and only on an individualized, occasional basis. In this chapter, I make the case that there is a need to routinely conceptualize cohorts as encompassing gay, lesbian, bisexual, straight, transgender, queer, and questioning students, while recognizing that these identifications have myriad and changing meanings, especially transculturally. Moreover, language curricula and teaching practices need to be rethought with this multisexual mix in mind.

'Supporting' Lesbian, Gay, and Transgender Students

Of those teachers who spoke about having gay, lesbian, or transgender students, the main concern was how to provide these students with support.

Some teachers decided to participate in the current study in the hope of learning more about the needs of their lesbian and gay students. A particular concern was how to respond when students came out to them. (Please note: for confidentiality, all names of participants, neighborhoods, and streets are pseudonyms.)

> 2.1 Maggie: I had a student ... who wanted to come out [as gay] here in the United States ... I didn't know that much about it but I said to him ... You're in the United States and there's free speech, but there still are a lot of people who are prejudiced. So I guess that's about all I knew was to say Take your time, and take it step by step. But- So I'm trying to learn more about how to support students.

It seems that even teachers who would like to respond to gay students in a supportive way may feel uninformed and unsure of how to do that, beyond advising them to proceed with caution, as Maggie did.

An administrator spoke of two students in her program who had come out to their teachers and classmates.

2.2 Janice: We had a student here a couple years ago who ... very honestly came out to the class and ... explained to them that he had a significant other in Sweden ... It just threw the whole class for such a loop ... We [teachers] were all very worried about this student. Because ... he was just feeling so, um, isolated, and I was having just such a hard time knowing how to support him ... [Other students] were really worried that they could get sick, or have AIDS ... [Eventually] he just kind of won their hearts. And I think that he saw that ... [the teachers] really liked him ... [and] would refuse to allow him to be isolated [...] It was a challenge for the teachers ... because ... he [said] I just had no idea that people would treat me the way they're treating me.

Openly gay students may be ostracized by their classmates, and as a result teachers may find themselves struggling to facilitate social integration in the classroom.

However, another student in the same program was received very differently by classmates.

2.3 Janice: But another time we had a, um, a female student ... who was also very out ... She was Taiwanese, and very into being like a guy ... In fact the first day we kicked her out of the girls' bathroom because we thought she WAS a guy ... She did everything to be able to be either [gender], and she got her ... state [identity] card and had 'male' written on it ... She was so proud ... that she had managed to do this. And she was SO WELL LIKED ... The students adored her.

Janice's account of this student, who seems to have been transgender, suggests that being out does not necessarily result in ostracism. Out queer students can in fact be popular with their peers and have a significant positive impact on students and teachers alike.

Unlike Janice, the majority of teachers who spoke about openly gay or queer students said these students had come out to them privately outside of class. A few teachers reported that this occurred regularly, often following in-class discussions of lesbian/gay topics (see also 7.12).

2.4 Alicia: Every time I've done a gay/lesbian unit at that [advanced language] level ... someone comes out. And it's usually that they come to my office to, um, ask me why we did the unit. And then they come out. When they feel a little bit safer [...] About one [student] a term. Both men and women ... I think that they're so used to being invisible that ... they wanna stay that way ... in class ... Only one woman ... came out in, uh, force [in the classroom] ... after the [gay/lesbian] unit. But most people ... don't want a lot of people to know, and they're afraid about what the repercussions will be.

In Alicia's experience, gay students usually had little interest in coming out to their classmates, preferring invisibility to potentially negative reactions.

Though Alicia was used to having students come out to her, and though in her classes she frequently came out as a lesbian herself (see 5.2), she was still surprised when one particular student came out to her after class.

> 2.5 Alicia: Early in a term … a student pushed me and pushed me [to come out in class, which I ended up doing] … He came out later on in the term … I remember another teacher who had [taught] him … had said … He's gonna have a hard time in [your] class because he's so … anti-gay … And then he turned out to be gay!

This scenario shows that teachers can misread students' sexual identities. It also highlights the potential importance to gay students of knowing openly gay teachers (see Chapter 5).

Moreover, if it is the case, as Alicia's experiences suggest, that most gay students are not out in their classes and that at least some of these students are not readily identifiable as gay by their teachers, then it follows that the proportion of students who are, in fact, gay is likely to be higher than many teachers realize.

A few teachers reported that, for some international and immigrant students, a primary motive for moving to the new host country was to be able to live in an environment where they could be openly gay.

> 2.6 Rachel: I think a lot of students come to this country in order to come out … [from] cultures where that's much more difficult to do, that is, this is perceived as a place where it's easier than it is … I would be grateful to be able to say Talk to Mark [an openly gay teacher/student-advisor], because I would know that there was an appropriate place for someone to go and ask questions.

Though the United States was generally seen by teachers in the study as a more welcoming environment for gay students than their home countries, Rachel pointed out that gay students might find life in the new country more challenging than they had anticipated. Rachel, like several other teachers, also pointed out that one way of creating learning environments that welcome openly gay and lesbian students was creating work environments that welcome openly gay and lesbian teachers, who could provide information and referrals to assist gay students in integrating into local gay communities.

At the same time, the point was also made that teachers should not assume that students' countries are necessarily less gay-friendly than the new host country.

> 2.7 Janice: The attitudes of our students [about homosexuality] are changing also. I mean those countries aren't stagnant, and they all have their own movements that are going on.

Janice's recognition that gay social movements are rapidly transforming many regions of the world contrasted with the view taken by most of the teachers in my study, who tended to characterize students' home countries as fairly inhospitable for gay people.

Potential Challenges Facing Lesbian and Gay Students

Though overall there was a general desire to support gay and lesbian students, there were few specific ideas as to what exactly this support might look like. Some felt unsure about how to support students who came out to them privately, while others found it challenging to support students who came out to their classmates and were then ostracized. To address these concerns effectively, better understandings are needed of some of the challenges that lesbian and gay students are likely to face in their day-to-day lives, both in and out of the classroom. In considering these students, there is a need to recognize "the very real ways in which lesbian and gay sexualities are subordinated, marginalized and constructed as 'other' both within the social formation at large and within schools themselves" (Redman, 1994, p. 144).

Kato's (1999) study of gay, lesbian, and bisexual international students studying in the United States sheds light on some of the pressures these students were under with regard to negotiating their sexual identity. A male student from Colombia was concerned about the possibility of being sent back to his country because of the "social cleansing squads that hunt [homosexuals] down and attack them"; a female student from Bermuda feared not being able to get a job when she returned if word reached home that she was a lesbian (pp. 3–4). Other students (from Europe) were having difficulties in the United States, which they found to be far more restrictive than their home countries.

> [T]he Danish student remarks that the United States feels very "old fashioned, uptight, and conservative" compared with his home country, and, therefore, he is more reluctant to come out [as gay] to people in this country. The woman from the Netherlands agrees, describing the feelings she had when she arrived and was confronted with some of the "ignorant attitudes and biases" against gays and lesbians. "I was sent back in time approximately ten years," she said.
>
> (Kato, 1999, p. 5)

Taking a broad sociological approach, Sears (2005) categorizes a number of countries according to whether their "LGBT educational policies and programs" and "state policies/cultural climate" are 'persecutorial,' 'homophobic,' 'heteronormative,' 'supportive,' or 'proactive'—with countries like Egypt, Mexico, and the United States found to be among the least supportive and Canada, New Zealand, and the Netherlands among the most supportive (p. xxviii). Though the in-school and out-of-school experiences of gay and lesbian language learners would be expected to vary greatly depending, in part, on the geopolitics of the region(s) in question, most of these learners have to grapple with at least some degree of anti-gay prejudice and discrimination, across the domains of work, family, school, and public life.

As to the in-school experiences of gay and lesbian language learners, the few studies that have been published thus far report alienation and isolation in the face of heavily heterosexualized curricula and classroom talk. For example, Jewell (1998) interviewed Jackie, a transgender student from Thailand studying English in Australia, about her textbooks. Not surprisingly, Jackie did not find the unit on families very engaging (p. 8); as Jewell explains, "the characters are all referenced in terms of their marital status and as parts of heterosexual nuclear families" (p. 8).

Jackie's reaction: "'I feel some uh very boring. I feel because not me. Not good for me. No good for me, because married ... Marry for me not need'" (p. 8). Jewell reports that Jackie would prefer it if "her chosen sexual identity" was visible in ESL materials; he quotes her as saying "Take my photograph ... they [other students] learn my mind ... learn my life ... they understand" (p. 9).

Jewell argues that "Jackie and other non-heterosexual students" need to be able to "have *their* experiences heard and shared, just like heterosexual students do" (1998, p. 2). This means being able to "display" their sociosexual identities to other students and to the teacher when discussing topics that are common in beginning-level language classes, such as "telling stories about his/her partner, ideal partner, ... hopes for the future" and so on (p. 12). He makes the point that heterosexual students would also benefit, as they would "gain an understanding of the multivariate forms of sociosexual identity with which they may come in contact in the ESL classroom and elsewhere" (p. 2).

A recent study of mostly bilingual youth at a Francophone high school in Canada found that gay students there were overwhelmingly "positioned as outsiders" (Dalley & Campbell, 2006, p. 23). Bernard—gay, white, and Canadian-born—reported that some of his peers considered it "almost a cool thing to hang around with a gay guy," which initially seemed positive but came to feel discriminatory as he was constantly being characterized as exotic. Zadun—gay, black, and a refugee from Somalia—spoke of his fear at being found out by his family: "They are going to kill me, my brothers" (p. 23). One lesbian student reportedly had to transfer out of the school because the environment was so oppressive. The discriminatory environment for gay and lesbian students was exacerbated by the near-complete lack of gay/lesbian themes or perspectives in the school curricula.

Anti-gay dynamics in the classroom may need to be addressed not only when a student comes out, as Janice indicated (2.2), but also when a student is perceived to be gay and taunted for it. A recent study shows how fifth-grade students in a literacy class in Brazil were constructing others as gay and therefore "deviant" (Moita-Lopes, 2006). In one such instance, two boys chatting in class were "deliberately positioning as gay another boy," which involved mocking the supposedly gay classmate by calling him (the Portuguese equivalent of) a "little fruit" (p. 37). The teacher in this case "was aware of the relevance of this topic [homosexuality] to the pupils, but did not know how to deal with it in class" (p. 38). Because taunting scenarios like this one can be destructive, Moita-Lopes (2006) argues, teachers need to be willing and able to address the topic of homoeroticism in classrooms.

Schools can be hostile places for lesbian and gay students. Kumashiro (2002) quotes the following statistics from a range of studies compiled on the Web site of the U.S.-based Gay, Lesbian, and Straight Education Network:

- 97% of students in public high schools report regularly hearing homophobic remarks.
- 80% of gay and lesbian youth report severe social isolation.
- 90% of gays and lesbians experience some form of victimization on account of their perceived or actual sexual orientation (Kumashiro, 2002, p. 171).

Of course, not only peers but also teachers can make homophobic remarks that adversely affect gay and lesbian students, as we shall see in Chapter 4.

While there is little research or documentation of attempts to create less discriminatory environments in language programs, Clemente and Higgins' (2005) study of youth at a university language center in Mexico suggests that such efforts are being undertaken. One of the youths, Arturo, considered the language center where he studied and taught English to be a sanctuary from the difficulties of his home life as he was not out to his family. At the center, Arturo said, "a high number of students are gay and that encourages me and makes me feel I am not alone anymore" (p. 14). Clemente and Higgins (2005) make the case that "the pursuit of English provides [Arturo] with a safe zone for exploring the contours of his sexuality and social class" (p. 2). Their study suggests that learning environments can become supportive spaces for gay students who may be experiencing social isolation elsewhere. However, no specifics are provided about the teaching practices that made, or helped to make, this possible.

Teaching Lesbian and Gay Students

A few teachers in my study described specific tasks or approaches they had used when taking into account gay and lesbian students.

Like a number of other teachers (see 3.22–3.24, 5.27), Paige regularly invited gay guest speakers to class. She described teaching strategies she used in following up their visits.

2.8 Paige: [I assign] some kind of journal type writing or a summary of the guest speakers with a response of their own opinion, to give them another chance to talk about what this has meant to them. And I'm careful about, um, what kind of questions I'll ask students so as to not out somebody or put them in a position where they'll feel uncomfortable … [Also] I don't ask students to read each other's writing when I'm doing lesbian and gay issues. It's just written either to themselves or to me … so that if they wanted to express, um, something that they didn't want other students to read they would feel permission to do that.

Paige's emphasis was ensuring that students would neither feel pressured to come out themselves nor encouraged to out others (see also 5.5). Her desire to protect the privacy of gay students was paramount and informed the way she set up learning tasks with gay themes and established a potential 'safe zone' for gay students through one-on-one interactions with her.

Once when a student came out in the relative privacy of a student–teacher dialogue journal, Paige had found it challenging to write a response.

2.9 Paige: [The student] was writing some pretty explicit sexual stuff, which I wasn't very comfortable with. So I wanted to respond to him positively for taking the risk of coming out to me, but I also needed to let him to know that I didn't want him to write this explicit sexual stuff. (P laughs) So it was actually pretty difficult, and trying to do this at a level of English that he would be able to understand.

Paige made a point of distinguishing gay identity from gay sex, encouraging the student to elaborate on the former but not the latter. Her account underscores that communicating these sorts of distinctions can be challenging due to language proficiency issues.

Unlike Paige, who tried to create an environment in which gay or lesbian students would not fear being outed, Claire (a teacher-educator) would make a point of identifying those students who seemed likely to be gay or lesbian.

> 2.10 Claire: Sometimes … with teachers [I] just say What do you think of so-and-so, she looks like a total dyke! … [I'll use] language that's kinda friendly and frank … And then straight people always get so uptight about that. Because they think Oh you're not supposed to judge anyone by their sexuality so you shouldn't even notice it! … It's a way to sort of skirt the issue … It's … not having the language or the comfort to really talk about differences.

In Claire's experience, even teachers who intended to be supportive of lesbian/gay students were reluctant to speculate about which of their students might be gay or lesbian, yet to Claire this was an ordinary part of 'getting to know students' and assessing their needs. She felt that if teachers overlooked or ignored a student's gayness, then they might not be attuned to certain challenges the student might be facing with classmates or with assignments.

Claire's position involved providing novice teachers with assistance and guidance. In the example below, she refers to two icons of lesbianism—triangles, a symbol that alleged homosexuals were forced to wear by the Nazis, and k.d. lang, a well-known Canadian singer.

> 2.11 Claire: Once I went into a class and … this wonderful Japanese woman … was … completely decked out head to toe in triangles and k.d. lang buttons and was just really in the throes of enjoying her identity and really BEING out … Every topic she chose was gay related. For an oral presentation, for a writing project, that kinda stuff. And the teachers weren't able to really give her direction on how to focus her topics. So I … went into class … and worked with her individually. And … had teachers be aware [of] … how are other students feeling about her … making them feel comfortable with her in the class … And really getting them to appreciate what she was doing, like how amazing this was.

Supporting gay students in the classroom could take the form of providing knowledgeable feedback on gay-themed assignments, facilitating group cohesion between openly gay students and their classmates, and framing outness in positive ways. Claire added that other students and staff often felt inspired by gay students who were out (see also 7.20).

A number of teachers were concerned that lesbian and gay students were having to study materials whose characters and subject matter were overwhelmingly, and usually exclusively, straight. Tina described her frustrated attempts to address this.

2.12 Tina: When I had a gay student in my [EFL] class I really looked at the book differently. And I really thought about what I was saying very differently. Like you'd open a book and there'd be a dialogue between … Bill and Susan planning a date for Saturday night. And you see that every single chapter, everything lists, you know, He gave his girlfriend flowers for Valentine's Day. And … you just realize that … all of the examples are so clearly … in that bias … [How] do you compensate? … [I tried to by saying] If a man's going to ask his girlfriend or his boyfriend depending on whatever. And, um, students would laugh … I wasn't sure is that helping, in the sense … [of] including another possibility. Or is that being sort of culturally imperialist, … saying … I have my views and I'm gonna make you listen to them. Or is that actually negative and it's opening up a door for people to laugh at … Or maybe … it makes that ONE PERSON in the back of the room feel better … I'm not really sure.

Tina's dilemma raises complex questions about challenging the pervasive heterosexuality within learning materials, while considering the implications of doing so in the context of postcolonialism.

Considering the Learning Needs of Gay and Lesbian Students

As we have seen, teachers attempted to consider the needs of gay/lesbian students by safeguarding the privacy of those who did not wish to be out, affirming those who did come out, and improvising to augment learning materials that were heavily heterosexualized. These efforts are important because, as Chan (1996) puts it, "Opening up educational institutions and educational materials to include the lives, stories, contributions, and existence of lesbians, gay men, and bisexuals is essential in moving from heterosexism to an open institution of learning" (p. 22).

Malinowitz (1995) recommends that teachers consider how lesbian/gay students might be experiencing class assignments and interactions (though below she is referring to writing, her questions could be applied to speaking as well). She asks,

> What factors might [lesbian and gay students] have to weigh when deciding whether or not to disclose their sexual identity in their writing, and what are the risks and costs of either choice? What tensions surround the naming of that identity, and what are the effects likely to be on writers who are asked to compose reflectively and critically?
>
> (p. xvii)

Hart (1988) notes that students' fears about being seen as gay might impede their development as writers: "[A lesbian student] may fear 'ripples' from the teacher or even more from her peers in the class. And so she will divert her first and best, her most vital idea, and the work of getting better at using language is getting undone" (p. 33). Malinowitz (1995) found that such fears are widespread.

> When I talk with lesbian and gay colleagues and students about the problems lesbian and gay student writers face in mainstream writing classes,

I most commonly hear references to 'voice'—or, to be more accurate, 'voiceless-ness.' Facing an audience of their peers and teacher, students feel afraid—afraid that they won't be listened to, that they will be ridiculed, beaten up, punished, ostracized, that their expression will be curtailed, that they will be relegated to the remove of Other, that they will be denied, either explicitly or implicitly, the oppor-tunity to articulate their 'real' thoughts ... Lesbian and gay students lack an audi-ence of their peers, a group whose 'reading schema' line up with their own.

(p. 131)

Malinowitz (1995) argues that, when "homophobic conditions" exist in class-rooms, gay and lesbian students are unlikely to risk coming out, which means that maintaining a sense of safety will take precedence over "experimenting with writ-ing" (p. 258). She further argues that "[t]he occasions when these sorts of decisions arise extend far beyond the obvious times when they may have the option of writ-ing about sexuality or relationships, since their lesbian or gay identity touches virtually all parts of their lives" (p. 258).

Many gay and lesbian students in Malinowitz's (1995) study said they avoided gay or lesbian topics for class assignments. This avoidance required a certain amount of effort "since 'personal experience' essays are common assignments and the mate-rial that comprises the rest of a person's life must be shuffled around to successfully enact the gay discursive deception" (p. 257). The discursive requirements of this sort of enactment would seem particularly challenging for those students who are writ-ing or speaking in a second or foreign language in which they are not fluent.

At the same time, gay and lesbian students tend to be very experienced at being cautious and counterhegemonic:

Because lesbian and gay men must constantly assess the consequences of being out and negotiate the terms of disclosure, often necessitating elaborate monitoring of what is said and even thought ("internalized homophobia"), a particular complication is woven into their processes of construing and constructing knowledge. Even for those who are most out, acts of making meaning involve constant confrontations with many of the premises and mandates of the dominant culture.

(Malinowitz, 1995, p. 24)

It would seem likely that these 'constant confrontations' would be exacerbated for those interacting in a second or a foreign language. There are few studies of these matters with student populations that are markedly multilingual or transnational. However, one recent study highlights the speech constraints that gay language learners can experience.

Ellwood (2006) conducted a research interview with Katsuyuki, a 20-year-old Japanese man studying English at an Australian university, and through her questions, inadvertently elicited what Katsuyuki called his "really big secret"—namely, that he was gay. In retrospect, Ellwood realized that during the interview the student had been trying to conceal his gayness, which meant he had been distorting many aspects of his life, such as his reasons for "deciding to come to Australia, wanting to learn English, being shy, having attained a certain level of proficiency in English, and having the personality that he felt he had" (p. 79). For example, when Katsuyuki was asked why he had decided to come to Australia, he first answered that he liked the friendliness of Australians, but after coming out to the researcher he was able to explain that, actually, in Australia there was the possibility of not only finding a (Caucasian) boyfriend, which he desired, but also obtaining a visa so that both of them could live and work in the same country (Ellwood, 2006). The sorts of issues that this student felt he could not speak openly about (such as why he was learning a second language) are fairly typical topics in language classes, which underscores the importance of creating classroom environments in which gay and lesbian students have the option of speaking openly about their lives if they wish to do so.

However, as Janice (2.3) and Claire (2.11) intimated, just because gay and lesbian students may be grappling with anti-gay discrimination in and out of class does not mean that teachers should "adopt a reductionist pedagogic approach that sees gays and lesbians as mere problems or victims" (Mac an Ghaill, 1994, p. 170). On the contrary, lesbian and gay students often develop creativity, resourcefulness, and resilience in order to negotiate the constraints that they often face, and as a result their self-expression and communication can be, as Malinowitz (1995) put it, "invigorated—not just stifled" (p. 113).

This last point can be illustrated by returning to the gay Japanese student mentioned above. In the final week of the term, Katsuyuki came out to the entire class by using his "gay identity as an attention-grabbing strategy to begin his [oral] presentation" (Ellwood, 2006, p. 81). As Ellwood observes, this student's public coming out represented a stark contrast to his nervous insistence, early in the term, that she keep his gayness a secret. For the end-of-term class presentation, the student creatively reframed his gay positioning from fearful victim to confident showman, which highlights the fact that choices about the degree and circumstances of outness are being continually made and remade (see Chapter 5). (See also King, 2008, for a study of Korean men who found being gay to be advantageous in learning English.)

Whether positive or negative, the perspectives, concerns, and experiences of gay and lesbian learners are rarely integrated into language learning materials, as Shardakova and Pavlenko (2004) note in a study of the identity options in foreign language textbooks. The authors recommend the inclusion of tasks that explore potentially "difficult encounters" that these learners may face when they travel or immigrate to a new country (p. 33). This sort of material could prove useful in teaching, especially since openly gay students may encounter negative reactions not only beyond the classroom but also within it (see 2.2).

Thinking Queerly and Transculturally about Sexual Identities

Nearly all of the teachers in this study spoke of gay, straight, and lesbian people as if the meanings of these descriptors were completely straightforward and unproblematic. However, a few teachers noted that sexual identities and the terms used to describe these are not necessarily clear-cut or fixed (see also 8.46).

2.13 Janice: Even … somebody who categorizes themselves as a straight person, like myself, … are much more open to thinking about possibilities of …

living with a woman someday. [...] I think that as a society ... we've made some movement that way. Of realizing that maybe we can't just categorize ourselves all in one.

2.14 Tina: My experience [of gay culture] has been kind of a playfulness with roles and ... definitions ... My mom will say one day she's a lesbian, and the next day she'll say she's bi, ... and then the next day she'll say she's omni-sexual. I'm like What does that mean! (T laughs)

One teacher alluded to the possibility that categories of sexual identity were not necessarily universal.

2.15 Mike: I think to a certain degree ... Asians as a generalization ... have a stereotype of ... flamboyant ... men who ... dress up [as women] ... They don't think the homosexual exists, a lot of them.

This comment raises the question of how students and teachers in the transcultural arenas of language education are likely to understand what it means to identify as gay, homosexual, transvestite, or transgender, and it highlights the fact that the practices and meanings associated with sexual identities are highly varied.

Ways of Theorizing Sexual Identities

As the preceding comment suggests, ways of conceptualizing and interpreting sexual identities are far from universal (see, e.g., Livia & Hall, 1997a). Britzman (2000) observes that in North America, for example, "sexuality is an identity, while in Brazil sexual cultures are fluid and not focused on claiming an identity" (p. 46). Valentine (1997), discussing Japan, makes a similar point:

[C]onceptualizing self in terms of sexuality is considered alien in Japan, as this makes doing into being, practice into essence, in that what you do defines what you are. In Japan, what you are, your self, tends to be defined through interaction, where you belong with others, your socially recognized networks of relationships.

(p. 107)

In the transnational arenas of language classes, then, teachers and learners are likely to have mixed understandings of what exactly is meant by notions such as 'sexual identity' or 'gay'; for some, the focus would be on individual identity and its expression or repression, while for others the focus would be more on intersubjectivity and social relations (a contrast which, incidentally, parallels a lesbian/gay versus queer theory framework; see Chapter 1).

Furthermore, interpreting others' sexual identifications is often marked with ambiguity and mismatched understandings, especially transculturally (Nelson, 2005). It has been observed that gay identity tends to be associated with people who fit a certain demographic. In North America, for example, "the identity of a middle class, gay, white man is seen as gay"—his class, race, and gender tend to remain unmarked (Fung, 1995, p. 128). However, people who identify as gay but who are not white, middle class, and so on, may be less likely to have their gayness perceived as a prominent aspect of their identity. For example, Fung, who describes himself as racially Chinese, culturally Trinidadian, gay, and living in Canada, explains that his "race, culture, and sexual orientation are seen to compete with each other" (p. 128).

The notion that multiple identities are competing or conflicting is a result of "interest-group pluralism," which, according to Phelan (1994), frames "private interest" as being in opposition to "common good" (p. 140). It accomplishes this by failing to acknowledge multiple, overlapping memberships in groups. In other words, each group is framed as if it were self-contained and distinct from other groups. There is pressure to choose one's "true self," or "primary allegiance" (p. 140). In light of this pressure, Butler (1993) points out that for many people coming out as gay may not be a viable option: "For whom does the term ['coming out'] present an impossible conflict between racial, ethnic, or religious affiliation and sexual politics?" (p. 227).

Thus, second and foreign language learners who are gay may not be readily recognized as such on campus or in the classroom, whether because they do not fit others' preconceived images of gay or they do not find it feasible to foreground their gay identity. In the case of immigrants and refugees, newcomers to a country are often heavily reliant on family and community support (see Morgan, 1997); those who are gay may be reluctant to come out because of the risk that such support might be withdrawn (see Dalley & Campbell, 2006).

Exactly what constitutes coming out is not necessarily clear-cut and can vary internationally. In the United States, Strongman (2002) observes, coming out is understood to be "a defining moment," a verbal "declaration," a "speech-act," which is not surprising since lesbian/gay discourses from that region emphasize "liberation through disclosure" (p. 181). Santiago (2002) calls this a form of "public exhibitionism," explaining that it may be "more rapid and efficient, yes, but certainly less wily" (p. 18). In Latin America, by contrast, coming out is often a slower, subtler, and less overtly verbalized process than it is in North America, according to Strongman (2002). Thus, in globalized language classes, what I have elsewhere called "a queer chaos of meanings" is perhaps to be expected, given the likelihood of mismatched understandings as to whether or not someone has in fact come out (Nelson, 2005).

Another important point is that sexual-identity discourses and practices are changing worldwide at a rapid rate, as Janice mentioned (see 2.7). Queer cultural productions such as films are quickly proliferating and receiving attention transnationally. According to Erni (2003), "From Singapore, Taiwan, the Philippines, Korea, and Hong Kong, [queer youth] have reported on the enormous usefulness of the Internet not only to make queer friends, but also to question and debate sexual politics, ... gay marriages (including 'sham marriages' ...), and all kinds of sexual curiosities" (p. 382). Erni (2003) also makes the point that, "[i]n the West, queer connotations have to be read off the text; but over here, the consistent, almost nonchalant, blurring of the line between homosociality and homoeroticism ... offers an open text for alternative imaginings" (p. 383), thereby emphasizing once again that, for some, sexual identifications may be characterized more by fluidity, ambiguity, and nuance than by directness and definitiveness. Also prevalent in Asia are "drag" and "codes of androgyny and camp" (Erni, 2003, p. 383), which may explain why Mike (2.15) made the comment that, for many of his Asian students, 'the homosexual' does not seem to exist.

Tan (2001), writing of sexual politics in Taiwan, differentiates 'kuer,' which derives from North American 'queer' and represents a defiantly subversive stance toward the mainstream, from 'tongzhi,' which derives from "common (*tong*) goal (*zhi*)" (p. 128)—a revolutionary term of address during Mao's China that in current usage denotes a "more reformist" approach to the cause of equality for sexual minorities (p. 134). Thus, understandings of 'what homosexuality is' are moving rapidly in transnational flows, producing myriad meanings and variations.

> There is no reason to expect that just because some Taiwanese and San Franciscans employ similar vocabulary or relationships models, then these words and models must carry the same personal or social significance, or that they will function in the respective societies in similar ways. We do not find in Taiwan a pristine Taiwanese homosexuality but a confluence of local and imported conceptions, underpinned by economic, social, and political systems, producing distinct and sometimes conflicting hybrid models of what (homo)sexuality 'is.'
> (Tan, 2001, pp. 124–125)

In queer research and activism, definitional quandaries abound. For example, a "queer teachers study group" that met in Canada over a 2-year period "could not come to any agreement" about what the terms gay and lesbian "really meant," which Sumara and Davis (1998) attribute to the "richly divergent life experiences among the group's members" (p. 207). What exactly is meant by 'gay,' not to mention 'queer,' is a highly contested question, perhaps especially transculturally. To put forward another example, Strongman (2002) considers it reductive that "[t]he rhetoric of the gay and lesbian ... movement in the United States unites under the single category of 'gay' such different sexual categories as an Indian *hijra* and a Mexican *joto*" (p. 177).

Another complicating aspect is that links between sexual identity and sexual activity can be rather tenuous (Weeks, 1987), as illustrated by the findings of a survey of U.S. university students:

> Perhaps the greatest surprise of the survey was discovering how loosely students' sexual identities were connected to their actual sexual experiences ... [15%] of students who said they were heterosexual had had sex with a person of the same gender ... [40%] of students who identified themselves as lesbian had had sex with a man within the last year, and two-thirds of gay male students reported having sex with a woman within the last year. About 30 percent of both gay- and lesbian-identified students had never had sex with a same-sex partner.
> (Stoller, 1994, pp. 202–203)

This sort of dissonance between sexual behavior and sexual identity reinforces the notion that "[s]exual identity may be ... less a matter of final discovery than perpetual reinvention" (Fuss, 1991, p. 7).

Lastly, ways of theorizing and understanding sexual identifications are increasingly complicated due to the growth of online environments globally: "representational notions of identity are perhaps even more problematic in network(ed) spaces than in the real world" (Alexander & Banks, 2004, p. 284). As Carlson (2001) observes, "[t]he worldwide information web and the global village may … provide opportunities to build new kinds of fluid, affinity-group communities and shapeshifting identities" (p. 306) such as the "cyborg queer" (p. 308). With the advent of 'queer cyberspace,' multimodal possibilities for sexual-identity constructions are undergoing rapid changes that are only just beginning to be investigated (Alexander & Banks, 2004; for an analysis of English language students' online discussions of homosexuality, see Nguyen & Kellogg, 2005).

For all of these reasons, then, language classes that encompass student and teacher cohorts across a range of geographic, cultural, and linguistic backgrounds are likely to comprise not only people of diverse sexual identities but also people with diverse understandings of what is signified by 'gay identity' or 'coming out.'

Rethinking Pedagogy with Multisexual Student Cohorts in Mind

Among the teachers in this study, there was little recognition of the diverse ways of theorizing, naming, and performing sexual identities, especially internationally. This may help to explain why, apart from a few notable exceptions, most teachers in my study had the view that gay and lesbian students were in their programs on only an occasional basis ("we had a gay student a couple years ago"). When these students came out privately to the teacher or publicly to the class (though the latter occurred only rarely), the teachers felt it was important to respond supportively, which often meant calling upon staff who were themselves gay in order to provide specialized support or guidance. While in some cases it may be feasible for openly gay teaching staff to provide counseling-style support to gay students or consultant-style expertise on gay subject matter to students (or their teachers), it seems unlikely that these strategies would be either widely applicable or pedagogically sufficient.

Overall, there was little recognition that gay students are not necessarily recognizable as such (perhaps especially cross-culturally), that student cohorts are routinely—not just occasionally—characterized by sexual diversity, or that any teaching ought to be undertaken with a multisexual student cohort in mind. Indeed, for some teachers, having students who were openly gay inspired empathy, without this leading to significant changes in curricula or teaching practices, while other teachers did begin to question their own pedagogical practices but felt uncertain about how to go about improving these.

I would argue that, in order to maximize the effectiveness of second and foreign language programs, there is a need to rethink and reframe teaching practices so that they do not presume, or produce, a monosexualized version of the world within and beyond the classroom. This means representing a range of sexual identifications within curricula and being open to exploring the nuanced meanings, norms, and expectations with regard to sexual identity that are associated with the language/culture being studied. It also means framing class activities and discussions in ways that will be conducive for learners of any sexual identity to actively participate and to share their perspectives.

Such efforts were being undertaken by some of the teachers in this study, as we shall see in the remaining chapters of this book.

CHAPTER 3
Engaging with Gay and Lesbian Themes

From the teachers' accounts, it is clear that lesbian and gay themes are increasingly arising in the teaching of language and culture, as multisexual discourses in wide circulation beyond the classroom steadily infuse curricula and classroom interactions. However, in some contexts, using gay and lesbian themes is still highly contested: teachers reported that at some educational institutions any mention of these themes was discouraged, if not outright forbidden. This chapter explores issues to do with the exclusion and inclusion of sexual diversity as subject matter in language classes. A case is made that this subject matter can be used to illuminate linguistic and cultural practices and norms and also to question and critique them.

A Popular Topic—Unless Prohibited

Many teachers in this study described instances in which they or their students had raised lesbian/gay themes in class, while others noted that, in some institutional contexts, talking about these themes was actively prohibited. This contrast and its implications are explored here.

A Popular Topic

Most teachers in this study reported that lesbian/gay themes were a regular part of their own classes, and some added that these themes were not uncommon in their colleagues' classes.

> 3.1 Paige: I'd say 50% of teachers [in this city] probably teach this topic sometimes … It's certainly typical enough that you can broach the topic with other teachers and not have them be shocked, and often have them say that they've at least mentioned it once. […] I've done it in … contemporary issues or American culture classes … [and] speaking and listening classes where students choose topics that they're interested in … It's come up in reading and writing classes as well.

Many teachers reported that, when they asked the class to generate class topics to study, the students often nominated gay or lesbian topics.

3.2 Janice   We've had three different classes doing gay and lesbian issues in one term. So it's a popular topic. The students request it.

A number of teachers reported that students regularly raised lesbian/gay issues in their written assignments or in class discussions.

3.3 Claire: It often comes up in our upper level classes when students are doing projects on … social issues. Somebody always wants to do something on gays in the military or gay marriage.

3.4 Sophie: [This term a student's] first essay was about … changing her attitudes towards homosexuals because two lesbians on the … bus helped her … with directions going somewhere.

Lesbian/gay themes would also feature in the form of brief remarks, without necessarily generating extended discussion.

3.5 Joan: Just about every class the issue of sexuality comes up in some way or another … Whether it's, um, pictures that were useful for the lesson that day or, um, attitudes that Americans have about sexuality or … homophobic remarks about other students.

Taken together, these teachers' accounts suggest that lesbian/gay themes are far more prevalent than is evident in mainstream ESL literature, where they are rarely even mentioned.

A Prohibited Topic

Several teachers reported that colleagues at other educational institutions were discouraged, even prohibited, from discussing these themes in class.

3.6 Tom: I do know of a couple of situations where [teachers] have wanted to provide information and have been told not to, which I think has been fairly shocking … [At another educational institution] they did a fabulous … flyer … What if I'm gay, where do I go, how do I know, what should I do about gay people, blah blah … [It was in] simple English with some good referrals … [But the program director told the staff] not [to] distribute this information to students … because it was not the kind of thing that we should be talking about in our classes … [I think it should be] the unmarked case. You wanna know where the dry cleaners are, you wanna know where the gay bar is, I mean that kind of normalcy to the whole situation. We're not there yet.

This example raises the question of how much leeway teachers do or do not have in terms of disseminating accessible, practical information on gay matters to gay and straight students alike.

Another teacher noted that, at some educational institutions, discussing gay perspectives or issues in the classroom is completely forbidden under any circumstances.

3.7 Mark: I have friends who teach at [a nearby educational institution], and their administrative dictate is This is not to be discussed in the classroom. So the teachers aren't allowed to bring it up as a topic, and they're … [in] a gay neighborhood. So the students walk outside the door and see men holding hands … They're a block from a gay bar! … [But] they have a conservative administration … They see it as promoting a lifestyle.

In those teaching settings where it is considered contentious even to acknowledge the existence of gay/lesbian people, students and teachers alike would find themselves in the strange position of not being allowed to mention, let alone discuss, any observations, practices, or opinions linked to non-heterosexual identities. In contexts like that Mark described, where any mention of the same-sex couples just beyond the classroom door would be censored, it is difficult to imagine being able to create open, welcoming forums to foster language learning.

On the subject of exclusion, a comparison was made between issues of race and issues of sexual identity.

3.8 Clay: If a teacher's responsibility is … to include everybody in the class, most people would immediately say You don't have a right to exclude people on the basis of race. But people will implicitly say that you do have a right to exclude people on the basis of sexual identity. By saying Well we don't talk about it.

This raises the point that, generally in language education, exclusionary practices are rarely regarded as such when sexual identity is their target. In other words, there is little recognition that refusing to acknowledge or engage with sexual diversity is an act of exclusion.

On Excluding Lesbian and Gay Themes

The fact that teachers reported strong interest among students in talking about sexual diversity in class is hardly surprising, given the pervasiveness of queer themes in the media, on the Internet, and elsewhere (Cruz-Malavé & Manalansan, 2002a). The fact that teachers also reported decisions by some program administrators to prohibit queer-themed conversations in language classes warrants some discussion.

As Auerbach and Burgess (1985) and others have noted, it is important to consider not just explicit, overt curricula but also 'hidden curricula' because "what is *excluded* from curricula is as important in shaping students' perceptions of reality as what is *included*" (p. 480). In the *TESOL Matters* article mentioned in Chapter 1, Vandrick (1997b) argues that the common practice of excluding homosexuality, bisexuality, and transgenderalism from ESL curricula, textbooks, and research itself constitutes a form of homophobia. However, in a letter-to-the-editor, a reader dis-agrees: "Homophobia is a bigotry and not the absence of discussion about homo-sexuals in the classroom or in texts" (Ford, 1997, p. 6). According to Friend (1993; as cited in Dalley & Campbell, 2006), both bigotry *and* absence are forms of homo-phobia: heterosexist discourses operate through 'negative inclusion,' whereby gays and lesbians are mentioned but only in negative terms, and also through 'system-atic exclusion,' whereby any acknowledgments of gay and lesbian existence are rou-tinely excluded. While Chapter 4 looks at instances of negative inclusion, this chapter considers systematic exclusion, which may be less readily apparent but is no less problematic.

As Chan (1996) explains it,

> Outright homophobia can take the form of censorship of materials and denial of exposure to gay, lesbian, and bisexual issues. Sometimes this can take the form of not presenting information on sexuality in all its forms. Other times, it means pretending that homosexuality, lesbians, gay men, and bisexuals sim-ply do not exist, at least not in the classroom. More extreme versions of homo-phobia include censorship of books with gay and lesbian characters.
>
> (p. 22)

Of course, when lesbian, gay, and bisexual perspectives are excluded from the classroom context this does not mean that sexual identities are excluded, for straight perspectives remain prevalent. This is why I have referred to the "monosexualising tendencies" that dominate the research literature and learning materials of language education (Nelson, 2006, p. 1). Representing only heterosexuality can be considered a form of heterosexism:

> [H]eterosexism ... operates through silences and absences as well as through verbal and physical abuse or through overt discrimination. Indeed, one form of heterosexism discriminates by failing to recognize differences. It posits a totally and unambiguously heterosexual world in much the same way as cer-tain forms of racism posit the universality of whiteness. In this way, the dom-inant form is made to appear 'normal' and 'natural' and the subordinate form perverse, remarkable or dangerous.
>
> (Epstein & Johnson, 1994, p. 198)

Representing the world as "totally and unambiguously heterosexual" has the effect of making heterosexuality seem natural and any other sexualities or sexual identities seem unnatural. (For similar arguments about how racism is perpetu-ated through education and through other 'elite' forces such as the media and gov-ernment, see van Dijk, 1993.)

In other words, the practice of avoiding "any representations that might reveal the actual diversity and complexity of sexual choice" has the effect of normalizing only heterosexuality (Watney, 1991, pp. 394–395). Thus, heterosexist discourses operate by ostracizing 'homosexuals' from depictions of everyday "family life" and "the ordinary workaday world" (p. 391). Applying this to education contexts, prohibiting any talk of homosexuality has the effect (whether intended or not) of normalizing, or naturalizing, heterosexuality and denaturalizing homosexuality. As I have argued elsewhere, in language education, "excluding queer perspectives and knowledges from our classrooms and our [research] literature is, in effect, a way of enforcing compulsory heterosexuality, which hardly seems an appropriate role for language educators and researchers" (Nelson, 2006, p. 7).

It is worth noting also that both inclusive and exclusive discourses can be operating simultaneously within a given setting. In the special journal issue on 'Queer inquiry in language education' (Nelson, 2006), within each of the five education sites under investigation (in Australia, Brazil, Canada, and Japan), gay or lesbian themes were talked about, but within each context there were also various forces—sometimes subtle, sometimes blatant—that were working against these class discussions and conversations even taking place. As Carlson (2001) puts it, "[w]hat cannot be talked about or represented is very much part of the conversation and representation process" (p. 298).

For teachers working in environments like those described by Tom (3.6) and Mark (3.7), it would hardly seem a viable option to take part in this study. Thus, this book, in recounting what was said in language classes about (homo)sexual identities, must be read against the backdrop of what was not said, what could not be said.

Using Gay and Lesbian Themes in Teaching Language and Culture

In teaching lesbian and gay themes, some teachers focused on issues of language, which usually meant vocabulary development, while others focused on issues of 'culture,' such as cultural productions, cultural diversity, or cultural norms.

Teaching Language Involves Gay-Related Vocabulary and Meanings

Several teachers gave examples of their attempts to supplement class materials that make no mention whatsoever of gay people. Most examples involved vocabulary, often as part of curricula on family, relationships, or dating, all common topics in many language learning materials. Below, one teacher recounts how she introduced additional vocabulary in a beginning-level class during an exercise on 'family.'

> 3.9 Alicia: [In the textbook] all they had was … grandparents, parents … brother … sister … are married, is single … So we were just doing more words and so somebody said … husband and wife … Then I said Some people, you know, can't get married … So for, you know, men and men, or women and women- and then I said gay and straight, and then wrote gay and straight on the board, and then talked about what it meant to be gay and what it meant to be straight … That gay people were, you know, men who loved men, and women who loved women … And people got it. And you can always know because some people … laugh and then shift and get really uncomfortable … [But] most of the class was … OK …

> I think there's one guy in class who's gay. I'm SURE he's gay. You know, there's … the whole radar thing that's going [on]… big time since the first day in class. So he … watched the whole thing … without breathing for awhile, I think … Nobody said anything rude … One of the things that they were interested in was the fact that I would use the same word ['partner'] for … a couple that was gay, and for a couple that was straight.

Teachers can supplement the limited vocabulary presented in textbooks, as Alicia did, by introducing words associated with a range of contemporary relationships, thereby framing gay relationships as part of the social fabric. In so doing, some teachers may find themselves closely gauging reactions to the subject matter, especially from students who might themselves be gay or who might say something negative.

Tina, a student teacher, provided another example of including gay terms when teaching family vocabulary in EFL classes.

> 3.10 Tina: [I] gave a family tree where you have … Aunt Ruth and Aunt Sue. And that even brings up a vocabulary question of how do you refer to people in your family who are, you know, in sort of a gay marriage or gay relationship … It works well with my family tree because my family tree definitely has several gay couples in it. So that even puts names and faces on them if I bring my photo albums … I've had a lot of people asking questions. But the point was family vocabulary. The point was not Let's talk about gay and lesbian relationships.

Teachers can attempt to normalize gay/lesbian themes by integrating these throughout the curriculum and drawing on examples from one's own life.

A few teachers noted that students need to learn not only what is said but also what is not said.

> 3.11 Mark: A male student … was talking about his boyfriend … So I had to explain that to this student that Well actually in this culture if you say 'boyfriend' that has a gay overtone to it … You would just say 'my friend,' you'd use other terms, a male wouldn't use 'boyfriend' just to say one of their buddies. So it does become part of the instruction … A man has to know he can't say 'boyfriend,' whereas a woman can say 'girlfriend' and it doesn't have those connotations attached to it.

This teacher considered it important to make sure students understood the gay connotations of their speech, which highlights the potential ambiguities of communicating about sexual identities, especially for language learners. One way in which this ambiguity often arises in language classes is through gendered pronouns. It may seem that a pronoun has been used in error—for instance, if a man says "I love him" (see Prologue)—but it may be the case that the speaker is simply speaking about a same-sex partner. Thus, the challenge would be to make students aware of those language acts that connote gayness but without framing gayness as negative.

On the Dearth of Lesbian/Gay Representations

Evident in Mark's explanation to a student of what 'boyfriend' means "in this culture" (see 3.11) is the fact that language needs to be understood within a sociocultural context. Teaching language can be understood to mean teaching language *in* culture, since these two domains are "codeterminable, the one offering explanation for the other" (Candlin, 1989, p. 10), or teaching language *as* culture (Kramsch, 1993), or even teaching 'languaculture' (Agar, 1994). Sarangi (1995) proposes that "it is ... instructive to approach the language-culture relationship in a discursive mode, because it is discourse that 'creates, recreates, focuses, modifies, and transmits both culture and language and their interaction'" (pp. 21–22, quoting Sherzer, 1987, p. 295).

'Discourse' has become a somewhat ambiguous term because it is used to describe texts, language types, systems of power/knowledge (Fairclough, 1992), and broad systems of meaning and interpretation (see Sunderland, 2004). As Foucault (1981) has famously put it, "[d]iscourse is not simply that which translates struggles or systems of domination, but is the thing for which and by which there is struggle, discourse is the power which is to be seized" (pp. 52–53). Pennycook (1994) distinguishes a Foucauldian framework from that of critical linguists (following Fairclough) as follows:

> It [Foucauldian analysis] is not concerned with how discourses (texts) reflect social reality, but how discourses produce social realities; it does not look for relationships between discourse and society/politics, but rather theorizes discourse as always/already political; it does not seek out an ultimate cause or basis for power and inequality, but rather focuses on the multiplicity of sites through which power operates; and it does not posit a reality outside discourse, but rather looks to the discursive production of truth.
>
> (Pennycook, 1994, p. 131)

It follows that classroom discourses about gay and lesbian people do not passively reflect social realities but actively constitutes those realities, and the social inequities associated with sexual diversity are not just described with language but produced through it.

As we have seen, some teachers in my study would update and expand the lexical range for describing relationships and families that appears in typical learning materials. Shardakova and Pavlenko (2004) critique foreign and second language textbooks (in their case, Russian) for promoting compulsive heterosexuality by constructing learners—and their imagined interlocutors—as almost exclusively straight. Also noted has been the general dearth of gay and lesbian representations in French-, Italian- and Japanese-language textbooks (De Vincenti et al., 2007) and transgender representations in English-language textbooks (Jewell, 1998). Shardakova and Pavlenko (2004) argue that such voids "obfuscate the lives of [...] sexual minorities, and thus disallow rich discussions of the status of these individuals in the two societies [L1 and L2]" (p. 38). They recommend expanding the "identity repertoires" in language textbooks by "offering more terms that signify currently 'hidden' racial and sexual identities" (p. 42).

Silencing Practices

A key tenet of poststructuralism is that what is excluded exists alongside what is included, what is not said exists alongside what is said. Silence is not apart from discourse but part of discourse:

> Silence itself—the things one declines to say, or is forbidden to name, the discretion that is required between different speakers—is less the absolute limit of discourse, the other side from which it is separated by a strict boundary, than an element that functions alongside the things said, with them and in relation to them ... There is no binary division to be made between what one says and what one does not say; we must try to determine the different ways of not saying such things, how those who can and those who cannot speak of them are distributed, which type of discourse is authorized or which form of discretion is required in either case.
>
> (Foucault, 1990, p. 27)

Thus, silence is understood to be multiple rather than singular, active rather than passive: "There is not one but many silences, and they are an integral part of the strategies that underlie and permeate discourse" (Foucault, 1990, p. 27).

At times, language learners may require explicit discussion of what is *not* usually said (or written) (see 2.9, 3.11, and 4.26). Thus, language learners and teachers may sometimes need to talk about the sorts of things Foucault mentions, such as what people mean by what they do not say, what is considered unacceptable or undesirable to say, and how these choices depend on one's interlocutors and the nature of one's relationship with them. At the same time, having these sorts of discussions can be somewhat fraught, given the complexities of learning what 'not to say.' According to Bourdieu (1991), the process of socialization includes more than just learning to say or not to say—it includes learning not even to *think* to say, or to participate in what Bourdieu calls 'discourses of denial.'

In terms of lesbian/gay themes in language education contexts, what is not said may indicate a zone of unthinkability. When Alicia taught the words 'gay,' 'straight,' and 'partner' in a beginning-level ESL class (see 3.9), it is possible that some students had been wanting to learn these words but had never once thought that it might be possible to raise the topic in an ESL class. Similarly, Mark may never have thought to ask the male student who was speaking of his boyfriend whether he was in fact speaking of his lover (see 3.11). Thus, integrating lesbian/gay themes means working within, and against, what Butler (1991) calls a "domain of unthinkability and unnameability" (p. 20), similar to Bourdieu's 'discourse of denial.'

To take this point further, in those language classes or programs in which references to anyone gay or anything gay-related are rare, it is possible to equate this particular absence or silence with a lack, a void, a non-event, but it is also possible to look at it as an activity, a fullness, a permeating presence, indicating that much is going on covertly, even unthinkingly, to ensure that any gay references are disallowed. This point may be illustrated through a quote from novelist Toni Morrison (albeit about a different subject):

> Looking at the scope of American literature, I can't help thinking that the question should never have been "Why am I, an Afro-American, absent from it?" … [but] "What intellectual feats had to be performed by the author or his critic to erase me … and what effect has that performance had on the work?" What are the strategies of escape from knowledge? Of willful oblivion?
> (Morrison, 1989, pp. 11–12, as quoted in Holland, 1994, p. 175)

Such questions reinforce the notion that silencing practices are active and involve the de-valuing of certain 'discursive agents' (see Jaworski, 1997).

Applying this thinking to my investigation here, the question is not "Why are gay/lesbian/queer perspectives and themes absent from so much language education literature (and some language programs)?," but rather "What feats have been, and are still being, performed by language-education practitioners to erase these perspectives and themes?" And, most crucially, "*What effects are these acts of erasure having on the teaching and learning of languages?*"

Yet in a way, at a rudimentary level it is difficult to imagine a language class without any references to same-sex relationships since grammatical errors to do with gender are a frequent occurrence for those learning a second or foreign language. It is not always clear whether a student is making a grammar, pronunciation, or spelling mistake, or is intentionally coming out. Similar to Mark's 'boyfriend' example (3.11), De Vincenti et al. (2007) give the example of a male student learning French saying "Mon petit ami est japonais" ("My boyfriend is Japanese"); a teacher might need to consider whether the student meant to refer to a male partner—or whether he meant to say instead "Ma petite amie est japonaise" ("My girlfriend is Japanese"), in which case the teacher might wish to point out the error. A similar example, also from a French language class, is provided by Ladenson (1998).

Teaching 'Culture' Involves Gay and Lesbian Themes

The teachers in my study reported that gay and lesbian themes arose in the course of studying not only 'language' but also 'culture.' This occurred in three main ways: using cultural productions or artifacts with gay themes as learning materials; teaching about sexual diversity as part of a broader focus on cultural diversity or multiculturalism; and making explicit culture-based rules, norms, and signifying practices associated with sexual identities.

As to the first point, cultural productions such as films and television programs are widely used as a common source of 'authentic' language learning materials. Because sexual diversity often features within cultural productions and the media, gay and lesbian themes sometimes would become the prominent aspect of a lesson even though this was not the teacher's intended focus.

Ursula, for example, felt uncomfortable teaching lesbian and gay themes (see 4.3 and 5.28), but these arose in class nonetheless. Her listening class was based on television programs; one week the class happened to watch an episode of a situation comedy

('Ellen') that received extensive media coverage because the lead character comes out as a lesbian. (Below Ursula refers to the television network's controversial decision to run a 'viewer discretion advised' warning immediately preceding the show.)

> 3.12 Ursula: Ellen's coming out party was actually in my class supposed to be a media unit but needless to say it took a huge turn ... The whole world was talking about it ... Their homework was to watch that and then we talked about it. And, you know, our friends and how people respond to that, was that controversial 'viewer discretion' offensive ... [This lesson] wasn't meant to be a thing about gay issues but it ended up being one.

There is clearly a need to consider how to accommodate and frame gay or lesbian content when its emergence in class is unexpected (see Chapter 7) or even undesired (see Chapter 4).

A number of teachers reported that it was common for sexual diversity to be incorporated into curriculum on cultural diversity.

> 3.13 Alicia: The curriculum ... usually centers around cultural diversity ... So ... somebody always comes up with gays and lesbians [as a topic] ... [W]hen they go on to other [post-ESL] classes they're gonna need to be able to discuss these kinds of things without having to make a face and without, um, laughing ... [So I tell them] If you wanna study ... in the United States you're gonna have to ... get past that kind of thing.

A number of other teachers also mentioned that their second-language students needed to become familiar with local norms and expectations concerning talking with, and about, lesbian/gay people so that they would not inadvertently offend an interlocutor. Claire called this 'political correctness.'

> 3.14 Claire: [Students] have a lot of questions and a lot of silliness around what they see [locally], who's gay, who isn't, lots of teasing back and forth between them ... That's an opportunity to say ... Look ... if you say that word you're really gonna get this kind of reaction ... We're just so much more trained to be politically correct and sensitive to that than our students who are just so honest and direct. (Claire laughs) ... I mean they'll just say things. And we have to tell them No no no, you can't just say things! (we laugh)

Claire emphasized that showing respect sometimes means silencing oneself, so learning a language involves learning the local or target norms of what not to do or say. Another teacher, Tom, made a similar point about the importance of learning what he called 'etiquette.'

Janice also made a similar point about the need for second-language students to learn what she called 'cultural fluency.'

3.15 Janice: I think that … what we're striving to do is teach cultural fluency. And I think that a big part of cultural fluency is to let students know very early on about vocabulary and about things that we consider to be OK and not OK. You know, telling jokes about, um, certain groups … Because a lot of our students … don't understand that. […] [It also means] being able to … understand where Americans are coming from. So … if they go to a bar … they can … figure out what's happening … Because a lot of our students, they don't even know that they've gone into a gay bar. Because they're just not oriented toward that.

Mike: In their own country they'll find a bar of all men and (M laughs) it won't be a gay bar, so they would think it was the same thing.

Thus, learning some local cultural practices associated with lesbian and gay people can help students make sense of what is going on around them.

Cultural Productions, Cultural Diversity, Cultural Norms

In studying 'culture,' which is common in second and foreign language programs, it is not surprising that issues of sexual identity sometimes arise. Indeed, queer theorists consider the homosexual/heterosexual binary to function as "a central category of knowledge," which structures social conventions and practices, and is as powerful and pervasive as other well-recognized binaries such as "bourgeois/proletariat and masculine/feminine" (Seidman, 1995, p. 132). Thus even teachers who, like Ursula (3.12), feel uncomfortable with lesbian/gay themes are likely to find themselves having to deal with these themes in the classroom, given their prevalence in the media and other public spheres of civil life. Moreover, as Alicia (3.13) reported, and as we shall see in Chapter 7, sexual diversity may arise within discussions of social diversity or multiculturalism, which tend to be common study topics in language education. Importantly, it is not only in 'Western' education contexts that what King (2002) calls 'global gay formations and local homosexualities' are becoming part of classroom discourse. For example, a recent study from a university in Taiwan reports that a student majoring in English wrote a research paper on the topic of "Gays and lesbians: Creating and raising their own family" (Hsu, 2006, p. 87); see also classroom studies from Brazil (Moita-Lopes, 2006) and Japan (Ó'Móchain, 2006), among others.

In addition to cultural productions and cultural diversity, language classes often discuss cultural norms. Teachers in my study referred to 'political correctness' (to be discussed further in Chapter 4) and 'cultural fluency' in explaining why they sought to develop their students' cultural knowledge about gay/lesbian matters. The teachers' reports of students' laughter, jokes and 'teasing' about gay people highlight the need to familiarize students with the social rules, usually implicit and unspoken, that determine what can and cannot be said—in this case, in relation to gay/lesbian/straight significations within the local (or target) culture.

In terms of how to approach these matters pedagogically, it is worth noting that in most of the teachers' accounts presented thus far, there seems to be a tendency to inform students of "the way we do things here" (Auerbach, 1995, p. 18). However, the case I wish to make is that a fairly straightforward, teacher-to-student transmission approach is not necessarily sufficient, since learning to identify and negotiate implicit social/sexual conventions and practices can be a complex process.

Some factors that need to be taken into account include whose cultural norms and expectations are being taught, and how (and by whom) cultural fluency is to be determined. Holliday's (1999) distinction between large and small cultures is pertinent here. With a 'large culture' approach the pedagogic focus is "'other' or 'foreign' directed"; students learn about "one, predefined, 'target' ethnic, national or international culture" within which they must operate (p. 259). However, with a 'small culture' approach, the pedagogic focus is on "searching for, demarcating and observing the interaction between several cultures within a target scenario" (p. 260). A similar point is made by Candlin (1989), who advocates a "focus on inter-cultural understanding rather than on cross-cultural accumulating" (p. 10) (see also Sarangi, 1995). (This distinction will be further illustrated in Chapters 6 and 8.)

With regard to teaching cultural norms, another important point is that descriptions of culture do not merely reflect culture but actively produce it. As Holliday (1999) explains it, "group members' statements *about* 'culture' or 'their culture' should be seen as products or artefacts *of* the culture, expressing how they socially construct their image of their own culture, rather than a direct description of their culture" (p. 253). In this sense, culture is not a static entity but a living, changing matrix of forces that is continually being co-created and transformed. This conceptualization of culture further underscores the point that addressing the cultural aspects of sexual identities may require some discussion – particularly if the goal is not to "[make] learners expert at following pre-set paths [but to] promote their own capacities to draw their own maps" (Candlin, 1987, p. 17). (This point will be elaborated on in Chapter 4, where I argue that in the intercultural arenas of language classes, what is called for is not so much telling students what constitutes potentially offensive or insulting speech, but teaching them how to manage and negotiate interactions in which rules about 'correctness' are not shared.)

Though studying cultural (and linguistic) norms may be an integral part of learning a second or foreign language, it can also be a fraught one. Some teachers may share Tina's concern that to acknowledge sexual diversity might be interpreted by students as "being sort of culturally imperialist, ... saying ... I have my views and I'm gonna make you listen to them" (see 2.12). O'Loughlin (2001) reports that some teachers "will not broach the topic of homosexuality in the classroom as they are concerned it will be offensive to learners from some cultural backgrounds" (p. 39). O'Loughlin considers this view problematic, pointing out that it may derive more from the teachers' own discomfort with the subject matter rather than their students' discomfort, and that it is patronizing to characterize language learners as ignorant of sexual diversity or incapable of forming their own opinions or exercising agency regarding this topic.

A similar argument is made by Chamberlain (2004), who notes that over the past few decades, "everyday English culture" has become much more "sexually overt" (p. 51); as an example, he cites the international distribution (in Argentina, Japan, many Arab countries, and elsewhere) of the US television show 'Friends', with its lesbian character (Ross's ex-wife). Given the sexualisation of English, teachers need to be willing to address what he calls 'vulgar English,' so that students are better prepared for potentially embarrassing or even threatening situations. His argument is that learners of English may need to learn about "vulgar language" and its gradations.

The important question, then, is not whether the sociosexual aspects of cultural practices ought to be addressed in the classroom, but how this might be done. Ó'Móchain (2006) takes up the issue of creating "context-appropriate" ways of discussing gender and sexuality within educational institutions or regions in which open discussions of sexuality are rare and not necessarily welcome. He sought to incorporate lesbian/gay themes into his EFL class in Japan, but to do so in a way that would challenge the notion that homosexuality is a 'Western' phenomenon (see also Valentine, 1997; Kumashiro, 2002). Ó'Móchain (2006) had his class analyze the life-history narratives of gay and lesbian students (and teachers) from the same region as the students in the class (western Japan), thereby focusing on "queer lives in the local context, not as something relevant to people far away whom students could never imagine meeting or interacting with, nor as something that could be over-simplified in dichotomizations of East and West" (p. 53). He recommends that foreign-language teachers make use of "narratives of real people whose geographical and sociohistorical backgrounds are similar to those of the students, and whose life experiences problematize dominant notions of 'normal' gender and sexuality" (p. 63); and he points out that such narratives are widely available on the Internet, or could be obtained by students through interviewing locals.

Toward Queer Inquiry

Teachers in my study spoke about using lesbian/gay themes in teaching language/culture, as we have seen, but they also spoke about related matters such as whether social tolerance should be considered a legitimate teaching aim; how gay/lesbian themes could be normalized and how the presumption of heterosexuality could itself become the subject matter; how sexual stereotypes could be challenged; and why it is limiting to consider sexual identity just a 'social issue' for the classroom.

Teaching Tolerance and Normalizing Gay/Lesbian Themes

Janice mentioned that exploring lesbian/gay themes in class could enhance not only students' cultural fluency (see 3.15) but also their 'personal growth.'

> 3.16 Janice: And then there's ... personal growth ... Because they [international students] are exposed to ... different ways of being when they're in the US.

In the above quote, Janice was referring to students, but she also observed that she herself had experienced significant personal development from thinking through the implications of sexual identity issues for language teaching (see 5.15).

Some teachers said, or intimated, that in teaching gay themes they hoped to foster greater tolerance for social diversity generally. It was Paige who made this point most explicitly.

3.17 Paige: I don't want people to be bigoted towards lesbians and gays or hateful toward them. Especially if it's coming out of ignorance. Or any kind of related hatred based on race or religion or ... that kind of thing. So whenever I bring topics like that up, I do hope to have people open their eyes wider and perhaps take on a more accepting or tolerant attitude ... [Also] it's really fun ... to talk about issues that students ... get really engaged in ... (P laughs) It makes for a very lively class.

To Paige, issues of sexual identity were understood to be issues of social justice. While changing attitudes was not her sole motivation for teaching gay/lesbian themes, which in themselves generated high student interest, it was a hoped-for result.

However, not all of the teachers in my study found gay and lesbian topics pleasurable and engaging, as Paige did.

3.18 Jo: It can be an uncomfortable topic ... There's always that [fear] that you're gonna get, um, a lot of negative resistance [from students]. [...] The more I teach the more I don't feel like I'm God and I can change their attitudes and I should change their attitudes ... I can't want my student to change. I mean if he feels ... that he wouldn't want his friend to be gay, I can't spend class time trying to convince him not. I mean that's not fair.

Jo's reluctance to use gay topics in class was linked to her fear that anti-gay attitudes would arise and need to be dealt with in some way, but she did not consider it her goal, or her role, to try to change students' attitudes.

Janice responded to Jo's comments as follows:

3.19 Janice: [That] can be counterproductive too ... the whole idea of having an agenda and getting your student to change. Because our students ... do suspect that there's an agenda. That's why I feel like this is a topic that shouldn't necessarily be a topic ... it should be an ongoing thing ... [Otherwise, it's like] only doing Black History during February. Why isn't it ... just ongoing? [...] [For example] in your Business English class, you can ... mention that [a local business is] run by gay people and ... it's a successful business.

Janice took the view that gay and lesbian themes and people ought to be mentioned throughout the curricula, not necessarily framed as a discrete topic of study.

Tina also spoke about integrating gay and lesbian themes throughout curricula and materials, but she emphasized the value of not making gayness the main issue.

3.20 Tina: [If it's] OK we're gonna talk about gay issues ... it can get so heavy that people are afraid to say anything or do anything. Or take risks in any way, or kind of be humorous about it. But ... I just think that's the whole idea, kind of working [gay] things in and having that not be the point. But having it be A point ... If you figure ... 10% of the world is gay, so 10% of your things should have something ... about gays or lesbians. Or even not the topic, not ABOUT gays or lesbians, but a family tree should have a [gay] couple.

For Tina it was important to incorporate lesbian/gay content throughout the curriculum, but to do so with a certain degree of levity so that participants were not silenced by a fear of offending.

Though most teachers in this study spoke about integrating lesbian/gay characters, perspectives, issues, or themes into classroom talk and tasks, one teacher drew students' attention to their own assumptions about the presumed heterosexuality of characters in a class reading.

3.21 Sophie: [In class] we read that poem about the woman whose lover left her, and there's no pronoun ... I said ... Was her lover male or female? And they said Well male, of course. And I said Well how do you know? And we went through the poem ... The only clues (S laughs) were that this person wore shorts and ate steak ... So it was not much, it was just ... Why ... assume that her lover is a man?

This example illustrates that rethinking language teaching practices in light of sexual identities and inequities can mean not just adding gay/lesbian subject matter but also making the heterosexual presumption itself a subject worth examining.

The Question of Educational Aims

The teachers quoted above raise some crucial questions about what the underlying aims are, or ought to be, with regard to sexual identities in language education.

Recall the comments by Paige (3.17) and Jo (3.18) about attitude change. On the one hand, Paige's desire to foster in her students "a more accepting or tolerant attitude" (about sexual diversity in particular and social diversity in general) seems to directly oppose Jo's declaration that she's "not God" and "can't want" to change her students' attitudes. The one teacher hopes to change students' attitudes and the other teacher does not; the one enjoys lesbian/gay themes and the other does not. On the other hand, the two teachers have something in common, in that both focus on students' attitudes, viewpoints, or feelings toward the subject matter at hand, rather than other aspects, such as the students' ability to communicate effectively or think critically about the subject matter.

If the underlying teaching aim is understood to be promoting tolerance, then some teachers, like Jo, are likely to find that problematic and may steer clear of lesbian/gay themes altogether. This may limit learning opportunities for students since sexual diversity features within day-to-day interactions across family, work, and public domains. If instead the underlying teaching aim is understood to be promoting language/culture learning, then for some teachers it may seem feasible to work with material or topics involving lesbian/gay characters and issues, same-sex relationships and families, and sexual identity practices and inequities. (This distinction should become clearer in Chapter 4, which examines the three main approaches that teachers took in responding to anti-gay comments in class.)

While most of the teachers in this study spoke of gay or lesbian 'topics' as if these were self-evident, discrete, bounded matters that in the course of teaching language might arise occasionally, regularly, or not at all, a few teachers understood sexualities and sexual identities, meanings and implications, to have more of a permeating presence throughout the curricula and classroom interactions.

Integrating Gay/Lesbian Themes Throughout the Curriculum

On the topic of integrating gay/lesbian themes throughout the curriculum, it was suggested that these themes might be mentioned in the context of discussing other themes (such as local businesses or family trees). Janice's (3.19) example (mentioning that a successful business was run by gay people) involved highlighting gayness, whereas Tina's (3.10) example (including a gay couple in a family tree) involved not making an issue of gayness but just 'slipping it in' as if it were ordinary. Tina cited the widely accepted statistic that at least 10% of a given population is not straight, a statistic which led Chan (1996) to observe that at every level of educational institutions—from preschool to advanced graduate studies—"one tenth of the population had previously been invisible or underrepresented" (p. 22).

Most teachers in my study set about addressing the dearth of gay/lesbian perspectives in curricula by bringing in those perspectives, which in some cases proved awkward. (Recall Tina's attempt to supplement the countless heterosexual dating references: "If a man's going to ask his girlfriend or his boyfriend depending on whatever" [2.12].) An alternative to adding absent representations (in this case, gay or lesbian relationships) is drawing attention to those that are generally unmarked but relentlessly present (straight relationships), as Sophie did above (3.21).

This shift in emphasis draws on a central tenet of poststructuralism—that dominant norms may appear to be stable and solid, but they actually require constant affirmation in order to continue as 'common sense' (Weedon, 1987). Thus, the prevalence of heterosexual representations is an indication not of how 'natural' heterosexuality is, but of just how much constant public affirmation is required to maintain heterosexual identity as a cohesive, naturalized identity.

Another option is to try not to impose presumptions of heterosexuality. Elsewhere I have relayed how a teacher of Italian as a foreign language began to change her teaching practices after reading queer theory:

> When having the class role-play various scenarios involving a family, she used to elicit volunteers for the parts of father, mother, and children, but this time she simply asked her students to form their own family groupings for the role-play. Much to her surprise, two students bounced up and said they would be portraying a family that consisted of two lesbians, then on went

the role-plays—which not only led to stimulating class discussions but also reinvigorated her own passion for teaching … I think [this anecdote] can be read as an inspiration for our field: rethinking our habitual heteronormative practices can open up new spaces for exploring language and learning.

(Nelson, 2006, p. 8)

What this teacher did, or rather, did not do, was quite simple, but it had the effect of opening up a space for students to role-play a family configuration outside the heteronormative model.

Challenging Stereotypes About Lesbian/Gay People

A number of teachers invited openly gay or lesbian guest speakers into their classes (especially conversation and speaking/listening classes, where guest speakers were a common teaching tool). Mark described a student's reaction to lesbian speakers who had been invited into a conversation class at the students' request.

> 3.22 Mark: I think it's really important for [students] to put a face to the issue … This one Korean woman … had a problem with the whole topic of gay and lesbian issues. And then these two women came to class [as guest speakers] and she really liked one of the women and had to deal with the fact that she liked her as a person and she was a lesbian. And that was a real learning experience for her so I thought that was real valuable.

Interacting with a lesbian guest speaker unsettled this student's negative view of 'lesbian/gay people' in the abstract.

Another teacher also reported that inviting a gay guest speaker into her conversation classes had the effect of challenging students' stereotypes.

> 3.23 Ursula: This friend of mine that comes [to class], he's a banker. And so he comes in his suit and they're always really shocked. And they say How does he keep a job like that? And so … those things are just really visual confrontations of their stereotypes … which I think is really helpful … [to] put a face on it.

Others, however, found that using gay guest speakers to challenge student stereotypes can be problematic.

> 3.24 Janice: One term we had, um, three different classes … doing, um, this topic. And one class brought in [a gay/lesbian youth group]. They were SO alternative looking. They were very young and they came in with lots of piercing and tattoos and the students were … really shocked. And [the teacher] felt like it just had not been successful … She felt like she just showed the sort of marginalized group that, um.
>
> Mike: She was trying to communicate was not a marginalized group.

> Janice: Yeah. Whereas the other classes that had brought in people who were, you know, parents, and all different kinds of, you know, that were not as easily identifiable [as gay or lesbian]. They found that that was more successful.

There is the possibility that gay guest speakers will conform to, rather than challenge, student stereotypes of gay people, which raises the question of which gay/lesbian representations are brought into curricula.

Within a unit of work on lesbian/gay culture, Mike took his students on a field trip (a common activity in this program). But again, questions of representation became problematic.

> 3.25 Mike: I think … people to people contact is the best thing … I took [a class] to [a gay/lesbian bookstore] and that was wonderful … The manager … talked a little too fast but he was trying hard … to really, you know, meet up with these students … Of course then he let (M laughs) us go into the bookstore and that was great too except (M laughs) they found the porno section right away … I suppose I have an agenda … I don't want them to see what I feel their stereotype might be … [which is gay men] always wanting sex.

If the aim is to confront student stereotypes through personalizing the issue, then it becomes problematic if what students see confirms rather than challenges their stereotypes.

The Notion of Stereotyping

As shown above, a number of the teachers sought to challenge students' stereotypes about lesbian and gay people by arranging face-to-face encounters. This approach is aligned with the widely held belief summarized below by Chan (1996):

> Psychological research indicates that it is far easier and more common to hold negative attitudes toward members of a stigmatized group if you do not know or feel connected to someone, if you cannot see their humanity and similarity to yourself. When … students are not familiar with lesbian and gay people, either in real life or as characters in books, it is easier to continue to hold negative attitudes toward [them].
>
> (p. 23)

However, the success of this approach seems to depend on the suitability—in this case, the (straight-appearing) respectability—of the group representatives being put forward. This highlights the limitations of what Britzman (1995) has called 'pedagogies of inclusion,' which she critiques for parading 'authentic' images of lesbians in the hope of transforming negative attitudes about them, while doing little to challenge the underlying systems that mark social difference.

By contrast, what I have called 'pedagogies of inquiry' (Nelson, 1999) might involve taking into account the effects of stereotyping on communication. R. Scollon and S. W. Scollon (1995) argue that stereotyping can impede communication—especially interculturally. This is because it takes "just one or two salient dimensions … to be the whole picture" (p. 156). Stereotyping "does not acknowledge internal differences within a group, and does not acknowledge exceptions to its general rule" (p. 156). When crucial differences are overlooked, mutual understanding may be falsely assumed (p. 161). In sum, overgeneralizing can lead to communication difficulties. If language learners have a certain mental image or stereotype of how a gay person looks, talks, or acts, as the teachers above have intimated, then they may (falsely) presume their interlocutors are straight and go ahead and say things that they would not say if they realized that they were, or could be, speaking to a gay or lesbian person (or about to have their assignment assessed by one; see Chapter 5).

In addition to the potential for miscommunication, a second aspect of stereotyping that could be explored pedagogically has to do with its social functions. The teachers in my study considered sexual stereotyping to be an exclusively negative phenomenon, but as Misson (1996) explains,

> [W]e all in one sense are stereotypes in that we present ourselves to be read as particular kinds of people … [W]e tend to assert our unanimity with particular groups by dressing and acting in particular ways. There are a lot of gay people who don't fit into, say, the camp stereotype, but there are also a lot who quite happily do, and who flaunt it as a sign of belonging, of group solidarity. So, one doesn't want to suggest that there is anything wrong or limited with people who fit the stereotype, at the same time as not wanting to suggest that the stereotype is the essential truth about gay people.
>
> (p. 124)

This quote hints at the idea of sexual identities as 'performative,' which will be elaborated upon in Chapter 5, but the point I wish to stress here is that it may be productive in the classroom to discuss not only the limitations of stereotyping but also its socially constructive functions or purposes (more on this in Chapter 7).

Saville-Troike (1982) observes that 'social typing' facilitates social interactions:

> Social 'typing' or categorization is probably a necessary part of our procedures for coping with the outside world … If we did not 'know' how to relate appropriately to different groups of people before we were acquainted with them personally, we would be socially ineffective … Social typing should thereby be seen as a potentially positive and in any case inevitable process. The typing may assume negative aspects, however … [and] become a means of disaffiliation or rejection, or of rationalizing prejudice.
>
> (p. 182)

She also makes the point that the judgments produced through stereotyping can provide valuable insights not about those being typed so much as those doing the typing (pp. 183–184).

It follows that in class, instead of merely including gay or lesbian 'representatives' in the hope of their making a positive impression on students, it may be useful to foster inquiry about the purposes and effects of stereotyping. That is, when inferences are made about people on the basis of their (actual or perceived) sexual identity, how is communication impeded or enhanced? It may also be helpful to shift the object of inquiry away from those being stereotyped (its objects) and onto those doing the stereotyping (its agents); for example, if you were surprised to discover that you actually liked a lesbian, or that gay men work as bankers, never mind what you have learned about lesbians or gay men—what have you learned about yourself? Another option would be for teachers to discuss with the class their own motives and difficulties in terms of finding, or creating, suitable gay or lesbian representatives (either in person or in learning materials) who, for example, display neither tattoos nor an interest in pornography.

The Trouble with Inclusion

Britzman (1995) argues that most work on gay/lesbian issues in education advocates 'pedagogies of inclusion,' introducing "authentic images of gays and lesbians" into the curriculum in order to provide information and change attitudes (p. 158). It is hoped that straight students will learn to tolerate those who are 'different' and that gay and lesbian students will gain self-esteem through exposure to positive role models (p. 158). This model seems to describe the approaches of many teachers in this study. However, according to Britzman (1995), an inclusion approach is problematic. To understand her argument, it is necessary to consider two ideas that are central to queer theory: first, that categories of sexual identity are interdependent and hierarchical; and second, that affirming sexual identities in effect upholds the hierarchical binary system of hetero/homosexuality. Each point will be elaborated below.

The aim of lesbian/gay identity politics is to legitimate homosexuality (see Chapter 1). This has been approached primarily in two ways: by asserting that lesbian/gay people are basically the same as straight people (liberalism), or by asserting that lesbian/gay people are fundamentally different from straight people (separatism) (Seidman, 1995). Queer theorists argue that both of these options are limited. The aim of queer theory is not to legitimate homosexuality by asserting either its sameness or its difference to heterosexuality but to draw attention to and question the practice of categorizing and classifying people according to sexual identity. In other words, with queer theory the main concern has shifted away from "the repression or expression of a homosexuality minority" toward developing "an analysis of the hetero/homosexual figure as a power/knowledge regime that shapes the ordering of desires, behaviors, and social institutions, and social relations—in a word, the constitution of the self and society" (Seidman, 1995, p. 128).

Queer theorists think of sexual identity not as a property but as a discursive relation (Fuss, 1989). This means that "the assertion of one identity category presupposes, incites, and excludes its opposite. The declaration of heterosexual selfhood elicits its opposite, indeed needs the homosexual in order to be coherent and bounded" (Seidman, 1995, p. 127). Heterosexuality would have no meaning without homosexuality (and vice versa). This is because "persons or objects acquire identities only in contrast to what they are not. The affirmation of an identity entails the production and exclusion of that which is different or the creation of otherness.

This otherness, though, is never truly excluded or silenced; it is present in identity and haunts it as its limit or impossibility" (Seidman, 1995, p. 130, citing Fuss, 1989).

Thus, producing an identity inevitably produces an 'other,' and that 'other' is always necessarily present, even when it is apparently silenced or excluded. Butler (1990) explains this paradox: "for heterosexuality to remain intact as a distinct social form, it *requires* an intelligible conception of homosexuality and also requires the prohibition of that conception in rendering it culturally unintelligible ... The 'unthinkable' is thus fully within culture, but fully excluded from *dominant* culture" (p. 77). Paradoxically, homosexuality must be made both intelligible *and* unintelligible, thinkable *and* unthinkable, at one and the same time. So heterosexuality requires homosexuality—even as it repudiates it. "To the extent that individuals feel compelled to define themselves as hetero-or-homosexual, they erect boundaries and protective identities which are self-limiting and socially controlling," which "inevitably give[s] rise to systems of dominance and hierarchy" (Seidman, 1995, pp. 126–127). Thus, the function of the straight/gay binary is not merely to describe sexual identities but to regulate them. It is not neutral but normative, or heteronormative (a concept that will be discussed in Chapter 4).

The second point about the straight/gay binary follows from the first. Although affirming marginalized sexual identities may appear to oppose systems of dominance, in a way it supports them. Following Foucault, Butler (1990) sees "marginalised identities [as] complicit with those identificatory regimes they seek to counter" (Jagose, 1996, p. 83). To put it another way, naming a group in order to protect it from discrimination seems, paradoxically, to make discrimination possible. Similarly, opposing discriminatory regimes may serve, paradoxically, to reinforce their dominant, hegemonic status. As Lather (1991) explains it, "overtly positional work, while at war with dominant systems of knowledge production, is also inscribed in what it hopes to transform" (pp. 25–26, drawing on Foucault, 1980). One of the tenets of poststructuralism, then, is the need to look at "the ways in which you are complicit with what you are so carefully and cleanly opposing" (Spivak, 1990, p. 122).

According to poststructuralist thinking, there is no outside of 'ideology,' no escape from regimes of power/knowledge. Indeed, there is the danger of simply replacing one oppressive regime with another, as Gore (1993) and other educators have noted. Pedagogically, the aim is to get beyond "'us versus them' and 'liberation' versus 'oppression'" in order to deal with "a multi-centered discourse with differential access to power" (Lather, 1991, p. 25). Power, in this sense, is conceptualized as "localized, decentered, diversified, and always contested" (Canagarajah, 1993, p. 211; see Foucault, 1980). Schenke (1996) applies these concepts to ELT, arguing that there is a need to "search out and challenge our implications, as teachers, in the very discourses of transformation we otherwise seek to contest" (p. 158), which again underscores the need for self-reflexivity about these matters.

A Whole Pedagogy

One teacher/teacher-educator who had taken part in the focus group at TESOL found it problematic that lesbian/gay subject matter and homophobia were being discussed merely as 'social issues.' In her view, matters to do with sexual identities permeate every aspect of teaching and were not merely 'issues' that came up on occasion. She tried to articulate a broader vision.

> 3.26 Tess: Isn't it a whole pedagogy? … It's more than just an issue, a social issue that is raised … I think it's easy for [straight teachers] to … say that it's an issue. But … you are located in a whole set of … social relations and … political concerns that … inform your whole curriculum. How you present what, … how you respond to students, … the questions you raise.

When matters of sexual identity are considered to be 'already/always' present throughout curricula, then it becomes important not only to include gay themes but to consider a host of choices, such as which content gets selected or rejected; how information is presented; what questions and tasks are put to students; what sorts of (verbal and nonverbal) messages are conveyed, and so on (these sorts of things are examined in Chapters 6–8).

Fostering Queer Inquiry

I have proposed elsewhere that a gay-identity framework is less suited to language education than a queer-informed approach: "Queer theory shifts the focus from gaining civil rights to analysing discursive and cultural practices, from affirming minority sexual identities to problematising all sexual identities. Pedagogies of inclusion thus become pedagogies of inquiry" (Nelson, 1999, p. 373). This argument draws on Britzman's (1995) critique of pedagogies that seek to teach (or even preach) inclusiveness as a means of promoting social tolerance. I make the case that

> inquiry may be more doable than inclusion because teachers are expected not to have all the answers but rather to frame questions, facilitate investigations, and explore what is not known … In terms of engaging learners and teachers whose experiences and viewpoints are diverse, a focus on analysis may be more effective than a focus on advocacy.
>
> (Nelson, 1999, p. 377)

With an inquiry approach, teachers are expected to model learning rather than to convey expert knowledge. As Freeman (1998) puts it, "[i]f teaching is about knowing, inquiry is about not-knowing" (p. 34). With regard to sexual diversity, an inquiry approach seems especially useful because teachers would not need to have particular expertise in gay or lesbian subject matter per se, but rather, could draw on their expertise in configuring discourses and life events into educational experiences.

In the language classroom, queer inquiry might involve such things as ethnographic investigations of actual interactions to analyze ways of communicating, and communicating about, sexual identities; critical analyses of the sociosexual dimensions and meanings of spoken and written texts; and even creative innovations that reimagine current conventions associated with sexual identity—in short, approaching the subject of sexual diversity with what Canagarajah (2006, p. 19) has called an "interrogating spirit."

CHAPTER 4
Tackling Homophobia, Heterosexism, and Heteronormativity

One of the main concerns for teachers in this study was how to respond when anti-gay views were expressed in their classes. This chapter analyzes the issues and dilemmas the teachers encountered, and the strategies they used, in responding to these anti-gay views. Quite a few teachers were concerned about homophobia; their pedagogic focus was exploring negative feelings or fears about gay and lesbian people. Other teachers focused on heterosexism, setting up debates and eliciting opinions about controversial social issues involving sexual minorities. A few teachers focused more on heteronormativity, analyzing discourse practices and sociolinguistic norms pertaining to sexual identities. Although the latter approach was the least evident among the teachers in this study, I show why it seems the most promising.

A Pedagogic Focus on Homophobia: Fear and Hatred

For those teachers whose classroom experiences of homophobia centered on the personal or psychological aspects, the main teaching issues were responding to anti-gay comments and anticipating students' discomfort.

Responding to Anti-gay Comments

Although the focus of this chapter is how teachers respond when students make homophobic comments, it should be acknowledged at the outset that some students have the opposite concern—that is, how to respond when their teachers make homophobic comments in class. Not surprisingly, none of the teachers reported that they themselves had done this, but one did describe an incident that an ESL student had recounted about another teacher.

> 4.1 Mark: This [gay] student was starting to develop a trust level with the teacher and then the teacher one day in class just used the word ['queer'] in a derogatory way ... And [the student] ... lost all the trust that he had built up with that teacher. [The student] felt it was very insulting, but he felt he couldn't say anything about it.

This incident underscores the importance of considering how students experience teachers' speech or actions with regard to sexual identities and how these experiences might affect their learning (see Chapters 6–8).

Turning now to the teachers' experiences, some who identified as lesbian or gay found it difficult to maintain a sense of emotional distance and self-protection when students made, or seemed about to make, homophobic comments.

Though lesbian/gay issues had come up several times in Mark's conversation classes, each time he felt a sense of apprehension.

> 4.2 Mark: Since I'm gay myself this is always kind of a nervous issue … OK, what's the reaction gonna be and how are you gonna deal with that reaction. And- And how I've gotten around that is I let THEM tell ME this is a topic they wanna talk about. I don't, as I see it, impose this topic on them … It makes me real nervous. Because … if there's some conflict … I'm really involved in it and it's hard for me to step back and say … Let's have a discussion here.

Mark was careful not to be seen to be 'imposing' gay subject matter on his students, which raises the question of whether gay or lesbian teachers especially might feel susceptible to being criticized for 'promoting' gay subject matter (or perhaps gayness?).

A sense of unease was echoed by several straight teachers, some of whom were hesitant to discuss lesbian/gay subject matter at all because doing so might lead to homophobic comments, which they would find disturbing.

> 4.3 Ursula: I'm kind of uncomfortable about exploring something and giving them a chance to say things I don't really wanna hear.

Others wanted to challenge homophobic comments but felt unsure about how to go about this.

> 4.4 Scott: Although I'm not gay myself, uh, we often talk about, uh, sexual identities and gender in the classroom … And … some of the nicest students I know have some of the most, you know, really intense homophobic comments to make. And when that comes up, when those often off-hand remarks or aside remarks or little jokes or stuff, I don't know quite how to jump in there and … challenge that.

Several teachers mentioned being surprised by which students would make homophobic remarks. Like other teachers, Scott noted that derogatory remarks are often made in a casual manner and formulated as humor. The apparent levity of the homophobic 'asides' may add to the difficulty of finding ways to challenge them.

The following comment encapsulated a central tension described by a number of teachers.

> 4.5 Rachel: On the one hand you're … absolutely committed to provide space for everybody in the class, to sort of be who they are and explore who they are in an honest way. And on the other hand, um, I don't feel like I have to provide space for racist or homophobic comments … In other words, it's not OK to denigrate other people … in class.

Many teachers wanted to find ways of addressing homophobia that would not discourage students from expressing themselves.

Too Distressed to Respond to Homophobia

Three teachers spoke in detail about how they had responded to overtly anti-gay comments in class. One was Helen, who was eager to learn more effective ways of teaching gay and lesbian themes and of dealing with homophobia in the classroom.

4.6 Helen: I don't know how to frame things. I don't know how to react to the homophobia that comes out. I don't even know that that's my place. But it's EXTREMELY uncomfortable for me when it does. And so I find myself really caught and in conflict about that … When something hits close to home for me, I don't exactly know how to be objective and to step back.

She recounted a distressing incident that had recently occurred in a writing class she was teaching. In that class Helen would present the students with short articles from the newspaper and ask that each student respond in writing to the article of their choice. One day, thinking that this class seemed "open," Helen included an article about gay rights, and that was the article that each student chose as their writing prompt. As Helen circulated and saw what they were writing, she became increasingly distressed by what she called their "caustic" attitudes to gay people.

4.7 Helen: I had 11 students that said They're all going to hell … That was so emotional for me … I wasn't expecting that.

As Helen circulated she did what she always did with this task, which was to offer "immediate feedback" on grammar and word choice in order to help the students find the language to express their thoughts.

4.8 Helen: [I was saying things like] Is this what you mean by this? No it's not strong enough. OK, what about this word. That's what I mean. OK. So it would get more and more condemnatory. But it got closer to their truth … And it was all negative, with the exception of one student.

Helen was in the difficult position of helping the students to say things that were personally very painful to her (she was crying as she recounted the experience).

4.9 Helen: I was really aware of being gay, of being a lesbian … and feeling like I had a secret. And feeling ashamed. Moving into my own homophobia, it was awful. And I thought I'm NOT doing this again. […] I treated it just as a grammar exercise and, uh, handed it back and did NOTHING with it. Because I just was too … disturbed by the homophobia. And I didn't feel strong enough to out myself. And I knew I'd have to out myself … to talk about it.

Helen felt she should have responded in some way to the homophobia but felt unable to do so because she had no emotional distance from the topic. Moreover, Helen felt that she would be unable to discuss the students' homophobic reactions—in any form and to any degree—unless she told them that she was a lesbian. In her view, the one action required the other. Yet, Helen was fearful that if she came out to students there could be negative career consequences.

> 4.10 Helen: There's always the possibility that subconsciously you could be rated down [by students in their course evaluations] ... because, you know, you're a dyke.

Helen faced the twin dilemmas of dealing with homophobia and at the same time negotiating her own sexual identity—to her, these were inseparable. She personalized the homophobia by seeing it as her students' 'truth' and forced herself to help them to express their 'truth' while hiding her own extreme distress about it. She evaluated her teaching as inadequate, both because she responded only to the grammar and not the thematic content of student texts and because she felt she had failed to act with integrity by not expressing her own 'truth.'

Unsure of How to Respond to Homophobia

In another writing class, a student wrote that he hated gays, but this teacher's response was very different than Helen's.

> 4.11 Gwen: I gave them the journal assignment, 'Write about a memory' ... [A student] wrote, um, about a dream that he's had ... He described meeting a woman, in just the most beautiful detail ... It was very engaging ... How he saw this woman and she was so beautiful and ... the moment that he met her he asked her to marry him. And ... she opened her mouth, but the voice that came out was a man's voice. And then his conclusion was really short and really terse, and he said ... It made me hate gays. But ... the tone of his essay was so different that his conclusion didn't seem like that was really what he was thinking ... It seemed more like a question ... sort of a getting himself off the hook or something, depending on how I would respond. I didn't see it really as a declaration of his hate of homosexuality ... [I think he wrote that he hates gays] so that I wouldn't label him in some way or ... [maybe] he wanted affirmation of some kind.

Gwen did not take the student's anti-gay statement at face value. She did not see it as a fixed position (or even a private struggle) so much as a desire to save face while 'testing' the teacher/reader to see how she would react to his raising the topic of same-sex desire.

Gwen faced a dilemma about how to respond in writing to the journal assignment.

> 4.12 Gwen: I ... would have just written ... That's not such an uncommon kind of dream ... sometimes my dreams are about men and

sometimes about women … But … I asked a more experienced teacher … [who said] Ah, don't become their therapist … I actually ended up … praising his writing. I wanted to show him encouragement implicitly through that.

Gwen hoped that responding only to the positive aspects of the writing would manage to convey a positive, supportive response to what she saw as his questioning stance regarding his own sexual identity.

Gwen felt this incident raised important issues that were central to her teaching.

4.13 Gwen: [How to respond] might seem really trivial to some people … [But] I think that [the students] are at an age … where you think a lot about sexual boundaries and things like that … Whenever I teach a class this is one of the things I feel the most strongly about too. Not defining things and putting things into, um, categories, but seeing things along a continuum … especially with regards to sexuality and gender.

Unlike most teachers in this study, Gwen did not see sexual identities as fixed, knowable, straightforward categories. In her view, acknowledging the flexibility and fluidity of definitions and categories is integral to teaching language.

Despite the clear contrast between Gwen's and Helen's experiences of students' anti-gay comments, their teaching practices had something significant in common: the homophobic thematic content in students' writing was not engaged with or followed up in any way. Even though each teacher had given considerable thought as to how they might respond, neither actually ended up addressing the homophobic comments. Thus, a student's perspective might be that their teachers simply ignored these comments.

Facilitating Inquiry about Homophobia

A third teacher described a classroom experience in which she responded to anti-gay comments in a very different way than Helen or Gwen. Tess, a teacher/teacher-educator, placed a high value on "taking students seriously" and encouraging them to "speak from where they're at," as she put it. In a class presentation on 'homosexuality,' a group of students put forward this scenario: "OK, you're living in an apartment and you discover that your roommate is gay, what do you do?" The class responded that they would "throw out" the roommate. The presenters then put forward a second scenario—"Somebody else comes to apply for the room in the apartment and you discover that person is gay [too]." The class said they would throw out that person too. This pattern continued, leading to what Tess called a "crescendo" of homophobia.

After a while, Tess wanted to intervene but without simply forbidding homophobic comments.

4.14 Tess: I thought to myself … How can I enter this debate with a question that won't be a moralistic We won't permit those kind of comments. Because they're obviously there! I mean, they're lived and they're real and they're invested in them! … And I said, um, What is generating the fear here? And everything went silent … And I said … What … exactly marks someone as gay and not gay? Why … is the gay body sexualized? And what is the fear in that moment that would make you throw that roommate out, and not let that one in? And there was a long silence … And … then somebody … started saying … What if they raped me … And then all this stuff started to come out. Like suddenly … the question was being explored in … a productive way … And I said … These are sometimes my fears … My fear here right now, however, … in a very opposite way listening to you speak, … is … feeling the- the hugeness of the volume of … homophobia. And I'm not even gay but I feel it as somebody sitting here right now.

Tess 'allowed' students to voice their homophobic views or feelings, but she did not stop there. By posing questions, she was able to reframe the focus from rejecting gays to fearing gays. Instead of dismissing this fear as unwarranted or unacceptable, she asked students to reflect on what motivated it and what its consequences might be for others. Her questions repositioned the vocal students from those who feared gay people into those whose homophobia was inciting fear in others. Tess positioned herself as someone who both felt homophobia and feared it and as someone who was not gay but who was affected nonetheless by homophobia (which broke down the us/them dichotomy between straight/gay). Also, she invited the class to take a step back from the role-play scenario in which they were engaged and to notice and reflect on the immediate effects of their words on others in the room.

Anticipating Students' Discomfort

A number of teachers reported that one teaching challenge was judging whether there would be sufficient class time to deal adequately with lesbian/gay themes, given the emotions these might engender among students. They also said that lesbian/gay themes are rarely, if ever, part of the official curriculum, so the onus was on teachers to develop ways of framing these themes through class activities.

4.15 Gwen: It's not normally built into the curriculum, discussing sexuality or issues of identity or whatever. So if you open [that] up it's like opening up a can of worms … You've got to make sure that it's dealt with right and it's a huge responsibility.

Many if not all of the teachers in this study clearly felt a strong sense of responsibility in relation to lesbian/gay subject matter. Teachers were reluctant to raise it unless they felt able to 'see it through.' There seemed to be an expectation that most students are homophobic, so discussing lesbian/gay topics will require a fair amount of class time so that students can explore the reasons underpinning their fears.

4.16 Alicia: If I don't think there's enough time for anybody to make a shift then I won't- I won't use anything [lesbian or gay] … In my experience more students have started out really reticent, kind of afraid, very judgmental about … gay people in general. And if I don't think there's enough time for people to explore their feelings, and to figure out why they think what they think, if it's cultural or, um, it's discomfort … then I don't wanna get into it at all.

However, Rachel put forward a contrasting view.

4.17 Rachel: I don't understand why we're always trying to protect the most conservative elements of society by not exposing their little minds to the fact that … there may be something that … they disagree with … I think people just worry too much. And that part of the heterosexism is really an untoward responsibility to the majority.

In Rachel's view, teachers tend to be overly careful not to threaten those who hold homophobic beliefs. She saw this excessive concern as part of the problem of heterosexism. This raises the question of whether teachers ought to be less concerned about the 'homophobic majority' and more concerned about those students who identify as gay or lesbian, or who are questioning their sexual identity.

The Limitations of a Pedagogic Focus on Homophobia

The contrasting concerns of the teachers quoted above can be better understood by considering the notion of homophobia. The term derives from the discipline of psychology and refers to fear or hatred of gay men and lesbians (Kitzinger, 1996). Acknowledging homophobia makes it possible to explore and even transform it. However, it has been argued that the term 'homophobia' is problematic. It "centers heterosexuality as the normal" (Britzman, 1995, p. 158). 'Homophobia' "'naturalizes' the hatred of same-sex love by pronouncing this hatred and fear as a somehow inescapable feature of the human psyche" (Pellegrini, 1992, p. 45). Because 'phobia' refers to a "pathological fear," the implication is that people who 'suffer' from homophobia need to be "protected and consoled" (Hinson, 1996, p. 243). Committing violent acts becomes understandable in light of the irrational fear from which the perpetrators suffer (Hinson, 1996; Kitzinger, 1996). Thus, doing or saying things that are homophobic is made to seem human, understandable, even worthy of a sympathetic response. With the term 'homophobia,' then, it is the comfort level of the individual who feels the fear or hatred that is the main focus.

Pedagogically, this translates into a primary focus on those who 'suffer' from having homophobic feelings, not those who suffer as a result of being hated or feared. Martindale (1997) notes that this tendency is widespread throughout education, where the "usual focus of concern" is not the difficulties that "sexual minorities" face as they try to put forward their perspectives but rather the resulting "distress" of the "ostensible 'general population'" (p. 70). Accordingly, students are rarely, if ever, taught how to 'defend' themselves and others from homophobic discrimination and harassment (Shardakova & Pavlenko, 2004; see also Auerbach, 1995). Instead, the focus tends to be making sure that students who are bothered by gay topics or people will not feel uncomfortable.

The pedagogic limitations of a focus on homophobia are also evident in the teaching accounts of Helen, Gwen, and Tess (see 4.6–4.14), each of whom responded in quite a personalized way when their students made gay-hating comments in writing or orally. Gwen decided to praise the positive aspects of the student's writing in the hope of providing a supportive response to the student as a person who was possibly questioning his own sexuality or perhaps testing her openness on the subject. Yet, this meant that in her written feedback on the student's text she made no comment about the marked difference in tone between the ('I hate gays') conclusion and the rest of the text—despite the fact that this intratextual dissonance had struck her as a reader.

Helen saw her role as assisting students in expressing their views. She did not discuss with the class the value of taking into account the likely views on the subject among readers in that particular setting (a U.S. university)—despite the fact that she herself had been shocked and deeply disturbed by the incongruence between her students' views and her own. Because Helen understood the students' anti-gay comments to be their authentic 'truth,' she seemed to feel it was not her place to challenge or question that truth—in fact, she felt duty-bound to assist them in choosing the vocabulary to express it, despite her own mounting distress about what they were actually saying. Helen felt unable to speak as a teacher about the homophobia without also speaking as a lesbian, yet in her assessment it was too dangerous professionally to speak as a lesbian teacher (an issue that will be elaborated in Chapter 5).

Unlike Helen and Gwen, Tess used lesbian/gay themes in a way that promoted inquiry. However, the object of inquiry was the students' own feelings; thus, the main emphasis seems to be on furthering what some teachers called "personal growth" (see 3.16). Such a deeply personal focus may not be a viable option in some classes, perhaps especially those with international cohorts, since some teachers and learners might find the 'confessional' mode unfamiliar, inappropriate, or undesirable.

In sum, I think the above teaching accounts show that teachers sometimes need to be able to 'step back,' as Helen and Mark each put it, so that they can respond to anti-gay comments in ways that are less akin to a counseling or psychological approach.

A Pedagogic Focus on Heterosexism: Debates and Controversies

For those teachers who set up class discussions and debates about heterosexism, the main teaching issues were framing lesbian/gay themes as controversial and turning nondiscrimination policy into pedagogy.

Framing Gay/Lesbian Issues as Controversial

As we saw in Chapter 3, a number of teachers reported that when students were asked to do written projects or oral presentations on social issues they often chose topics such as "gays in the military or gay marriage" (see 3.3). This next teacher had her students write a research paper on a "controversial topic" of their choice.

4.18 Rhonda: [Each term] there will be one or two who will write a paper on a gay issue. Because it's in the media, it's in their faces, and some of them are thinking about it … Trying to represent both sides of the issue with the strongest arguments on both sides … exposes the students to some of the opinions, some of the information that's out there … in magazines or … on the net … I think it's a very productive experience for them, um, to look at both sides.

A student teacher described a similar activity she had used in an EFL class. Aware that most of her students had negative attitudes about gay people, she set up a structured debate about gay marriage.

4.19 Tina: I had a homogeneous group of very conservative Catholic people in a culture where you don't really talk about gay and lesbian issues unless you're joking … So what I've done … is to assign roles or positions to students so that if you're bringing up a controversial issue … both sides gets equal time. And … that worked really well in a speed debate format … where the point was to debate. The point wasn't a conversation … If I'd asked everyone in that room What do you think about gay marriage? maybe out of 15, two might have been kind of open to considering the idea. But in the debate they won hands down, … the pro-gay marriage side … They came up with really creative reasons why it was a good idea, and the other side couldn't … because they weren't really thinking, they weren't being creative … Whether you're changing really what they think or not, they're … hearing that … out of their own mouths … I think it made them think a little bit. And so that was … how I got around that problem of opening things up for gay bashing.

The students were not asked to voice their own views but simply to 'act the part' of someone with a given opinion. Because Tina anticipated homophobic attitudes, she set up a task that would ensure that those attitudes would be expressed *and* challenged—and challenged by the students themselves, not by her. Tina considered this task successful because it generated creative thinking.

Rachel, a teacher-educator, observed a class in which the student teacher framed lesbian/gay subject matter in a way that, not surprisingly, generated homophobic responses.

4.20 Rachel: The worst hour I ever had in an ESL class was watching … [a student teacher use a] values clarification [task in which] … people learn … [the] language of negotiation because they have to reach consensus over … contentious issues … It … was a who lives and [who] dies … sort of thing … And one of the people was 'the homosexual.' And so for an hour we all sat there while various people from around the world said He should die … It was really horrifying. Without any sort of self-consciousness on her part. First of all she assumed … that nobody in her class was gay. And second of all that it would be alright for everybody in that room to hear people for an hour talking about how homosexuals should die! … It's therefore become a great example in [teacher-education classes] of, um, what it means to not think about these issues, and what you subject people to, and what it means for you to assume things about your students.

Rachel was disturbed that the student teacher she observed had no consideration for students—of any sexual identity—who might find it undesirable to be subjected to a barrage of anti-gay comments.

Rachel suggested that teachers use heterosexism as a tool for creating social cohesion, especially interculturally.

4.21 Rachel: [It's as if teachers think] I finally hit the universality of the human experience, which is that everybody's sexist and heterosexist, you know. (R laughs) And so all these little sexist jokes or these little, you know, like Oh he said boyfriend ha ha ha … People use misogyny and heterosexism as a sort of safe thing to do in their classes. Because it'll be seen as universal … [We need to] break it down, so that people see that for what it is. And ask themselves why are they doing that.

Understanding heterosexism as a social act that serves a social function, Rachel observed that heterosexist humor can serve to unify a disparate group of learners because it is something that people from diverse countries are likely to understand and find amusing.

The Possibilities and Limitations of a Pedagogic Focus on Heterosexism

Unlike the teaching accounts in the first section of this chapter, which focused on homophobia, the above accounts focused on heterosexism. Like 'racism' and 'sexism,' 'heterosexism' refers to the systematic institutionalization of discrimination, in this case based on sexual identity. The focus is sociopolitical rather than psychological. 'Heterosexism' places the onus on "the agents of oppression" rather than "the oppressed" (Blumenfeld, 1992, p. 15). In other words, 'heterosexism' does not locate the problem in negative feelings about gay people (as does 'homophobia') but in acts, policies, and structures that limit the freedom or opportunities available to people on the basis of their being (or being perceived to be) gay. These constraints occur across many zones of public life—they are not isolated incidents but part of a system of domination in which one group (straight people) has power over, and commits injustices against, another group (gay, bisexual, and lesbian people).

Pedagogically, a focus on heterosexism makes it possible to discuss contemporary issues of broad social relevance, to make connections between systems of discrimination (see 5.22), and to acknowledge that it is not only people who identify as gay, lesbian, or bisexual who are discriminated against but also those who are *perceived* to be gay, lesbian, or bisexual because they "do their gender in ways that conflict with dominant hegemonic patterns—those who do their masculinity or femininity in non-traditional ways" (Hinson, 1996, p. 243).

However, as the teaching practices reported on above indicate, framing lesbian/gay themes as controversial tends to reduce complex social issues to only 'two sides'—with the implication that one is right and one is wrong. It also invites anti-gay comments, which may not be appreciated by some students, as Rachel notes about the live-or-die debate. In fact, Malinowitz (1995) quotes a gay student who, having experienced a similar class discussion, said with sarcasm "I love hearing the question of whether or not I should be allowed to exist tossed around in a 'lively debate'" (p. 5).

At the same time, to take up Rachel's point (4.21), theorizing heterosexism as socially purposeful action could make it possible for teachers to reflect on why they use heterosexism, so that they can then explore alternative ways of achieving goals such as fostering group cohesion. Also, a focus on inquiry rather than debate could make it possible to explore questions like the following (below Malinowitz is using the term 'homophobia,' but the same questions could be asked of 'heterosexism'):

> Homophobia is bad; we want it to go away. But what exactly *is* that thing—or those disparate things—that we call 'homophobia'? In what forms does it exist? … What gives it such power in so many spheres of human activity? … What do people get out of homophobia in our society?
>
> (Malinowitz, 1995, p. 75)

Thus, instead of ignoring, accepting, or seeking to counter homophobia or heterosexism, the aim could be to open up the broader meanings of these notions by understanding them to be ways of making sense of experience.

In language classes, the pedagogic focus might then become how homophobic or heterosexist meanings are communicated and interpreted and what effects these have on communicative interactions and social relations.

From Debate to Discussion and Inquiry

In fact, a few teachers did speak of the problematic aspects of framing lesbian/gay issues as controversial issues.

4.22 Paige: I don't really like approaching issues that deal with … human rights as a controversy … Talking about, you know, whether any group of people has a right to be who they are and have the basic rights that we hope to all have. Um, that's not something that's debatable, in my mind. So … I don't like setting up the [gay] topic in terms of a debate … It's more asking questions and, um, trying to get them to explore what they know, and what they don't know, and what they might want to know. And getting them some information.

Paige saw her role as eliciting students' questions and providing them with the information they sought, which she considered neutral activities—unlike a debate.

One teacher/teacher-educator spoke specifically about heterosexism as subject matter, but she described an open-ended discussion rather than a debate (the article she refers to below is Nelson [1993]).

> 4.23 Tess: I've used Cynthia's article on heterosexism in ESL and taken it into my ESL classrooms ... as well as ... teacher ed classrooms, people who are training to be ESL teachers ... What's so interesting to me is that the ESL students are far more progressive in their reading of that article than the teachers in training are [...] [ESL students have discussed whether] a lesbian identity is ... an alternative to ... [oppressive socioeconomic] structures [in Korea, say], ... whether this is, um, a trendy identity or whether it's a real identity, and whether it's a possible option and how possible is it. So it was an intersection of ... a race space with a gender space with a generational space ... And that kind of discussion never came out in the teacher ed classes. Never.

Tess was able to frame these discussions in ways that moved beyond 'two-sided' debate, and in doing so she found that ESL students were much more open than ESL teachers-in-training to discussing the complexities of lesbian identities internationally.

Facilitating Inquiry about Heterosexism

Preferring discussion to debate, Paige focused on eliciting students' knowledge and interests and then providing information, while Tess focused more on open-ended inquiry, exploring multidimensional aspects of identity that students raised concerning such things as the viability of lesbian identities in countries like Korea.

Benesch (1999) recounts a discussion from an English for Academic Purposes class that she was teaching and her attempts to promote 'dialogic critical thinking' (citing Gieve, 1998), which involves examining and debating assumptions. Benesch assigned a newspaper article about the 1998 murder of an openly gay university student, Matthew Shepard, in the United States. While reading it, one student muttered that he hated gay people. During the class discussion of the article, Benesch intervened twice in order to encourage students to "examine certain assumptions further" (p. 578):

> I asked the students to question the assumption on which many of their contributions seemed to be based: that homosexuals are primarily interested in making sexual overtures to and converting heterosexuals. Could this notion be based on fears some students had already raised rather than on a real threat? I asked. My other challenge was to ask the students to consider the social origins of their fears as well as alternatives to killing or beating up someone as a way of dealing with those fears. The two interventions were intended to connect the Shepard case, experiences and concerns students had described, and more abstract notions of tolerance and social justice.
>
> (Benesch, 1999, p. 578)

This lesson was considered successful because it connected texts, newsworthy events, and ways of thinking and behaving but also, as the author goes on to explain, because it led to several students changing their attitudes after realizing that their contempt for gay men stemmed from their own fear and embarrassment. This again raises the important question of what teachers are aiming to accomplish when engaging with the topic of heterosexism.

Framing Nondiscrimination Policy as Pedagogy

Promoting greater tolerance—of lesbian and gay people in particular and of subjugated peoples in general—was a goal shared by some teachers in this study (see 3.17).

Liz pointed out that discrimination based, among other things, on sexual orientation was officially prohibited at her educational institution and that informing students of the illegality of heterosexist speech would be one way to discourage, or even prohibit, such comments.

> 4.24 Liz: The department head was explaining that … we needed to be aware of [the university's nondiscriminatory policy statement] because there had been some racial and ethnic issues … where students had- had come close to attacking each other on certain topics. And we had to, um, be aware that not only was it a teaching issue but it was a legal issue … [When I asked about sexual orientation] she said This program will not tolerate any harassment of students or teachers based on sexual orientation … [So] you can ask questions like that, get the backing from your administration, and then take it into the classroom as … [a] nondiscrimination [issue]. You wouldn't tolerate racial comments … [or] gender discriminatory comments from your students … If you're uncomfortable … fronting the issue as a gay/lesbian issue, you can couch it as a nondiscriminatory issue and as a safe space in the classroom issue.

Another teacher made a similar point about putting policy to the service of pedagogy.

> 4.25 Jill: In the district I work in they have … a little poster that everybody can have in their rooms. It's No sexist, racist or homophobic language or, behavior will be tolerated here. And … it's just something that you can refer to any time you see any of that disrespectful stuff. And it's so nice now that the homophobia part is on it.

However, what is considered acceptable or unacceptable is not always so straightforward or clear-cut, as Tina pointed out in describing her EFL teaching experiences.

> 4.26 Tina: [Students] see things in movies and they come to class and they say Oh yeah all those fags … And how do you deal with that … I don't

know if you can bring it up as a culture point, saying that in American culture that's not acceptable. Because it's not in- in my American culture. But there are a lot of American cultures in which that is acceptable. And, um, they might run into that. And so I always brought it up as a personal issue. I just said, You're talking about my family and I'm really offended by that … I found that to be better than trying to argue an abstract point about Well that's not acceptable and these kinds of words are offensive to many people. That … just lost them.

Tina pointed out that 'American cultures' are plural and encompass mixed norms in relation to homophobia.

Clay responded to Tina's comment above by distinguishing rules of the culture from rules of the classroom.

4.27 Clay: I think try to establish some ground rules for discussion … [I know of an] English class taught in sort of a Freirean approach. And, uh, the teacher … spends a lot of time establishing ground rules for discussion that exclude hateful, uh, jokes … And it gets worked out in relation to all kinds of topics, not just a single topic … I wouldn't personally present it as a … rule in the culture because … the culture's variable and- and different groups have different rules. But as sort of a rule of the classroom. This is the way in this class we try to express respect. I mean I'm not trying to say it's a straightforward matter. In this particular class the teacher's … working on it all the time. And they actually talk about OK … in this topic what is disrespectful speech and what constitutes that. So I mean you end up having to … deal with this issue over and over again. But then you don't have to say OK now … we're gonna … narrow the discussion of this topic, whereas other topics people can say anything they want.

Clay emphasized the need for classroom rules to be negotiated and clarified— not just once but on an ongoing basis. Teacher and learners together can explore what constitutes disrespectful speech. In this way, shared understandings are not presumed, and no particular subject matter is singled out as uniquely sensitive.

The Notion of Making Classrooms Safe

Common to the above accounts is a desire to make the classroom a 'safe' space, as Liz (4.24) put it, which is an understandable goal given some of the problems that have been documented in education contexts. In language education literature, 26 ESL and EFL teachers signed a letter to the editor of *TESOL Matters* saying they had witnessed lesbian and gay students being "ridiculed and taunted in class" (Anderson et al., 1997; see also Moita-Lopes, 2006; Saint Pierre, 1994). Dalley and Campbell's (2006) study of youth at a bilingual high school in Canada found that discourses of heteronormativity were dominant in the classrooms and corridors of the school—despite the much-touted school motto of 'unity in diversity' (the effects of this sort of environment on gay and lesbian students were discussed in Chapter 2).

In education research, many gay and lesbian students report that it is not uncommon for their teachers to "simply ignore the harassment and humiliation" to which their classmates subject them (Sears, 1987, p. 91). Hinson's (1996) study of Australian high schools found that "it was widely believed that teachers and students would be victimised or even bashed if they were perceived to be gay or lesbian," yet teachers and principals were the least outspoken about heterosexist violence than about any other form of violence (p. 248).

Hinson (1996) defines "heterosexist violence" as "physical, verbal, visual or sexual forms of violence directed against individuals or groups on the basis of their perceived sexual preferences" (p. 241). Incidentally, Sedgwick (1990) takes a much broader view—that forbidding people "the authority to describe and name their own sexual desire" in itself constitutes a profound form of "intimate violence" (p. 26). But to return to Hinson's study, she explains that most schools tend to "psychologise" the problem and attempt behavior management at the level of the individual (p. 242). She goes on to explain why this "micro-structuralist" approach to heterosexist violence is inadequate. (Below she uses Australian English slang terms for 'lesbian' and 'gay man.')

> Violence is not socially random. It is patterned—in terms of who does what to whom. Violence is not simply innate and inevitable. It is sanctioned and maintained in some social contexts more than others. A teenage boy in 'trouble' in a court room, for instance, is unlikely to yell out "Lezzo!" or "Poofta!" to his judge. Those who do violence 'know' who they can do what to and in what context. Even where violence is highly sanctioned, this is only so in relation to certain 'kinds' of people.
>
> (Hinson, 1996, pp. 242–243)

Hinson (1996) recommends that educators theorize heterosexist violence in schools as a social behavior that is maintained and sanctioned through "violence-maintaining practices" (p. 247). Considering the problem in this way, the key is not to simply replace these practices with 'correct' ones but rather to take a self-reflexive approach (p. 247). Hinson recommends that educators ask themselves, on an ongoing basis, "*to what extent are violence-maintaining practices being supported or resisted in any given context?*" (p. 248).

This discussion leads to three important implications for language education. First, rather than attempting to 'correct' the heterosexist speech or behavior of the odd student on an individual and occasional basis, there is a need to reconsider pedagogy and policy in terms of whether these uphold violence-maintaining practices (in this case, against sexual minorities) or actively challenge these practices. In other words, instead of locating the problem in an individual student who is understood to 'be homophobic' and in need of 'correction,' the problem is located in the educational practices and discourses across a given institution or program, which are understood to be either reinforcing heterosexism or challenging it.

The second point follows from the first. Questions about how to address homophobia or heterosexism should not be left to individual teachers to work out but ought to be taken up by groups of teachers, administrators, and other stakeholders through a process of exchange and debate; furthermore, the aim would not be to come up with a fixed policy to 'solve' the problem once and for all but to engage in a process of reflection and experimentation that casts matters of sexual diversity and inequity as sufficiently important to require ongoing collegial attention. On that point I should mention that, for many teachers, participating in this study was their first opportunity to articulate their own experiences, and to hear those of their colleagues or coworkers, about sexual identities and language teaching. Many of the teachers told me that taking part was very valuable, and they hoped to have more opportunities for collegial discussions and professional development on these matters.

Third, second- and foreign-language learners do not necessarily already know the dominant 'rules of usage' and the positive or negative connotations of terms such as 'lezzo,' a point that was hinted at by Clay (4.27) and will be elaborated further on in this chapter.

Dealing with Discomfort

Discomfort is probably far more prevalent in language classes than actual violence. As we have seen in this chapter, a number of teachers in this study felt discomfort when dealing with lesbian/gay themes or homophobia in the classroom. Jones and Jack (1994) report that ESL teachers attending Jones's workshops, on including gay and lesbian literature in the curriculum, feared being attacked by students, parents, or administrators for incorporating gay/lesbian themes. Some teachers may prefer to avoid sexual identities in particular and social identities in general as subject matter as it is likely to generate a degree of discomfort. In hooks' (1994) analysis, teacher reluctance to consider "race, sex, and class is often rooted in the fear that classrooms will be uncontrollable, that emotions and passions will not be contained" (p. 39).

For some people, lesbian/gay themes seem especially provocative or emotionally "charged" (Malinowitz, 1995, p. 42). The potentially contentious nature of lesbian/gay themes may be exacerbated within the intercultural arenas of language education. Not only may teachers and learners have different points of view about a given topic (see Duff & Uchida, 1997, discussing EFL), but they may not have the same expectations about what sorts of topics are even appropriate to discuss in a classroom context (see Jones, 1996, also discussing EFL). Furthermore, teachers and learners may have different approaches to face-saving during contentious or discomfiting discussions (see R. Scollon & S. W. Scollon, 1995).

Also, critically examining social identities as subject matter can disrupt one's location in terms of class, gender, and ethnic relations, which can threaten one's familiar ways of coping with everyday life (Simon, 1992). This sort of disruption is not merely a private matter but can affect students' relationships with others. Among second-language students in particular, there may be "reluctance to transgress linguistic, cultural, gendered, and classed norms that sustain supportive social networks in a competitive and impersonal economy often hostile to newcomers" (Morgan, 1997, p. 440).

Some teachers, like Ursula (4.3), prefer to avoid subject matter or tasks that might evoke fear or discomfort (for themselves or their students). Yet, it has been argued that these emotions may simply be part of the learning process. Fear may indicate "that a particularly significant moment of learning may be at hand, in which old investments are about to be questioned, modified, or possibly displaced" (Simon, 1992, p. 81). This may especially be the case when students are engaged with the subject matter. Discomfort may actually facilitate learning rather than impede it (see Johnson, 1995). As Schenke (1996) puts it, "To unsettle familiar stories is, after all, to take risks," which means that class discussions "are not always 'safe' places" (p. 157). Simon (1992) notes that "classroom language practices are not only a mode of social organization but, also potentially, a mode of disorganization" (p. 92). This is because people are constantly taking up new discursive positions, which means "the point of departure" is not static but changing (p. 92).

If pedagogy is understood as "a space within which meanings are posed and contested" (Simon, 1992, p. 69), if language is understood to involve negotiating and contesting meanings, and if differential power relations that exist beyond the classroom are understood to exist within it as well, then is it possible to avoid fear or discomfort? The question may not be whether these feelings are desirable or undesirable, but how to respond when these arise. Britzman (1995) calls into question the notion that a classroom—presumably, an environment in which thinking is encouraged—could be considered 'safe,' since intellectual exploration can have the effect of unsettling one's habitual thinking and emotional equilibrium. Boostrom (1998) cautions that 'safe space' metaphors in education serve to "censor critical reflection" rather than encourage "the friction of dialogue"; his argument is that "teachers need to manage conflict, not prohibit it" (p. 407). As I have put it elsewhere (in a teacher-researcher dialogue chapter), "Do we need to make our classes safe spaces for gay and lesbian topics and people? Or for questioning and unsettling our understandings of straight, gay, and lesbian topics and people?" (Ó'Móchain, Mitchell, & Nelson, 2003, p. 138).

Rather than attempting to make the classroom a safe space, the focus could be on "working out ethical relations" (Britzman, 1995, p. 164)—or perhaps developing a "community of solidarity" (Simon, 1992, p. 67) or a "community of communities" (Weeks, 1990, p. 98). The important thing is that the emphasis should not be on sheltering students from danger or discomfort so much as learning to turn each other into allies, following Phelan (1994). This approach echoes that described by Clay (4.27)—establishing, through discussion, agreed rules of the classroom about what exactly constitutes respectful or disrespectful speech in a given context. In other words, issues of heterosexist discrimination could be linked specifically to matters of language, an approach that is elaborated in the final section of this chapter.

A Pedagogic Focus on Heteronormativity: Discourse Practices

A few teachers reported classroom approaches that neither sought to deepen understandings of gay/lesbian people nor to debate sexual issues but instead engaged directly with discourses and discourse practices as a way of analyzing heteronormativity.

Foregrounding Discourse Practices

Claire reported on a dilemma that a novice teacher under her supervision had discussed with her. The teacher felt disconcerted that her students were writing about another teacher who had come out as gay. The disconcerted teacher, who was averse to talking about gay matters generally, felt imposed upon by having to respond to her students' writings about this topic. Claire advised the teacher to try to respond in a less 'personal' way: first, by stepping back from her own perspective and recognizing that there are other ways of looking at the issue and, second, by focusing on the text *as a text*, for example, assessing how well the argument was developed rather than whether she happens to agree with it.

> 4.28 Claire: Like try to look at it as an issue as opposed to what her personal perspective might be on it … Step back and say Has this person supported their argument? I mean … look at it almost rhetorically. And, um, educating her about what the perspectives are on the issue, that there's something a little more going on here besides just religion and besides what your perspective is. Open up a dialogue.

Claire's advice was often sought by teachers who felt unsure of how to respond when their students wrote anti-gay arguments.

> 4.29 Claire: [A student] might take an angle that gay people should, uh, not be allowed to get married because they're not capable of raising children … [I advise teachers] to tell students Look I'm the reader and … your angle is gonna turn me off …, so how could you reconsider that?

Again Claire's advice highlighted the relational nature of writing and reading. She recommended that teachers discuss how their own views might affect their reading and evaluation of an anti-gay argument.

A similar point was made by Rachel, a teacher-educator who wrote learning materials. When she incorporated lesbian/gay themes into these materials, she tried to frame tasks in a way that emphasized the writer's purpose and audience.

> 4.30 Rachel: If people [students] want to write, um, homophobic stuff they have to understand that they're … representing a series of values for a community. That these aren't given.

Rachel made the point that when students write homophobic things they are not merely expressing an individual viewpoint, they are taking a stance that is associated with a group of people, that has historical and political dimensions, and that is linked to a set of values.

This point is illustrated by the experiences of a teacher-educator/administrator who, whenever he organized EFL teaching conferences, would make a point of including gay/lesbian issues as a topic on the program.

> 4.31 Eric: I have had … very interesting talks with [outraged] teachers who said … in the front of the [EFL] conference office, How can you

put this [topic] on [the conference program]? … We don't talk about this! Or These people need to be killed. I mean, I heard that. And then privately coming back when they saw I had also a back room where they could talk to me, saying Oh I'm so thankful that you had it on the program! … How do you use it in your classroom?

The same teachers who in a public situation vehemently objected to the subject matter were in a private situation grateful and inquisitive. In this case, homophobic speech may well have been what Rachel described (below) as "a display for one's peers."

4.32 Rachel: I think … racist and homophobic comments often come from … a display for one's peers. Because … people police each other, police themselves. And are keeping themselves in line. And so you might as well name it as, um, you know, this is what you imagine is the rhetorical stance of a group of people, and it is just a rhetorical stance and it's attached to a group of people.

Rachel pointed out that discriminatory speech or text is regulating and regulated. Conceptualizing homophobic or heterosexist comments as rhetorical stances may make it possible for teachers to diffuse their power by attending to them as textual productions and analyzing the points of view or interests that particular discursive positionings represent.

One teacher made the point that comments casting straight people as 'normal' also warrant some discussion.

4.33 Liz: I think that the issue starts before you necessarily have to bring in the [gay/lesbian] topic per se. For example, you're working on a reading passage and the word 'spouse' is used and a student asks you … Does that mean normal, like a man and woman? And you address the issue of his evaluating 'spouse' as being a 'normal' word for a 'normal' male–female relationship.

This example shows that teachers can highlight the linguistic nuances through which heterosexuality comes to be normalized.

Analyzing Heteronormative Discourses

Though none of the teachers in my study used the term 'heteronormativity'—a term from queer theory—I think the above accounts point to its potential usefulness in addressing what the teachers called homophobia or heterosexism. 'Heteronormativity' refers to "the normalising processes which support heterosexuality as the elemental form of human association, as the very model of inter-gender relations, as the indivisible basis of all community"; the emphasis is on how heterosexuality, and only heterosexuality, is made to seem normal or natural (Warner, 1993, p. xxi). The case I put forward here is that heteronormativity could prove a useful concept in language teaching because of a shared concern with sociolinguistic and sociocultural norms, discursive representations, discourse practices, texts, and systems of meaning making.

As this chapter has shown, most teachers in this study wanted to encourage students to express their feelings or thoughts but at the same time were reluctant to subject themselves or their students to viewpoints that could be considered offensive to gay people. Overall (with a few notable exceptions), there was little sense that homophobic utterances might constitute opportunities to explore matters of language, discourse, and culture. Such moments were more likely to be avoided, cut short, or endured than explored, opened up, or exploited in a pedagogic sense. When discussions of homophobia or heterosexism were considered valuable, it was usually because teachers felt that students were learning to become more tolerant or accepting of gay people, or were at least being exposed to arguments for tolerance.

Ironically, it may be exactly those moments when language teachers feel that something inappropriate or uncomfortable is occurring that can serve as a rich source of teaching and learning. In a study of how EFL teachers and learners in Hong Kong perceived a government AIDS-education campaign, Jones (1996) reported that non-Chinese teachers sometimes found their students' comments on the topic off-putting.

> 'When my students start talking about things like this, I just turn off,' one teacher in this study admitted. 'I just can't stand their attitudes.' The results of this research suggest that what this teacher perceives as her students' inappropriate attitudes arise from a complex system of framing involving ideas not just about AIDS but about language itself. It is, therefore, at such moments that we as language teachers must resolutely 'turn on,' must look behind what is being said and, together with our students, begin to unravel the web of cultural models that enclose us and the topics that we talk about.
>
> (Jones, 1996, pp. 118–119)

It follows that exploring, rather than shunning, homophobic attitudes that teachers find disconcerting can lead to insights not just about the subject matter at hand but about the ways in which language and culture operate. The workings of cultural discourses may be especially evident during discussions that involve discomfort, disagreement, or disjuncture. As Candlin (1987) puts it, "moments of conflict are potentially … revelatory … of the discoursal and pragmatic resources of the participants" (p. 415), which is why such moments can be productive in language classes.

In discussing lesbian/gay themes in the intercultural arenas of language classes, moments of conflict, disagreement, or discomfort are perhaps to be expected. This is especially the case given the vast changes that are rapidly taking place worldwide with regard to the visibility and legitimacy of historically subjugated sexual identities and communities (as discussed in Chapter 2). Sexual diversity discourses are being transformed in significant ways, which is exactly why language learners may find it useful to unpack them. As I have argued elsewhere,

It is precisely those aspects of culture that are in flux, that are being contested, that are most likely to confuse students. How to negotiate competing discourses may be exactly what language students need to learn. In ESL contexts, the fact that discussing lesbian and queer themes can be complex culturally is precisely why doing so can be productive pedagogically. Not productive in the sense of furthering a gay agenda or a campaign for gay rights—but in terms of enhancing the ability to understand, participate in, and negotiate discursive practices.

(Ó'Móchain et al., 2003, p. 136)

Meaning making involves an ongoing process of evaluating what one is hearing and reading (and saying and writing) (Lemke, 1995, p. 34, following Bourdieu, 1991). There are "*dominant* norms of evaluation" that are accepted as natural by most people, and "everyone knows up to a point what those dominant norms are and speaks and evaluates at least in relation to them if not always strictly according to them" (Lemke, 1995, pp. 34–35). Yet second (or foreign) language learners are likely to have varying degrees of familiarity with 'what everybody knows' in the local (or 'target') context. It may therefore be a mistake to presume that language learners already have the knowledge and ability to evaluate utterances in accordance with norms that are dominant.

The idea that in a given classroom, or on a given campus, 'no homophobia will be tolerated' (see 4.24, 4.25) is neither a long-established principle across the United States nor a universally accepted notion. This idea is based on particular understandings of gay or lesbian identity, of what constitutes harassment or discriminatory language or behavior against members of this group, of what it means to tolerate or to refuse to tolerate these acts, and so on. There is the question of how students might understand these notions and what they have to do with learning a second or a foreign language. There is also the question of whose 'rules' or values predominate in the classroom and how this gets determined.

Yet, in my study there was a general tendency for teachers to discourage students from expressing homophobic comments, rather than to clarify and discuss such things as what meanings or connotations the student intended to convey, whether the student understood that their utterance was likely to be interpreted as homophobic in the local context, whether the student shared the teacher's understanding of what in fact constitutes homophobia, or why some people might make homophobic comments and why others might wish they would not.

Much like cultural norms (discussed in Chapter 3), norms of language use are not facts but are "open to challenge and to change" (Cameron, 1995, p. 235). It can be problematic to teach "the language of 'appropriateness'" because that "has the effect of treating norms as facts, of obscuring their contingency and thus of blunting critical responses to them" (p. 235). Another reason for caution is that, when researchers or teachers (or students) attempt to objectify "what form of language is appropriate for a given speaker in a given setting," they may be drawing on their own stereotypes of that particular community or situation (Barrett, 1997, pp. 185–186). It may be necessary, therefore, to find nontransmissive ways of exploring what does or does not constitute discriminatory speech, as Clay indicated (4.27).

Thus, instead of asking "What can I do or say so the student will not make (or continue to make) homophobic remarks?," the questions for teachers become as follows:

- On what basis has the student evaluated this particular context/situation/group of interlocutors as one in which saying (or writing) X seems to them to be acceptable or desirable?
- To what extent does the student's evaluation align with, or diverge from, my own evaluation or that of others in the class?
- Is the student cognizant that some people in some contexts would find that remark inappropriate or even offensive?
- What broader discourses and ideas are shaping this communicative event or interaction?
- Does the student have the linguistic resources to identify a communicative rift on this subject and to take steps toward repairing it?
- Are any aspects of this homophobic instance or exchange worth exploring as a means of illuminating language/culture/communication?

Thus, the aim is not to encourage learners to adopt dominant norms of evaluation or to "conform[ing] to the norms of the culturally hegemonic strata" (Thomas, 1983, p. 110) but to ensure that learners are sufficiently informed to be able to evaluate their own (and others') speech and actions in relation to those norms.

This openness is important because even teachers who consider their approach to be critical or "progressive" might seek to expose error and reveal truth (Simon, 1992, pp. 46–48). Gore (1993) has cautioned that even critical pedagogies can become "regimes of truth" (p. 2) that produce "effects of domination" (p. 145). However, a truly critical approach to teaching "must remain open and indeterminate," attempting to "take people beyond the world they already know but in a way that does not insist on a fixed set of altered meanings" (Simon, 1992, p. 47).

Queer Approaches to Language Teaching

As we have seen in this chapter, several teachers in this study reported that their educational institutions had adopted antihomophobic and other antidiscriminatory policies, which could be brought into the classroom as a means of discouraging homophobic remarks. To poststructuralists, however, oppression and liberation are not mutually exclusive but are "co-implicated in ever shifting patterns," so there is a need to continually question the configuration of oppression and liberation as opposites (Usher & Edwards, 1994, p. 226). Hence, postmodernism attempts to expose hegemonic knowledges and practices but not by simply opposing these since doing that is to remain caught up in their power (Usher & Edwards, 1994). This distinction suggests that the point is to not to eliminate but to illuminate power differentials: As Foucault (1982) puts it, "A society without power relations can only be an abstraction … [T]he analysis, elaboration, and bringing into question of power relations … is a permanent political task inherent in all social existence" (pp. 222–223). Thus, the aim of poststructuralist pedagogies is not so much to challenge oppressive power relations as to trace their effects (Lather, 1991). This suggests that homophobic or heterosexist remarks can be conceived as opportunities to foreground the power relations that give rise to, and are reinforced by, such remarks—and the effects that these broader forces have on day-to-day interactions and social relations.

On this point, Misson (1996) makes a pedagogic case for examining the consequences of anti-gay discourses on the material conditions of people's day-to-day lives, such as reinforcing (and even creating) rigid gender roles and disrupting friendships and family relationships. He recommends asking students to consider the potential consequences, to them and to others, of participating in homophobic discourses, as well as the benefits of not doing so.

Several teachers in my study mentioned the need to inform learners of the local norms of 'political correctness' (e.g., 3.14). On this subject it is worth turning to Cameron (1995), who makes the case that some people find the emphasis on 'politically correct' language objectionable, not because they dislike the values, ethics, or politics that such language represents, but because they dislike having less "control over the meaning of their own discourse" (pp. 119–120). (An example she gives is that having to choose between 'chair' or 'chairman' to describe a woman in that position means having to choose between a feminist or a conservative position—no neutral option exists [pp. 119–120].)

For language learners, whose control over the meaning of their own discourse is by definition somewhat tenuous, the politicized dimension of words associated with sexual identities may be unfamiliar and even bewildering. For example, some learners might be perplexed as to why it would be considered problematic to tease and laugh about people being gay or to use 'normal' as a synonym for 'straight.' Thus, the pedagogic goal, I would argue, is not to stop students from saying something offensive or even necessarily to reach agreement on which (or whose) rules are preferred but to look at how interlocutors identify and manage interactions in which rules about 'correctness' or 'appropriacy' are not shared. In other words, the focus is not necessarily on addressing homophobia per se but on addressing the issues such content raises about the processes of communication, discourse practice, and meaning making.

Curran (2006) makes the point that, when students ask questions in class about gay people (such as, "Are gays born that way or is it because of the environment?"), teachers might feel tempted to provide answers and information, but it may be more effective to have the students critically examine their own questions in terms of the heteronormative assumptions therein. This could involve unpacking the "sociocultural-political contexts in which the question was asked," "possible motivations behind the question," and the "range of possible reactions and responses to the question, along with the factors that may contribute to such" (p. 93). Curran notes that this is a valuable way of deconstructing the 'heterosexual hegemony,' to which I would add that it is a valuable way of deconstructing the workings of language in social interactions. Thus, critically examining heteronormativity can lead to broader questions of language use.

Conversely, taking a language-focused approach can be a practical way of examining how heteronormativity is operating in a given situation or text. Teaching practices already in common usage can be applied to the realm of sexual identities, as illustrated by Moita-Lopes (2006). He shows how a standard critical-literacy approach can be applied to texts with gay or lesbian themes; the 'interactional positionings' constructed within a text can be interrogated through questions such as "Who are the writers/speakers in the interaction? Who are the potential readers/hearers (projected interlocutors)? Are their sexualities indicated? ... Are other social identities indicated in the text?" (p. 42). Moita-Lopes (2006) also suggests that the inequitable construction of sociosexual identities can be analyzed when several texts covering the same subject matter are juxtaposed—for example, contrasting the coverage of a 'gay sex scandal' in a mainstream weekly magazine versus a gay magazine.

In this chapter, I have argued that within the intercultural, international arenas of language classrooms, where there are few shared 'truths,' it may not be effective to merely point to a poster that says "no homophobia tolerated here" in order to 'remind' students that their behavior is inappropriate. Instead, there may be a need to discuss what constitutes homophobic speech in various situations, or what the possible effects of such speech might be. Thus, the teaching aim would not be promoting social tolerance toward gay people but rather equipping students with ways of analyzing the production and negotiation of sociosexual meanings and norms.

Such a focus has two important implications. The first is that in addition to addressing homophobic comments on a one-off, spontaneous basis, as most teachers in this study were struggling to do, there is a need to build into the planned curricula some attention to the ways in which sexual identities and inequities feature in linguistic interactions and textual practices. The second implication is that in addition to developing ways of challenging the homophobic comments of students—which was a main focus for the teachers in this study—there is a need to challenge the policies and practices of educational administrators, material developers, and other stakeholders whenever these discourage open discussions of the sociosexual dimensions of language, literacy, discourse, and culture. In other words, what needs to be addressed is not just students' homophobic comments but the heteronormative thinking that underpins the language teaching industry as a whole.

CHAPTER 5
Negotiating Sexual Identities in the Classroom

Many teachers in my study found representing their own sexual identities in class to be a complex process, perhaps especially when lesbian and gay themes were being discussed. With this subject matter, teachers' and learners' attention tended to be drawn to how their own and others' sexual identities were being perceived. This chapter first looks at teachers' responses when students asked if they (or a colleague) were gay. It then examines gay and lesbian teachers' reasons for and against coming out in class as well as some self-representation issues that straight teachers experienced when teaching lesbian/gay themes. I suggest that the sexual identity dilemmas and negotiations of teachers—whether gay or straight, in or out—can inform language pedagogies by offering insights into self-representation, the emphasis being not who is gay (or who is out), but why and how systems of difference (in this case, sexual difference) are constructed and imbued with meaning.

When Students Ask If Teachers Are Gay

Several teachers reported that, during units of work on lesbian/gay themes, a student had asked directly whether their teacher (or another teacher) was lesbian (or gay). The teachers' responses to this and similar classroom situations were varied.

Responding to Questions about Whether Teachers Are Gay

A classroom incident was reported in which a student asked a teacher if she was a lesbian.

5.1 Janice: Julie had a student who ... thought it was just really funny in the middle of class, and he did this repeatedly, to say Julie, are you a lesbian? (Mike laughs) And it was just totally not funny ... He almost got kicked out of school. Because I feel like that was just not acceptable and ... we owe that to him. To let him know that ... (Mike is laughing) The thing about it was that he never thought that was not funny ... He had one more time and he would be out, dismissed, and out of the country ... He did not get it up until the very end.

Janice considered this student's query to be so offensive as to warrant a disciplining response, yet the situation seemed to be highly amusing to the student himself (and, interestingly, to Janice's colleague Mike).

While Julie's student was given a clear message that it was not appropriate to ask his teacher if she was a lesbian, Alicia's student received a very different response to that question.

> 5.2 Alicia: [My students] pretty much ask me anything … And so [a student] said … You like women, huh. And I said What? And he said OK no no no, he said Never mind, never mind, never mind. And some people were kind of listening and so I thought I want him to ask the question again so that I can answer it for the whole class. And so I asked him to ask me again and … I said Yes. And we got into this big discussion about it … And we talked about different words for that … Some students were appalled … Two women … from Somalia were devastated that this would be true … [Especially one of them. But] by the end of the term she was OK. And when I saw her the next term she was very happy to see me and hugged me.

Alicia could have avoided the student's question, or answered it privately, but she made a point of having the student ask his question in front of the entire class, which ensured that all of the students were part of the discussion that followed. In recounting this classroom incident Alicia's tone was matter-of-fact; she did not seem to have experienced any discomfort or sense of dilemma about her decision to come out as a lesbian to her students.

Mark recounted an incident that had occurred in another teacher's class.

> 5.3 Mark: Ursula was doing a topic of sexual orientation in her class and one of the students asked Is Mark gay? And she didn't know what to say … so she said I don't know. Which wasn't true. And so the student said So then it's not true … And she said Well then if you don't know then it's probably not true and it's a rumor so we should stop this rumor. So it became very uncomfortable for her and so she talked to me about it … So I put out a statement over email [to the teaching staff] saying If this should come up in your classes just have the students come and talk to me … It caused a- kind of a backlash … the response from the teachers was No this is not appropriate. We don't discuss sexual orientation, we don't discuss sexuality … The other option was … Yes you can tell [the students] that I'm gay … But some people … felt uncomfortable doing that as well. And then some other teachers … responded to that saying Well you can tell them I'm gay too. And then one of the other staff who's not gay said Oh you can tell them I'm gay too! (laughter) … [She said she was] just trying to make the point of how unimportant this is. Or … how unimportant this SHOULD be … But … what people weren't seeing is that people talk

about ... their so-called sexual orientation all the time. In the class they talk about their husband ... their children ... What did you do at the holidays? ... What are you doing on the weekend?

By recommending that the student stop the 'rumor' that Mark was gay, Ursula conveyed the message that there was something negative or undesirable about insinuating that someone might be gay, and the subject was relegated to the realm of gossip, unworthy of class time. However, when Mark suggested to his colleagues that if a student asked whether he were gay they could either have the student come talk to him, or simply answer affirmatively, there was strong sentiment against discussing the topic with students at all. Some teachers equated it with the topic of sexuality, which they felt was taboo, some wanted to safeguard the privacy of gay colleagues, and others seemed to think the subject of sexual identity was trivial or irrelevant to the main business at hand.

5.4 Mark: One of the people who said NO we just don't talk about those things ... about a month later ... she saw this person ... [whom] she kind of recognized ... And she ... said Do you have some connection with the ESL program? And he said Yeah I was a volunteer [conversation partner]. And so they were discussing, and he said Is Mark gay? Just, you know, out of nowhere ... And she was shocked. She said How- How dare you ask that question? And he just kind of looked at her like ... What's wrong with that question?

Clearly, teachers were not agreed as to whether or not a direct question about someone's (homo)sexual identity was acceptable. For some, such a question was inconsequential, while for others it was fairly fraught.

One teacher, Paige, said she made this variability a subject of discussion in class. Here, Paige was describing how she followed up visits from openly gay guest speakers.

5.5 Paige: I'll often explicitly talk about social conventions in the United States about asking people if someone is gay. And when that's considered acceptable and when it's not ... Part of that is thinking of gay students in the room ... I don't really want everybody to start joking around and saying Are you gay, are you gay?

Paige acknowledged that asking whether someone is gay could be considered acceptable or unacceptable depending on factors such as setting, situation, interlocutor, and so on, and she framed these multiple possibilities as a subject worthy of class attention.

Using Sexual-Identity Questions to Explore Language/Discourse/Culture

As we have seen above, when students ask teachers about their (homo)sexual identity, or that of their colleagues, teachers took two main approaches. One approach was to close the topic (or attempt to close it) by responding with clear discomfort or even disapproval, while another approach was to simply answer the question and then invite discussion. However, given the heteronormativity that pervades some school environments, many teachers may not feel they are in a position to provide an honest, straightforward answer when questioned about their own, or another teacher's, sexual identity.

In their study of a Francophone Canadian high school and the heteronormative discourses predominant in that environment, Dalley and Campbell (2006) report a lunchtime scenario in which a male student questioned a male teacher about his sexuality.

> Leo explained [to Mr. Choquette] … that there was a rumour among the students that he [Mr. Choquette] was gay. Leo said he had 'defended' Mr. Choquette's reputation so now he had the right to know. Although Mr. Choquette objected vigorously at this invasion into his personal life, Leo was insistent and eventually Mr. Choquette denied being gay … Later the same day, this teacher confided to [the researcher] that if he had continued to refuse to answer Leo, that would have confirmed the rumours and he would have been labeled a 'fag.'
>
> (p. 24)

This teacher told the researcher that he was, in fact, gay and felt very frustrated and angry at having to be closeted at the school. The authors note that "the power of heteronormativity at [the school] seemed to place the authority of straight students above that of teachers suspected of homosexuality" (p. 24).

The lack of authority and respect given to teachers perceived to be gay or lesbian has also been noted by Mitchell, who reports that "Some gays and lesbians may never have the chance to teach ESL at all" (Ó'Móchain et al., 2003, p. 131). This is because in some contexts their applications to teacher training programs may be rejected on the basis of their sexual identity, on the grounds that it would be difficult to find student-teaching positions for gay applicants since some "public and private schools are unwilling to accept gay student teachers" (p. 131).

For those teachers who, for whatever reason, do not wish to provide a straightforward answer when asked directly about their sexual identity, an alternative would be to turn the focus onto the types of answers that were feasible in the given context, as Evans (2002) illustrates.

> That day in class, a student had raised his hand to ask the question … "Are you a lesbian?" … [The teacher] answered "*Do you think this school is a place in which someone could answer 'yes' to that question and feel safe?*" [italics added]… [The teacher's] response illustrated how her feelings of discomfort about responding to that question were related to larger social structures.
>
> (pp. 175–176)

Language teachers might reframe such a question in a way that highlights issues of language, discourse, culture, or communication. Discussion could be generated on a number of related topics, such as what factors make a question such as "Are you a lesbian?" desirable or undesirable, acceptable or unacceptable; how people find out what others' sexual identities are; how such a question might be introduced, phrased, or intoned differently to achieve a different effect; or in which situations/settings/countries such a question is more likely, or less likely, to be asked.

Such discussions might be useful because language learners and teachers may well have divergent understandings of whether, or how, to ask questions such as "Is so-and-so gay?" or "Are you gay?" Given the cultural and linguistic diversity that characterizes second and foreign language classes, learners and teachers are likely to hold diverse understandings of what should or should not be discussed, by whom, and how.

> Not only may participants [in ELT classes] bring different attitudes to different topics, they may also bring different expectations about the forms of discourse and rules of interaction appropriate to these topics. This fact should not be seen as a barrier to education, but as an opportunity ... For what we teach when we teach language is not just the mechanical encoding and decoding of linguistic information, but also the way speakers of different languages fit this information into different social and ideological frameworks.
>
> (Jones, 1996, p. 118)

Points of divergence can be "explored or exploited for purposes of learning and teaching" (Kumaravadivelu, 1994, p. 41).

Also, as Paige's (5.5) strategy highlights, class discussions of the local conventions about asking whether someone is gay could be initiated by a teacher in anticipation of—not just in response to—a student's query.

Responding to Questions about Teachers' Marital Status

Far more frequent than direct questions about sexual identity were direct questions about marital status.

> 5.6 Jody: [Students often ask] Oh are you married? You know, and legally no, I can't be ... [But I keep] my silence as a teacher out of fear of students' reactions, maybe being fired, colleagues' reactions ... [For me] that's just emotionally ... extremely damaging. (J laughs) ... It makes my, uh, teaching life very complex ... I wanna be honest. I don't wanna participate in my own oppression.

For Jody, being asked if she was married raised the emotionally charged dilemma of whether or not to risk coming out to students, given the potentially negative career consequences if she answered honestly.

Using Marital-Status Questions to Explore Social Issues

Being asked if one is married seems to be an extremely common occurrence for many ESL teachers (see Nelson, 1993, 2005; Snelbecker, 1994). For queer teachers, the question can be somewhat fraught. Some may feel, as Phelan (1994) has described it, that

> [they] live in a constant either/or situation: either one is 'in the closet,' passing for straight and experiencing the loss of self that that entails, or one is 'out' and facing the harassment, economic deprivation, threat of violence, and loss of family support that so often follow.
>
> (p. 71)

Hence, the sense of dilemma that many gay teachers seem to experience—not once, but repeatedly:

> Coming out is a process, never a once for all time act. Many, perhaps most of us move in and out of the closet several times a day, depending on where we are and who we are with: at home, at work, with family, with trusted friends. There are longer term patterns, too: it is not uncommon for gay people to move from a situation in which they have been relatively open about themselves to one in which they have felt constrained to silence [such as teaching].
>
> (Spraggs, 1994, p. 180)

Curran (2006) recounts how he addressed the marital status question, within an ESL class that he was teaching in Australia, in a way that generated discussion of some broader social issues. During an introductory activity on the first day of class, he was asked whether he was married and he said he was not. The next day he initiated a follow-up activity:

> [I had the students] list the sorts of questions that people typically ask each other, and to identify any topics that were potentially sensitive, problematic, or offensive. The class identified family and marriage as the topics most likely to be sensitive and they discussed possible reasons for this, which led to a group brainstorm of the range of family forms that is found in Australia. I mentioned that there had been an increase in families with lesbian, gay, or bisexual parents, and I named several local schools that had a significant number of children with such parents. This ... led to a discussion of same-sex relationships and same-sex marriage. I eventually guided the discussion back to the original question that had prompted the day's activities ("Are you married?") and explained that I had found it difficult to answer because I was gay.
>
> (Curran, 2006, p. 87)

Even teachers who are not gay themselves, or who choose not to come out, could follow up questions about marital status by facilitating a discussion of broader issues to do with family configurations, as Curran did.

Sexual Identities as Performative

Coming out, or disclosing one's 'true' gay self, has been characterized by the identity-based lesbian/gay movement as a means of fostering personal integrity and mobilizing for civil rights. However, as discussed in Chapter 1, poststructuralists contest the notion of self-disclosure, arguing that there is no preexisting unitary self to be revealed, no 'butterfly emerging from the chrysalis' (Malinowitz, 1995). Identity is understood to be "a process, perpetually in construction, perpetually contradictory, perpetually open to change" (Belsey, 1980, p. 132). If identity is "a matter of 'becoming' as well as of 'being'" (Hall, 1990, p. 225), then 'becoming out' might be a more accurate term than 'coming out' (Phelan, 1994). But what exactly does it mean to come (or become) 'out'—"Out of what? Into what?" (Malinowitz, 1995, p. 75).

In queer theory, a key concept, taken from linguistics (Austin, 1975), is performativity—the notion that utterances act upon the world rather than just describe it. Butler (1990, 1991) argues that sexual identities (like gender identities) are not 'authentic' or descriptive but performative. That is, sexual identities are not expressions of prior truths but are instead the effects of repeated discursive or semiotic acts (though these effects then claim to 'represent' prior truths) (Butler, 1991).

Cameron (1995) extends Butler's analysis beyond gender and sexual identities, arguing that the notion of performativity could be applied to "any apparently fixed and substantive social identity label" (p. 16). In Cameron's (1995) summation, "Sociolinguistics says that how you act depends on who you are; critical theory says that who you are [and are taken to be] depends on how you act" (pp. 15–16).

The notion of performativity makes it possible to attend to how heterosexuality, not just homosexuality, is 'produced.' It is through repeated discursive acts that "the illusion of a seamless heterosexual identity" is produced (Butler, 1991, p. 18). Producing a 'seamless' or unified identity that then appears 'natural' requires ongoing effort. In order to maintain its dominant, naturalized status, heterosexuality requires constant reinforcement: "that heterosexuality is always in the act of elaborating itself is evidence that it is perpetually at risk, that is, that it 'knows' its own possibility of becoming undone" (Butler, 1991, p. 23)—which is why it has to be marked by language users "so assiduously and repetitively" (Cameron, 1995, p. 17).

The performativity of identities is a useful notion pedagogically, perhaps especially in classes with a language/culture focus, because it makes it possible to examine the linguistic/semiotic acts whereby sexual identities (in this case) are constituted and communicated. The notion of performativity also underscores how teacher identity can itself become pedagogy (Morgan, 2004), which is exemplified in Curran's (2006) example of coming out in class and which will be further illustrated in the next section.

On Lesbian and Gay Teachers Coming Out to Students

Of those teachers in my study who identified as gay or lesbian, most had not come out in class, even when teaching gay or lesbian themes. Only a few reported having come out in class, yet there was much discussion nonetheless about coming out dilemmas.

Coming Out Inadvertently

Several teachers explained that when they were in their local gay neighborhood or at a gay event it was not uncommon to encounter ESL students from their programs.

5.7 Tom: [At gay venues] I routinely run into [ESL] students ... And so I just don't make any beans *[sic]* about it ... A student once saw me [in the gay neighborhood] and said ... What are YOU doing here? And I said What are YOU doing here? You know, ha ha ha. (C laughs)

Thus, even gay and lesbian teachers who do not choose to be out in the classroom may feel 'outed' when students see them taking part in the local gay/lesbian social scene.

Considering Coming Out

Coming out is not necessarily a clear-cut, verbalized event.

5.8 David: I do each term try to work in some gay material, some gay task, to just get the students talking about it for one, two, three days in the term ... I imagine by doing that I'm kind of indirectly disclosing to my students that I'm gay ... I'm sure by bringing up the topic most of them probably suspect it.

The notion that introducing gay themes is itself a gay signifier raises the question of what exactly constitutes 'coming out,' especially in classroom situations.

Nancy regularly taught lesbian/gay themes without coming out but was questioning this choice.

5.9 Nancy: I bring [lesbian/gay themes] up in the classroom every term in whatever course I happen to be teaching—writing ... or reading or ... listening/speaking ... But I always have a very strong delineation between bringing up the topic and including myself in the topic. (laughter) ... It's hard for me to ... be self-disclosing because, um, I've ... been around longer than it's been kind of a fashionable thing ... So, uh, this is my question ... When we are talking about, uh, sexual awareness, sexual images, how personal does it need to get? [...] Is it required ... to raise awareness of, uh, gay people? Is it dishonesty if you don't include yourself when you're teaching?

Paula: ... If you were doing controversial issues like abortion ... and you'd had an abortion ... is that ... something you would share?

Nancy: ... But to me that's a very different ball park because that's ... one discrete thing. I mean, this [being a lesbian] is integral in every aspect of my BEING, my whole LIFE ...

Kath: ... If I don't talk about it because I'm afraid, then that's one thing. If I don't talk about it because ... it's not the appropriate time to, ... that's something else. But I think ... what's on the table right now ... is ... How do you handle that personal fear?

In this discussion, the notion that, for gay teachers, self-disclosure was a social obligation was set against the notion that it was a fashionable trend; the notion that sexual identity was integral to every part of life was set against the notion that it was a private part of life; and the notion that coming out was at times inappropriate or at least unnecessary was set against the notion that it was at times desirable but too frightening to pursue.

A gay teacher educator, Ira, spoke about the importance of finding ways to address that fear.

> 5.10 Ira: I can see ... young gay men and lesbians [in my teacher-education classes] ... I don't want them to go through what I went through ... I want them equipped ... with the tools that they need and ... the integrity to- to go out there and ... not feel that sense of, um, dissociation from themselves ... That sense of I'm here as a teacher but I've left my sexuality outside the classroom ... You can ... see it in their eyes ... I see myself so clearly because nobody ever addressed [this] when I was training.

Ira's observation raises the question of how teacher-education programs might address the particular challenges that lesbian and gay student-teachers may face in the classroom.

Although for Tom coming out as gay to students in his program was not a pressing issue, he was supportive when teachers under his supervision did want to come out.

> 5.11 Tom: My being gay is just a portion of my personality and who I am as a person, and not at this point in my life the single most defining feature. That's not always the case with people who ... have been out for a fairly short period of time. It's a lot more important to them personally ... As a supervisor ... my question is ... Is it your need or their need? Um, if it's your need, look at that ... [If] you still wanna do it, go for it ... Probably ... a third to a half of our teaching staff is gay ... As a teacher trainer and a supervisor my concern is basically only that ... [coming out] is ... a conscious and intentional choice on the part of the teacher.

As Tom indicates, a substantial proportion of teachers potentially face decisions about whether to come out. He recommends that teachers who are considering coming out think through the pedagogic purpose of doing so.

Straight Teachers 'Come Out'

Gay teachers' grapplings with the coming out dilemma can be perplexing to straight teachers. As the TESOL focus group discussion came to a close, a participating teacher made the following comment.

> 5.12 Scott: [I don't] stand in front of my class and say Good morning, I'm Scott Smith and I'm a heterosexual. So why should anyone else have to state, you know, overtly their, um, sexual orientation?

To this teacher, 'announcing' one's sexual identity was not something straight teachers did, so it seemed odd to him that gay and lesbian teachers would consider this an option, or perhaps an obligation.

However, many teachers in my study noted that it was not unusual for teachers to come out as straight to their students through the course of teaching—not by saying "I'm straight," but by mentioning their spouse or other family members or their holiday or weekend activities (see 5.3). Tina observed a conversation class in which the students had been talking about restaurants when the (female) teacher made an off-hand mention of her male partner.

> 5.13 Tina: [The teacher said] Oh my fiancé took me to a restaurant! I'm engaged! ... If you're a gay student, that's really shoving somebody's sexual preference in your face ... Just flaunting your ... heterosexuality ... If you were a lesbian and you did that ... the administration and students would be all over you—Me and my partner! ... It would be really different.

Tina objected to the double standard that made it generally unacceptable for a female teacher to make a similar comment about a female partner (for example, "My lover took me to a restaurant. I'm planning to move in with her!"). This classroom instance illustrates how straight teachers 'come out' spontaneously as part of discussing whatever topic is at hand, not by making an explicit pronouncement of their sexual identity. Thus, straightness is generally the unmarked case.

Classroom Discourse as Routinely Heterosexual

Even though straight teachers routinely 'revealed' their sexual identity through the course of day-to-day teaching, gay or lesbian teachers who did the same thing felt they were risking the disapproval of students, colleagues, and/or administrators. Some educators have argued that this double standard is inequitable, even absurd.

> [The National Union of Teachers in the United Kingdom] cannot proclaim that lesbians and gays are entitled to equal opportunities in education and society and in the same breath say that so long as they are teachers, they must keep quiet about their sexual identity. Not, at the very least, until it bans its other members from wearing wedding rings and telling classroom anecdotes about their spouses.
>
> (Spraggs, 1994, p. 193)

The heterosexualized nature of much classroom discourse is not always recognized as such, particularly not by straight people. Few feel the need to identify as straight, as that is "the unspoken norm" (Phelan, 1994, p. xiv), "the great unsaid" (Weeks, 1987, p. 31). In the same way that men tend to be considered "free from or not determined by gender relations" (Flax, 1989, p. 59), heterosexual people tend to be seen as free from, or not determined by, sexual identity (Mac an Ghaill, 1994). In general, members of 'dominating groups' tend not to identify (nor to be identified) with the group. Instead, they consider themselves unique individuals. However, members of 'dominated groups' do tend to consider themselves (and are considered by others) as members of the group (Goffman, 1963). In the field of linguistics, according to Poynton (1997), there is little acknowledgment that

> everyone is raced, gendered, classed, generationed, sexualised, and so on. Individuals may not see themselves in terms of such 'identities' if they are part of the dominant group who defines what is normative, but they can be certain that others will. Where difference is what those at the centre see, privilege is what is highly visible from the margins … [including] the sexual privilege of the heterosexual (particularly the married, heterosexual adult).
>
> (pp. 15–16)

Although heterosexuality is pervasive, it is rarely constructed as (hetero)sexual identity, so it often remains unmarked—at least, among heterosexuals. Straight people often fail to see the myriad ways in which heterosexuality permeates daily conversation: "Husband, wife, wedding ring, kids, anniversaries, in-laws, boy/girl friend: all are the currency of everyday social intercourse for the heterosexual" (Harris, 1990, p. 103). To gay people though (or to those raised in gay families, as Tina was [see 2.14]), heterosexuality is often highly visible as a sexual identity.

Furthermore, the myriad, routine ways in which heterosexual identity is announced are not always recognized as value laden. Harris (1990) points out that "[e]very comment we [teachers] make, every text we use, involves the transmission of some value or belief … If I choose to wear a wedding ring, I am saying that I support the convention of marriage, in much the same way as I would be advertising my conformity to any other social institution by wearing its badge" (p. 36).

Many teachers in straight relationships feel free not only to wear wedding rings to class but also to talk about their partner or spouse to their students. There are numerous examples of this in language education literature, but to name just one, Morgan (2004) recounts how, at a class lunch in a restaurant, a student reached into her husband's wallet for money to pay their portion of the bill, and another student commented that the wife controls the family finances. In an attempt to save face for the husband, who appeared uncomfortable, Morgan began telling the group about his own wife and her "preeminent role in family financial matters" (p. 181).

To teachers in my study there was nothing problematic about revealing one's relationship status in the course of teaching; what was problematic was that it was often only straight teachers who felt able to do this. This double standard may be perpetuated at least in part because heterosexuality is less likely to be recognized as a sexual identity, or even to be associated with sexuality: "The sexualization of straight subjectivity is frequently not acknowledged" (Mac an Ghaill, 1994, p. 165).

Coming Out to Draw on One's Lived Experience

Several teachers said they came out in order to make it possible to speak in class about their own experiences, either in spontaneous ways throughout the curriculum or when teaching a lesbian/gay unit.

Paige explained how she responded when straight teachers challenged her decision to come out as a lesbian in her classes.

5.14 Paige: I've had coworkers who have said ... it wasn't right for teachers to come out [as lesbian or gay] and they shouldn't share their personal lives with students and feeling that it was never appropriate for them to do that ... I've just asked them to think about how often they've talked about their husband or wife in the classroom, or their kids, or mentioning that, you know, they have a partner ... I ... try to give them examples of how being a lesbian is such an integral part of my life that not including that means that I censor SO much of who I am and what I can bring to a classroom that it changes my teaching completely ... I think one of the things that good teachers often do is bring up spontaneous examples related to something they're teaching. And I can almost never do that if I don't come out. Unless I change all the characters and the story and use different pronouns ... I [also] ... say to teachers ... [that] I'm not talking about my sex life to students.

Teachers, whether straight, bisexual, or gay, need to be able to draw on aspects of their family life in the course of teaching.

In Paige's view, the discomfort or disapproval of some colleagues about out lesbian teachers stems from a tendency to sexualize lesbianism and gayness but not straightness. This view was corroborated by Janice, who had felt perplexed and disconcerted when she first heard of 'lesbians and gays in ESL' as a topic for professional discussion (below she refers to Carscadden et al., 1992 [see Nelson, 1993]).

5.15 Janice: I can remember ... [hearing about] your presentation at TESOL ['We are your colleagues: Lesbians and gays in ESL'] thinking WHY in the WORLD? ... What ... are they doing?! What is this about? ... Now I'm embarrassed ... that I had such a narrow view of it. But I kept thinking What does this whole SEX thing have to do with ESL?

Paige gave an example of a class in which she decided to come out as a lesbian so that she could draw on her own experience of the subject matter.

5.16 Paige: [In my] Business English class ... the students were very interested in ... how women who were mothers balanced their work lives with their home lives ... My students ... wanted me to talk about my experience of being a working mother ... To do that I needed to come out because I couldn't leave out the fact that I had a partner who was helping me do this and pretend that I was a single mother.

According to Claire, gay and lesbian teachers in her program had similar reasons for wanting to come out.

5.17 Claire: We ask students to … share who they are and we don't share who we are … And other people come out in the classroom as straight just by virtue of … small talk about their weekends … Sometimes … [teachers] come out because it's really appropriate in the context of a unit … [for example] on family … There's a reading about [a gay family] in this collection of readings about what makes a family … A gay man … [taught] the class … and then a lesbian [did] … [But] then a straight person had the class (Claire laughs) and it became … considerably less dynamic because they couldn't add this [coming out as gay].

In Claire's experience, some gay teachers wanted to be able to be as open about their lives as their straight colleagues and students were. Also, the curriculum could be expanded and enlivened when gay teachers shared their lived experiences of topics such as family.

Paige reported that coming out also enhanced the quality of her relationships with students.

5.18 Paige: I had one student write … about how, um, she had been divorced in her country, and felt really stigmatized because of that. And that she REALLY appreciated … my being honest with them and talking about my experience and, um, it just, it made her feel really validated and, um, comfortable … [My coming out] lets [students] have a shared sense of identity in a way I think with the teacher, like Oh I can see … that you share this similar situation of being stigmatized or prejudiced against so maybe you can understand me better.

Coming out can strengthen rapport with students and help them to feel comfortable expressing their own experiences of social discrimination.

Drawing on Lived Experience as a Teaching Tool

A high school English (not ESL) teacher in the United Kingdom, who is a lesbian, describes what it is like to teach without coming out: "I conduct my interactions … through a deliberately constructed self-presentation that is not merely asexual but excludes or drastically distorts almost every aspect of my daily life, affectional, intellectual, political and aesthetic" (Spraggs, 1994, p. 180). As another educator puts it,

To live in the closet, in this void, is to be constantly aware of what one is *not* saying, is *not* doing, is *not* experiencing or receiving, because you are afraid to be fully, publicly yourself. In the classroom, it often means avoiding authors or themes that might cast you as a teacher or student in a questionable light.
(Bennett, 1982, p. 5)

Thus, decisions about curricula are sometimes determined by teachers' fear of being seen to be gay.

Spraggs (1994) argues that lesbian and gay teachers, like straight teachers, should be able to come out in the classroom if they so wish. Her argument, like Paige's (5.14 and 5.16), is based on the importance of being able to draw on one's experiences while teaching.

It is not a teacher's business to emphasize continually her or his own opinions, let alone to press pupils to agree with them. But to assert that most teachers efface their own personalities when teaching is manifest nonsense, and to suggest that it is desirable that they should seek to do so is to disregard many of the realities of the classroom situation. An anecdote from life may drum home a point … far more effectively than any amount of impersonal exposition. Moreover, in a context in which pupils are pressured continually to expose their own experiences and thoughts, whether in classroom discussion, story writing or formal essay, the assumption by the teacher of self-protective silence and aloofness is neither pedagogically useful nor morally appealing.

(Spraggs, 1994, pp. 183–184)

Spraggs points out that expecting students to disclose their experiences and opinions while teachers do just the opposite is problematic ethically and pedagogically. Furthermore, as Mercer (1995) argues, "one legitimate goal for a teacher is to make information *memorable*," and a way of accomplishing this is to recount interesting narratives (p. 27). When teachers are not free to draw on their own lives, their ability to share interesting stories may be somewhat limited.

In second and foreign language classes, teachers' life experiences and points of view may be more prominent compared with other educational subjects, given the likelihood that it is the teacher who is presumed to be most familiar with the 'target' culture/language (see 5.25). Duff and Uchida (1997) note the "self-disclosure and contrived intimacy and familiarity that characterized many conversational EFL classes with young foreign teachers" (p. 463). Even though self-disclosure does not appeal to all teachers, it is often expected of them (p. 463). The degree of difficulty this poses for gay and lesbian teachers may depend in part on how central or peripheral sexual identity is in their lives. Being a lesbian was an integral part of Paige's life (5.14) (and Nancy's [see 5.9]), whereas being a gay man was only a 'portion' of Tom's personality (5.11).

For Paige, coming out in the Business English class made it possible to share her own experiences of the subject matter, which was working mothers (5.16); for the teachers in Claire's program, coming out made it possible to augment and energize the unit on families (5.17). These accounts illustrate Fuss' (1991) argument that "To be out is really to be in—inside the realm of the visible, the speakable, the culturally intelligible" (p. 4). They also suggest that out gay teachers can be seen as a resource because they can contribute 'real-life' experiences and perspectives that are typically underrepresented (if represented at all) in language materials and curricula.

A shared experience of oppression can help to establish rapport with students, even if the forms of oppression are different, as Paige reported (5.18) (see also Mittler & Blumenthal, 1994). A similar point was made in Maher and Tetreault's

(1994) study of U.S. tertiary-level 'feminist classrooms,' which described a lecturer who regularly came out as a lesbian in her classes: "her disclosures create a climate that can embrace a range of differences, so that student experiences can be validated or remain concealed; in a sense, she articulates the unspoken identities of the diverse, sometimes oppressed, groups in her classroom" (p. 241). By coming out, the teacher's aim was not necessarily to encourage students to disclose their own identities or experiences, but rather to validate "both student experiences and their concealments" (p. 242).

In a 1963 study of managing 'stigmatized' identities, Goffman argues that all societies have identity norms (though some have more than others), but few people, if any, meet every norm; as a result, almost everyone is engaged, at least to a degree, in managing the stigmatized aspects of their own (and others') identities (pp. 128–131). Moreover, given the power and the number of social norms, most people grapple at times with decisions about whether, and to what extent, to 'pass' (i.e., not to disclose the stigmatized identity). Passing affects not only the stigmatized person and the strangers with whom she or he interacts but also those who are close to the stigmatized person (p. 97). Furthermore, there is a "pervasive two-role social process in which every individual participates in both roles [being stigmatized and stigmatizing], at least in some connections and in some phases of life" (p. 138). Thus, virtually everyone at times experiences being stigmatized, faces decisions about 'passing,' interacts with others who are passing, and stigmatizes others. Given the challenges of doing these things in a second or foreign language/culture, it would seem valuable to have teaching staff who are able and willing to explore such issues in class. Thus, having openly gay and lesbian teachers (among others) would be an asset.

Coming Out to Challenge Homophobia and Encourage Critical Thinking

In addition to being able to draw on experience and connect with students, teachers sometimes came out in order to counter students' homophobia and to foster critical thinking.

> 5.19 Paige: If we're doing a [lesbian/gay] unit ... there are often homophobic comments ... If I hear a few comments like that ... I'll purposely come out sooner because ... it doesn't feel fair to the students that they're not able to make a knowledgeable choice on what kind of comments they make and how that might be hurting their teacher ... 'Cause they might be really embarrassed if they found out afterwards that they had said this about their teacher ... not realizing that she was gay.

Thus, coming out can be a face-saving gesture for one's students, who may be making homophobic comments without considering the possibility that their teacher could be a lesbian.

Another teacher, Kath, explained why she came out in her beginning level speaking/listening class.

5.20 Kath: It was three days in a row where they had been giving reports about favorite movies and guys going He really liked … Arnold Schwarzenegger … Oh you gay, oh you fag, oh you really love him don't you, hee hee hee … I was tired of these kinds of comments happening and I said Well you guys seem to really like to talk about, um, gay people, so we're going to have a gay speaker (laughter) … I had them brainstorm questions … Then I [left the room briefly and returned] … and talked to them … It did resolve having all those comments in the classroom … I felt more rapport with most students … It seems to get passed on so that's all right because I have a supportive administration.

Kath felt that coming out had positive results—no more gay teasing and better rapport with students. Kath described a second instance when she came out, but in a different way and for a different reason.

5.21 Kath: I need to be personal with people. It's how I connect … I come out all the time and it's … really promoted discussion … [and] critical thinking … This last term I came out because … they were saying … How do we change racism? We all think racism is bad. And they said Education … It was like so pat … And I said … I've been a- a lesbian … in … the feminist movement since 1971. And it is not … so SIMPLE … I mean, what do you mean by education? … [I got] them to go more into depth, to do more critical thinking … [by] being able to talk about … my history of- of [community] organizing.

In this case, coming out made it possible for Kath to draw on her knowledge of lesbian feminist activism as a means of bringing more depth and complexity to the class discussion of racism.

Another teacher also considered coming out to be a pedagogic tool for highlighting connections between diverse cultural groups and systems of oppression.

5.22 Carmen: We're always teaching cross-cultural awareness … but we leave out the sexual orientation part of it … One term by the end of the class I could come out to my students and they had no choice but to accept me because of what they had already learned. I said, you know, What is racism, and what causes racism? and they said Fear and lack of education. And they could apply that to homophobia … and … they thought Wow, because of what I know I- I have to accept this on some level.

Coming Out to Raise Awareness of Audience

Relevant to language education are published accounts by teachers who frame their coming out as more of a communication issue. One such account is by Malinowitz (1992), a tertiary-level composition teacher. When students write about gay topics, Malinowitz cautions them not to assume that their reader (teacher or classmate) is not gay (or HIV-positive), and she asks them to consider how a gay or lesbian reader might react to their writing: "Stunned, they began to consider questions of audience and tone in new ways, and to recognize some of the assumptions embedded within their simple 'us/them' dichotomy" (p. 3). Such considerations are critical to student writers for they must learn to "clarify the complex intentions, possible reinterpretations and reader-responses, and consequences that they will have to negotiate" (Malinowitz, 1995, p. 42).

This point is illustrated by Destandau's account of teaching English for Academic Purposes (Destandau et al., 1995). She reports that a student giving an oral presentation said that the U.S. city in which they were located had "too many gays," which made several students hiss and shift uncomfortably. Classroom incidents like this one prompted Destandau to begin telling students that she is a lesbian (see Chapter 1). She reports that her coming out helped students to develop a greater awareness of their audience, a key objective in both academic writing (in order to anticipate readers' expectations and reactions) and in academic speaking (in order to craft arguments that will persuade, rather than alienate, the audience).

On Lesbian and Gay Teachers Not Coming Out to Students

Most gay- and lesbian-identified teachers in this study had not come out in their classes. A few teachers articulated their reasons for not coming out, which are presented here.

Risks of Coming Out

For Alicia, who did sometimes come out (see 2.5 and 5.2), an important consideration was the students' language-proficiency level.

> 5.23 Alicia: [In] low-level classes I rarely come out because there's no reason to … The language level is so low that we're … discussing fruits and vegetables … and stuff like that so it doesn't matter … [Also] you can't, um, discuss it … They just can't tell you what they're thinking or … feeling.

Alicia sought to shield students from the potential frustration of having reactions that they could not adequately express in the second language.

Ira made the point that coming out could threaten one's sense of security, materially as well as emotionally.

> 5.24 Ira: [When teaching in] a highly commercial environment … there are substantial risks … with coming out. I mean these are not just fears about self-revelation. They're fears about job security … They're real, very real for many people. […] And the other thing is see we're taught that … our professional success … is dependent on … not revealing ourselves … So it actually is a great internal struggle to actually say … I am gay. Because it goes against all my intuitions about self-preservation and, um, survival. So … it's never easy.

Ira's comment raises questions about the extent to which language teachers feel they must maintain a straight persona in order to succeed professionally and how the pressure to 'act straight' can constrain teaching practices, and thereby learning outcomes (we saw an example of this in Chapter 4, with Helen [see 4.9]).

Coming Out Dilemmas

Alicia's and Ira's concerns highlight the fact that sexual identities are often what Vandrick (1997a) has called 'hidden identities.' Goffman (1963), in his study of how 'stigmatized identities' are 'managed,' makes a useful observation on what it is like to have stigmatized attributes that are not necessarily evident to others: "To display or not to display; to tell or not to tell; to let on or not to let on; to lie or not to lie; and in each case, to whom, how, when, and where" (p. 42)—facing these constant choices, rather than being "spontaneously involved *within* the situation," a person tends to become extremely "situation conscious" (p. 111), "a scanner of possibilities" (p. 88). Situations that are for others "unthinking routines" become "management problems" for the person who is attempting to gauge conditions of disclosure (p. 88). Thus, the need for deliberation, planning, and reflection before coming out to students as gay contrasts sharply with the spontaneity, frequency, and insouciance typically associated with 'coming out as straight' (see 5.13).

Given the risks that are often associated with coming out, few gay people "are not deliberately in the closet with someone personally or economically or institutionally important to them"—and this is the case even for those gay people who are very out in most circumstances (Sedgwick, 1990, pp. 67–68). One reason is that it is not always possible to predict how others might react to the knowledge that one is gay. Furthermore, it is not necessarily the case that people simply 'decide' who will, and who will not, be informed that one is gay—there is often a degree of uncertainty about who does or does not know:

> Even an out gay person deals daily with interlocutors about whom she doesn't know whether they know or not; it is equally difficult to guess for any given interlocutor whether, if they did know, the knowledge would seem very important.
>
> (Sedgwick, 1990, p. 68)

Coping with these uncertainties and ambiguities may contribute to the intensity some teachers experience when teaching gay themes.

These uncertainties and ambiguities can be exacerbated in the international, intercultural arenas of language education. In a study of foreign and indigenous women teaching EFL in Japan, Simon-Maeda (2004) found that lesbian EFL teachers struggle to obtain and maintain teaching positions as a result of the "homophobic atmosphere prevailing in Japan" (p. 423). Due to the difficulty of finding lesbian teachers who were willing for their interview data to be published (given their career fears if they were to be identified), Simon-Maeda (2004) turned to a lesbian network on the Internet. She presents the following 'composite summary' of the online responses she received to her request for work stories from lesbian and queer EFL teachers:

Since coming to Japan, I am not out in my daily life, and it's pretty strange for me … Maybe my shyness and reluctance to talk about my personal life is related to my having been a lesbian all my adult life. Maybe I hate hearing people talk about their personal lives at work because I know that, even if I do, it won't be received in the same way … What am I afraid of? That people's attitudes toward me might change. That my contract might not be renewed. That I might be laughed at. That I might become a more public figure. That I might always be viewed only as 'the lesbian' rather than the multifaceted person I am. That I might be seen as a controversial person.

(p. 423)

Simon-Maeda argues that it is highly problematic when educators feel they must "divorce their pedagogical ideals and practices from their lesbian, queer, or bisexual subjectivities" because they end up "isolating themselves and depriving students of the opportunity to reflect on sexuality issues" (pp. 423–424).

From the accounts of lesbian- and gay-identified teachers in this study it is clear that there are more than the two options of either coming out explicitly or not coming out at all. Griffin's (1992) study of 13 lesbian and gay educators (from preschool through high school) in the United States found that they 'managed' their sexual identities at school by "passing," "covering," "being implicitly out," or "being explicitly out" and that these were seen as a continuum, with 'passing' the "safest" (pp. 175–176). The educators believed that students (and their parents) and colleagues would be more likely to infer that they (the educators) were gay or lesbian if they were seen to be "talking to gay or lesbian students" who approached them for "counseling," "teaching classroom lessons on homophobia, sex stereotyping, lesbian/gay writers," or "objecting to gay jokes or homophobic slurs among students or colleagues" (pp. 180–181). This raises questions about whether language educators might feel pressure to avoid certain activities, such as talking with openly gay students, teaching gay material, or challenging homophobia, for fear of being perceived as gay or lesbian, and if so, how these concerns shape or limit their teaching practices.

Pressures of Being an Out Teacher

In Claire's experience, teachers of international students are sometimes reluctant to come out as gay or lesbian because of the pressures of being positioned as a cultural representative.

5.25 Claire: [ESL] teachers … have this extra duty of kind of being a cultural informant for our students … We are often their only contact with native speakers. Especially … foreign students … [Teachers feel they must be] Everywoman, Everyman … Mr. and Miss America … I think it comes from students asking … Do Americans do this? or What's the American family like? or How do people date? … Suddenly you're in this role to … know all this stuff … So if I come out as a gay teacher then have I really done my job? … And then is it the gay America I should be representing, you know? (Claire laughs)

> I mean ... now I'm not only the only American, I'm the only lesbian they've ever met. (We laugh) ... I think the pressure gets kind of huge. And then once you're out do you have to be a good lesbian ... It does really up the ante.

As Claire observes, students tend to expect their language teachers to be 'representatives' or 'informants' of the new culture, and as such to convey knowledge about the social conventions associated with such things as (heterosexual) dating. This role of informant may make it all the more daunting for teachers to make a point of challenging the presumption that they have first-hand knowledge of straight customs and conventions.

Ira spoke of similar pressures and tensions that might lead gay and lesbian teachers not to come out to students.

> 5.26 Ira: [In the TESOL focus group] we were discussing ... coming out as being, uh, definitely something very positive, uh, for teachers. But I've actually found in some ways ... that you can actually become more vulnerable because you're putting yourself in a position where lots of things are being projected onto you ... lots of anxieties ... You have to carry the weight of people's ... homophobia. [...] And eros. So ... the coming out gesture ... is not necessarily going to take you into a- a better space. It's very, very complex. Because actually you're relinquishing control over disclosure. Once you've done it, you've done it. There's no going back. [...] Up until that moment of disclosure I am not a gay man in the classroom ... It's from that moment that I start the performance.

Outing oneself may lead to a loss of control over one's image, by being 'demonized,' or hypersexualized, in the eyes of others. Also, there is a certain finality associated with the act of coming out, as well as pressure to 'fit' the identity, to reiterate the 'performance.'

(Sexual) Identities as Regulatory

Claire's comment points to the irony of expecting gay teachers to teach straight customs of the 'target' culture—and to do so without disclosing their own gayness (see Hirst, 1981). At the same time, as Claire observed, a teacher who has come out may feel pressure to become what Blinick (1994) calls "a super teacher—having to be extra good, extra dedicated to prove how wonderful lesbian teachers are" (p. 142). Thus, coming out can bring a new set of potential difficulties.

As Ira noted, an out teacher may have to deal with others' homophobic anxieties:

> [M]any people fear coming out in school (and elsewhere) because they don't want to watch themselves being reread within that cultural fiction of demonization; it can be overwhelming to contemplate the gulf between what one may signify to others and how one experiences oneself.
>
> (Malinowitz, 1995, p. 74)

Out teachers may also have to, as Ira put it, "carry the weight of people's eros" (see 5.26). Whereas straightness tends to be undersexualized, gayness tends to be hypersexualized (Hinson, 1996). All in all, coming out is not necessarily a liberating act.

Claire's and Ira's comments underscore the regulatory function of identities. According to Bourdieu (1991), identifying as a member of a community or a group by definition carries with it a requirement to act in a certain way. In this view, "to give a social definition an identity" is "to *signify* to someone what he *[sic]* is and how he should conduct himself as a consequence" (p. 120). How a group envisages and represents itself contributes to the group's reality since the process of categorization "tends to produce what it designates" (p. 133). In other words, theory about the reality shapes the reality. This means that "self-determination does not necessarily result from self-naming, since the names themselves have their own historicity, which precedes our use of them" (Livia & Hall, 1997b, p. 12, citing Butler, 1993).

This raises a point I have made elsewhere about the paradoxes of sexual identities, which under a queer theory framework are understood to be socially constraining as well as socially constructive:

> Sexual identities can exclude as well as include, limit as well as liberate (Fuss, 1991). Solidifying fluid sexualities into fixed sexual identities that can then be taxonomised may have more to do with social control than empowerment. After all, the purpose of the straight/gay binary is not merely to describe sexual identities but to regulate them; in other words, the binary is not neutral but normative.
>
> (Nelson, 1999, p. 376)

Thus, with coming out, instead of having to hide one's sexual identity by speaking as a straight person (or as an asexual person), there is a new imperative to speak and to conduct oneself 'as a lesbian.'

Claire's concern that language teachers feel they must represent the target or local culture (in this case, 'America')—and, if they come out, then the gay population ('gay America') (see 5.25)—raises important questions about who speaks for whom. Coming out makes it possible to speak *as* a gay person instead of just *about* gay people. However, to poststructuralists, the notion of 'speaking as' is still problematic.

> The question of 'speaking *as*' involves a distancing from oneself. The moment I have to think of the ways in which I will speak as an Indian, or as a feminist, [or] ... as a woman. What I am doing is trying to generalise myself, make myself a representative ... There are many subject positions which one must inhabit; one is not just one thing.
>
> (Spivak, 1990, pp. 59–60)

The multiplicity of identities and subjectivities that an individual must negotiate underscores the complexities of coming out, and the potential risks of being reread by others in a narrow framing.

Another potentially constraining aspect of sexual identities is alluded to by Ellwood (2006). In the article, she describes her own sexual identity as fluid and open, but when interviewing an ESL student from Japan who told her he was gay, she found that

> my lack of fixed identification as a gay person aligns me, by default, with the normative—that is, hegemonic heterosexuality. In light of Katsuyuki's strong claim to a gay identity, I felt that, unless I stated otherwise, I was being positioned as always/already heterosexual.
>
> (p. 77)

Thus, those who identify as bisexual, are questioning their sexual identity or who simply do not relate to sexual identity as a category of identity may feel that unless they come out as gay they are presumed to be straight.

This may in part account for the general rarity of bisexual, questioning, and fluidly identified perspectives among teachers in this study (see 2.13 and 8.46). Those who did not strongly identify as either gay or straight may have felt hesitant to describe their experiences or articulate their own identifications or dis-identifications, perhaps especially when surrounded by colleagues in the focus groups who were identifying themselves as straight, lesbian, or gay; this underscores the fact that 'speaking out' about gay and lesbian existence does not mean that there is an end to silencing—only that silencing takes new forms (following Foucault, 1990).

Talburt (2000a) is critical of the way in which much education literature on the subject of coming out seems to reify it: "Following calls for gay and lesbian voice and visibility, there is an imperative—indeed, an obligation—for teachers to figure themselves as classroom texts, to represent and embody a category of sexuality so that their very presence is pedagogical" (p. 55). But Talburt critiques what she calls the "'personalization' of pedagogy" (p. 56). By deliberately choosing not to come out, she says, teachers can create "a pedagogy of questioning in which expectations are never fulfilled but always rearranged" (p. 74). This argument is illustrated by an associate professor at a U.S. university who identified as a lesbian (and taught English as well as lesbian and gay studies) but chose not to come out in her classes. The teacher sought to "engage students with the subject matter rather with herself as a subject who matters" (p. 70); thus, the teaching text was not the teacher's identity but "the process of inquiry" (p. 69).

Straight Teachers and Lesbian/Gay Themes

Although it was predominantly lesbian or gay teachers who experienced dilemmas about how much to reveal to students about their own sexual identity, quite a few straight teachers talked about identity issues that arose for them in teaching lesbian/gay themes.

Straight Teachers: 'Outsiders' Versus 'Lucky'

Several teachers said they felt somewhat uncomfortable when gay themes arose, describing themselves as 'outsiders.'

5.27 Jo: I like to have [gay or lesbian] guest speakers come in because I don't know everything, and I'm not gay, so that makes me feel like I might even be more of an outsider.

5.28 Ursula: I feel very much like I'm an outsider talking about this. And sometimes that feels uncomfortable for me. Which is one of the reasons why I will only do it [teach lesbian/gay topics] when they [the students] absolutely vote for that topic.

Some straight teachers avoid gay themes altogether, while others avoid talking about these themes themselves by relegating that task to gay guest speakers.

The opposite view was also put forward—that teaching lesbian/gay themes was probably easier for straight teachers than for gay teachers.

5.29 Janice: I feel really lucky to be straight and do it [teach lesbian/gay themes]. Because there isn't this feeling like you're having to prove yourself.

Mike: You don't have to feel like you're defending yourself.

Janice: Yeah. [...]

Mike: The thing is ... you guys can even say you're straight and that's fine ... And you should do that I suppose ... [It] gives you even more credibility to ... talk about your ... knowledge of gay and lesbian culture and, uh, to not have it questioned by the students. But me, if they found out that I was gay ... then they would go Oh well he's got an agenda.

Janice and Mike noted that straight teachers do not have to prove or defend themselves when engaging with gay themes. Ironically, it is not gay teachers but straight teachers who can speak with authority and credibility about their own lesbian/gay knowledge—because the motives of straight teachers would not be seen as suspect.

Straight and Gay Positionings

When straight teachers frame themselves (or are framed by others) as outsiders, the implication is that gay/lesbian themes are peripheral to their own personal and professional lives, so they are not well positioned to teach it. Such subject matter should be left to authentic 'insiders,' that is, gay teachers, who are presumed to be more knowledgeable. On the other hand, when gay teachers frame themselves (or are framed by others) as teachers motivated by 'an agenda,' the implication is that gay/lesbian subject matter is of interest for personal or political reasons instead of pedagogic ones, so they are not well positioned to teach it. Such subject matter should be left to neutral outsiders, that is, straight teachers, who are presumed to have less invested in the subject and therefore to be more objective and less 'self-serving.' To me, each of these views is problematic.

The notion that teachers are only equipped to teach subject matter in which they themselves have a direct, subjective, 'insider,' expert, or autobiographical knowledge would severely, absurdly, and unnecessarily limit what teachers were able to teach (see Giroux, 1993b, pp. 92–93, on the dangers of a 'discourse of authenticity'; see also Livia & Hall, 1997b). "[R]ace, class, gender, and sexuality (among others) all inflect all of our lives" (Phelan, 1994, p. 72), which means that everyone participates in these social relations, and one is simultaneously privileged along certain axes of social positioning while marginalized along others (Flax, 1989). Furthermore, it is not necessary to identify as a member of a particular group to be able to speak about one's own positioning in relation to that group. As Giroux (1993a) explains it, referring to himself:

[A]s a heterosexual, white, middle-, and working-class educator, I cannot, for example, speak for African-Americans or women. But I can speak self reflectively from … my own location about the issues of racism and sexism as ethical, political, and public issues which implicate in their web of social relations all those who inhabit public life, though from different spheres of privilege and subordination.
(p. 369)

Straight teachers can approach discussions of lesbian/gay themes from a whole range of perspectives with regard to sexual identity. This might involve, for example, mentioning their own discomfort with homophobia—as we saw in Chapter 4 with Tess, who shared her fears about the "huge volume" of homophobia that was almost palpable in the classroom (4.14)—or talking about gay family members, as we saw in Chapter 3 with Tina, who showed the class photos of her lesbian aunts (3.10).

A critical question is who has the power to decide whose subjectivities will be 'allowed' into the classroom and whose will not.

Whether 'straight' or 'queer,' everyone lives, daily, a relation to the heterosexual norm both within and outside the school. These relations vary hugely according to both social position and the particularities of individual biographies … The crucial condition, here, is who has, or acquires, the power to install their own criteria into legislative or other institutional frameworks.
(Epstein & Johnson, 1994, p. 221)

Importantly, it is not just gay teachers who have a stake in questions about who is 'allowed' to come out and who decides.

Sedgwick (1990) identifies two beliefs that are contradictory but widespread (in what she vaguely calls "the West"): The belief that some people are *really* gay (the "minoritizing view") and the belief that anybody not currently gay could become so (the "universalizing view") (pp. 1, 85, and 88). Thus, same-sex desire is "at once marginal and central" (p. 22). Britzman (1995) applies these ideas to education, arguing that "minoritising discourses" frame sexual identities as relevant only to gay people, whereas "universalising discourses" "begin with a view of identity as a category of social relations" (p. 157). In a 'universalizing view,' then, questions about negotiating sexual identities are potentially relevant to anyone.

This broad relevance is due, in part, to the fact that the "gay closet is not a feature only of the lives of gay people" (Sedgwick, 1990, p. 68). Goffman (1963) explains that people who are not themselves stigmatized in a particular regard may "serve as a protective circle" for someone who is (p. 97). Those who do not identify as gay, lesbian, or bisexual, but who are close to someone who does, are affected by homophobia and heterosexism, as are those who are perceived as gay by others, whether or not they actually identify as gay themselves (Hinson, 1996). If outness is not a viable option for gay teachers, then on some level there is pressure on all teachers to ensure that they do not appear gay. This is because the "silencing of any social group ... wields an imperative for all members of a society to consciously position themselves outside the sphere of culpability" (Malinowitz, 1995, p. 28).

Just as questions about negotiating one's sexual identity while teaching gay content are not necessarily significant only to gay teachers, neither are they necessarily significant to all gay teachers. No doubt there are gay teachers who have no interest in teaching gay content and who experience no sense of incongruity about not being out in the classroom. (The fact that such views are not well represented in this study may be because teachers with these beliefs did not feel drawn to participate.)

Several teachers in my study suggested that gay and lesbian teachers were probably more likely than straight teachers to raise or respond to gay and lesbian themes, despite the complexities these teachers often face when negotiating their own sexual identities or addressing homophobia in the classroom. Goffman (1963) notes that, although it seems unfair, it is typically the 'stigmatized'—not the 'stigmatizing'—who are expected to bear the main responsibility for elevating the status of the stigmatized group. He asks, "Why should those who have the stigma, *more so than those who don't*, be given the responsibility of presenting and enforcing a fair-minded stand and improving the lot of the category as a whole?" (p. 113).

Although several straight teachers in my study said they felt like outsiders when dealing with gay themes, none of the gay teachers in this study expressed any reservations whatsoever about straight teachers dealing with gay themes. On the contrary, what concerned gay teachers was straight teachers being unwilling to approach gay themes, administrators forbidding teachers (or students) to raise gay themes, and colleagues objecting to gay teachers coming out in class.

Straight Teachers Negotiating Sexual Identity

For some straight teachers, negotiating their sexual identity in class was not always straightforward. In Tess's experience, introducing lesbian/gay topics in class led invariably to a degree of self-consciousness among participants about each other's sexual identities (below Tess refers to Nelson, 1993).

5.30 Tess: When I give out your article [on heterosexism in ESL] ... it's a renegotiation of my identity ... There's a very literal reading ... a very correspondence reading ... Then you must be gay because you're handing this out ... They know I have a kid and I'm not married and then suddenly Oh is it because you're really lesbian? ... Sometimes I'll front end it by saying ... I'm sorry if I'm gonna be direct but I wanna ask this question ... Having given this article ... how does it shift our

own identities in the classroom? And that works quite well ... It's
taking those risks. And you don't know where it's gonna go.

Introducing gay themes may give rise to dilemmas of self-representation, and
these dilemmas can be framed as a topic of discussion. (In this instance, Tess did
not say whether or not she would tell the students that she is straight, but in another
class example she did tell them [see 4.14].)

For Tina, a student teacher, a spontaneous remark she made in class ended up
becoming something of an event, in her EFL classroom (which was located in a
small town) and with her supervisor.

> 5.31 Tina: [In class a student said] I saw you with your boyfriend! ... My immediate
> reaction was to feel uncomfortable because I didn't want my students to
> know that I was dating or who I was dating ... And so I dodged it and
> I said Well how do you know he's my boyfriend? ... You saw me with
> Maria ... two weeks ago, and you didn't assume she was my girlfriend.
> And [the student] was completely at a loss for words. And I said Maybe
> Maria's my girlfriend ... You didn't know I was a lesbian? ... [My tone]
> was really serious. And the class ... didn't know what to do ... I said,
> I don't talk about my personal life in class and I don't ask you about yours,
> but since you asked ... OK, open your books to page whatever. And ...
> class just resumed normally ... So from then on ... every couple days a
> student would go You're not really a lesbian are you? I'm like Yeah ... is
> that a problem? And- and they were really at a loss for words.

During a moment of discomfort at feeling exposed, Tina challenged the
presumption that a woman and a man seen socializing were understood to be
involved romantically, but two women seen socializing were not.

The question–answer pattern described above continued over several weeks,
until one of the students saw Tina being openly affectionate with her boyfriend
and reported this to the class. Tina thought that getting the students to question
their assumptions about her sexual identity had been a valuable learning experience
for them. However, her supervisor saw it differently.

> 5.32 Tina: [My supervisor] thought that that was detrimental. Because ... I'm
> reinforcing that it's ... something to joke about ... That it's not really
> questioning their assumptions if it turns out that their assumptions
> were right in the first place. But my argument is as a straight woman
> how can I question their assumption ... that everyone's straight.

Her supervisor's concern was that she had trivialized lesbianism rather than
fostered understanding or critical thinking. Tina disagreed.

> 5.33 Tina: [My supervisor] was saying any sort of joking about such a serious
> topic [was not OK] ... [But] all the gay people I know ... that's what

you do, you laugh about it … [Being dogmatic] seems so counter … to what I've experienced of gay culture. I mean you're always redefining relationships … your concept of family … your ways of socializing … I don't think you get anywhere by saying (using a deep, monotone voice) *You should believe that gays and lesbians are totally fine* … I think … you get … farther with humor … I really think that … just slipping it in as really normal is one of the most important things.

In Tina's experience, gay culture involves redefining social norms, experimenting with identity practices, and using humor to transform narrow-mindedness, so she preferred a fluid, playful approach to lesbian/gay themes in the classroom.

Challenging the Presumption of Heterosexuality

Dalley and Campbell's (2006) study of high school students shows how a group of girls—who, in private, apparently did not consider themselves lesbians—deliberately presented themselves in public as defiantly out lesbians. Doing so made it more possible, the authors argue, for the girls to speak their minds, given the sexist environment of the school. Similarly, Tina's 'coming out' also had an element of defiance and seemed to be part of her attempts to counter the heterosexism she encountered in EFL classes (see 4.26) and materials (see 2.12).

It is interesting to note the 'coming out' contrasts between Tina and most of the lesbian and gay teachers in this study: Whereas she was spontaneous, they had undertaken careful deliberating and planning; whereas she seemed to almost dare her students to find it strange, surprising, or noteworthy that their teacher was a lesbian, they anticipated reactions from their students and allowed time for these to be discussed; and whereas she seemed matter-of-fact and off-hand, they seemed purposeful and focused.

Goffman's (1963) analysis of social stigmas can illuminate this contrast. When those who are not gay themselves but are close to gay people attempt to 'make gayness normal,' they tend to simply ignore the social stigma often associated with gayness, which Goffman (1963) calls 'normalizing.' However, when those who are gay themselves come out, they tend to present themselves as 'ordinary'—but without ignoring the stigma, which he calls 'normifying.' The difference, then, is that a teacher like Tina, who did not genuinely identify as gay, would pretend to be gay in a way that ignored, or failed to acknowledge, any possible stigmatizing effects.

Tina's 'coming out' (5.31) also raises the question of how teachers (of any sexual identity) might respond when they are presumed by students to be straight. On this subject it is worth considering the reflections of a group of (straight) tertiary-level composition teachers who had had their students write about 'homosexuality.'

When students assume, as in our case they did, that their teacher is heterosexual, that teacher might ask students what it would mean to them if she were lesbian, and why heterosexuals in general tend to assume other people are straight until proven otherwise. We can attempt to explore the ways heterosexuality is made to seem inevitable, a given.

(Berg, Kowaleski, Le Guin, Weinauer, & Wolfe, 1989, p. 32)

In second and foreign language classes, the presumption of heterosexuality can be framed as a potential barrier to effective communication, whether spoken or written. From a communication standpoint, it can be risky to assume that one's interlocutors, or audience, are necessarily straight, to disregard certain verbal or nonverbal messages that suggest otherwise, or to overlook opportunities to repair mistaken assumptions. This means that, rather than being concerned to save face for students who had mistakenly assumed their teacher was straight, teachers might wish to highlight the possible effects on social relations of mistaken assumptions about sexual identity as well as possible ways of repairing these sorts of communication breakdowns.

In fact, in second or foreign language classes the ambiguities associated with sexual identities may be particularly confusing. In Nelson (2004b), I show definite mismatches between how several ESL teachers chose to represent their sexual identities in the classroom versus how these choices were interpreted by their students. Thus, with regard to the identity-negotiation choices discussed in this chapter, there is not necessarily a straightforward correlation between teachers' intentions and their students' understandings, as we shall see in Chapters 6–8.

Self-Representation Quandaries as Subject Matter

The teachers quoted in this chapter illustrate a central paradox about identities in general and sexual identities in particular. On the one hand, identities can be limiting, as Claire (5.25) and Ira (5.26) noted. Identities regulate behavior (Bourdieu, 1991) and reinforce hierarchies of dominance (Butler, 1990). Queer theorists note that the notion of a gay identity is indispensable to those who are heavily invested in defining themselves as not gay (Sedgwick, 1990); similarly, Brandt (1986) argues that, even if race is not a fixed reality, it is a social category that gets defined through racism.

But on the other hand, identities can be socially constructive, as Kath (5.21) and Paige (5.18) intimated. Identities enable or produce "social collectivities, moral bonds, and political agency" (Seidman, 1993, p. 134) and function as acts of resistance (hooks, 1994; Weeks, 1987). Without some degree of essentialism (see Chapter 1), it would not be possible to develop a lesbian/gay movement or to research lesbian/gay issues (Malinowitz, 1995). Thus, there is a "tension between the political and pedagogic need for identity and the contingency of sexual identities" (Phillips, 1996, p. 106).

In order to connote a "fixing" of identity that is provisional (Phelan, 1994), the terms "working identities" (McLaren & Lankshear, 1993, p. 386) and "strategic essentialism" (Spivak, 1990) have been proposed. Phelan (1994), discussing sexual politics, advocates what she calls a "continual shuffling between the need for categories and the recognition of their incompleteness" (p. 154). This means taking a flexible view of identity categories and maintaining a certain distance from them so that they are not overly constraining. Thus, the very "instability of analytical categories" can be considered a resource (Harding, 1989, p. 18). As Seidman (1993) explains it, if "[we] cannot elude categories of identity … then the issue is less their affirmation or subversion than analyzing the kinds of identities that are socially produced and their manifold social significance" (p. 134). This way of thinking has much potential pedagogically.

Burbules (1997) argues that teachers often focus on the tolerance of difference, or the celebration of difference, but a more productive focus would be "the critical re-examination of difference, the questioning of our own systems of difference, and what they mean for ourselves and for other people" (p. 111). Thus, in this case, the pedagogic emphasis would not necessarily be on whether to name one's own (or another's) sexual identity but rather how and why sociosexual differences are constituted and made to matter.

Questions about self-representation are highly relevant in language classes in particular.

> Literacy ... is about the practice of representation as a means of organizing, inscribing, and containing meaning ... [L]iteracy becomes critical to the degree that it *makes problematic the very structure and practice of representation* [italics added]; that is, it focuses attention on the importance of acknowledging that meaning is not fixed and that to be literate is to undertake a dialogue with others who speak from different histories, locations, and experiences.
>
> (Giroux, 1993a, pp. 367–368)

The key issue is not so much whether teachers come out (as gay or straight) in the classroom but the extent to which their own insights and quandaries about sexual-identity negotiations are informing their curricula and their teaching practices by shedding light on questions of identity and representation generally. Theorizing sexual identities as 'situated practices' can make it possible to explore with students such questions as "under what circumstances one might identify oneself as *this* or *that*" (Sumara & Davis, 1998, p. 216). In other words, whether or not participants choose to explicitly name their own sexual identities, they can create a pedagogic focus on the *processes* of identity negotiation, which would draw attention to the linguistic nuances, ambiguities, and consequences of how identities are communicated in various situations and settings.

PART III
Inside Three Classes

Introduction to Part III

Class discussions featuring lesbian or gay themes are the focus of the next three chapters, which examine ESL classes at three different educational institutions in two U.S. cities. Before looking inside the classes, I outline some key procedures and principles that guided the data collection and analysis.

Observing Classes

Drawing on professional contacts, I made arrangements to observe the classes of three English language teachers—Tony, Gina, and Roxanne. Each had a Master's degree in the field and at least 12 years' experience teaching English in the United States and in Asia or Europe. Also, each had previously taught lesbian or gay themes and thought it likely (or at least not unlikely) that such themes might arise in their current (intermediate- or advanced-level) class. With the backing of the relevant administrators, the three teachers agreed to participate in the study, pending the agreement of their students.

On my first day in each class, I introduced myself as an ESL teacher who was conducting a research project about identities in language classes (my project had, of course, already been sanctioned by the ethics committee of my own university). At that stage I did not talk about sexual identities in particular because one of my main objectives was to find out whether or how someone in the class would introduce this topic. All of the students in the three classes agreed in writing to let me observe and audiotape their class, with some also volunteering to be interviewed.

I decided to audiotape the class sessions so that I could conduct "retrospective analysis" rather than rely on "instant coding" during class time (Edwards & Westgate, 1994, p. 61). I spent approximately two consecutive weeks in each class, which meant that I was able to observe a "'natural cycle' of classroom encounters" (Edwards & Westgate, 1994, p. 102)—which in each class amounted to all or most of a single unit of work on a particular theme. I did not conduct systematic observation of classes in the sense of having preestablished categories or questions (see Allwright, 1988; Edwards & Westgate, 1994). While observing, I would take notes, mainly about who was saying what but also about things like what was being written on the board, participants' body language (e.g., gestures), the apparent mood in the room (e.g., extremely still), and the seating arrangements.

The problem with observing classes is, of course, that the presence of an observer necessarily changes the phenomenon under observation. In an attempt to counter this, a common strategy is "to allow the researcher's presence to become, over time, so familiar a feature of the setting that observer and equipment are 'hardly noticed'" (Edwards & Westgate, 1994, p. 77). In each class, I tried to minimize my presence by maintaining a nonexpressive demeanor at all times, avoiding direct eye contact, sitting off to the side or in the back of the room, and taking notes nonstop (so that it would not be apparent which events I found especially interesting).

In Tony's classroom, which was quite small, my presence seemed marked and, at times, mildly intrusive; in Gina's, where observers were a common occurrence, once I had introduced myself and the study there was no further recognition of my presence; and in Roxanne's, which had the largest number of students, there was a comfortable sense of being welcomed but left to my own devices. All three teachers felt I had helped them to ignore me by appearing nonreactive in class. I should also mention that the class transcripts (especially Gina's) are somewhat incomplete, as class transcripts tend to be, due to a combination of factors such as frequent laughter, overlapping turns, simultaneous conversations, and seating distance from the tape recorder.

Interviewing Teachers

I interviewed each teacher a number of times—before, during, and after my 2-week observation period in their class. Initial interviews were semistructured; I asked about such things as the students' backgrounds and goals, the course objectives and curriculum, their own career background, and so on. For most of the interviews, though, I simply invited the teachers to describe any 'critical moments' from class, that is, any moments that were particularly memorable or problematic (following Candlin [1987, p. 415], who suggests that, for researchers, "interactional *cruces*," or moments of conflict, can be especially revelatory). The teachers typically discussed what had just happened that day, what they were planning for the next day, how well they felt the class was going, and what the class as a whole and particular students seemed to need. Our interviews at times touched on their previous experiences teaching gay/lesbian themes; their own sexual identity negotiations in the classroom; and their experiences teaching students whom they knew, or thought, to be gay, lesbian, or bisexual.

In one interview each with Gina and Roxanne, but not with Tony (who had no private office space), it proved feasible to use a research technique called 'stimulated recall':

> *Stimulated recall* is a technique in which the researcher records and transcribes parts of a lesson and then gets the teacher (and, where possible, the students) to comment on what was happening at the time that the teaching and learning took place … [This] enables teachers and students … to present their various interpretations of what is going on in the classroom, and for these interpretations to be linked explicitly to the points in the lesson which gave rise to them.
>
> (Nunan, 1992, p. 94)

I selected and roughly transcribed those parts of class sessions that included gay or lesbian content so that I could show the interviewee the class transcripts and play the relevant parts of the audiotape, stopping it whenever they had something to say about their thoughts or feelings at the time. Incidentally, the teachers were not told beforehand that they would be asked to provide a retrospective account of the gay-themed class discussions since foreknowledge might have affected their performance in class (Nunan, 1992).

In my interactions with the teachers, in order to minimize my potential influence on classroom activity, I did not offer evaluative feedback (negative or positive) on what was happening in the classes. At first teachers found this disconcerting, but in the end each mentioned that it had helped them to feel less self-conscious about being observed. I should also mention that I invited the teachers to comment on my written analysis of their classes (which Silverman [1993] calls "respondent validation," p. 156), but none took this up. (If they had, their comments would have provided more data but would not necessarily have made the existing data more valid [Silverman, 1993].)

Interviewing Students

I interviewed all 28 students who volunteered (10 from Tony's class, 7 from Gina's class, and 11 from Roxanne's class), which amounted to close to half of the 63 students in the three classes. Students were given the option of being interviewed in pairs instead of individually in an attempt to make the interviews less threatening, especially for those students who, as refugees (or children of refugees), might find it uncomfortable to enter a small, enclosed space to meet a virtual stranger with audiotaping equipment (as Morgan [1997] points out, some ESL students associate observing, recording, and documenting with surveillance).

The student interviews were semistructured. After explaining at the outset that I would not be discussing their interview with their classmates or teacher, I requested some brief introductory information (e.g., where they were from, how long they had been in the United States, their educational goals). I then asked what they had thought of the class session, or sessions, which had included gay or lesbian themes. Interviews lasted between one half hour and several hours, depending on students' willingness and availability. The stimulated recall technique described above was not used with Tony's students as room access on his small campus was extremely limited, but it was used with all of Gina's students and with three of Roxanne's students (those who had time for extended follow-up interviews). The technique proved especially effective at generating discussion with the students, who were, without exception, eager to hear the tape and read the transcript.

(In addition to interviewing teachers and students, I also collected copies of all class handouts and student writing [with teacher feedback] that were in circulation during my 2-week observation period in each class; however, these written materials are referred to only minimally in this book as the main focus is on the oral class discussions and interviews.)

Analyzing Teaching Practices

Though teaching practices are obviously shaped by broader institutional and geopolitical contexts (e.g., Layder, 1993), my investigative focus in Chapters 6–8 remains on what occurs inside the classroom, once again for largely pragmatic reasons. In negotiating permission from representatives of the host institutions before collecting any data, I agreed not to divulge certain details about the classroom sites under study, not only the names of the institutions (which is standard practice) but also additional potentially identifying information such as in which U.S. cities these were located (a less typical request).

Chapters 6–8 each analyze selected portions of class discussions that took place in one or two class sessions. Particular attention has been paid to those moments or issues that the participants either considered significant or experienced in notably divergent ways. My choices about analytic focus have also been informed by those issues that mattered most to the teachers who took part in my focus groups and interviews (see Chapters 2–5).

Because this book is the first to examine sexual identities and language-teaching practices, it seemed important to identify and explore key issues that emerged as noteworthy or problematic within each class. As a result, each chapter is somewhat different in emphasis and structure. Drawing rather loosely on Lemke (1985), the main categories guiding my analysis are as follows:

- Contextualization: How are gay/lesbian themes introduced or integrated into the class?
- Activity structures: What do participants (usually the teacher) ask others to do with lesbian/gay/bisexual themes?
- Thematic content: What is said about gay/bisexual/lesbian people or issues?
- Identity theories: What ways of theorizing sexual identities are operating, and what effects do these seem to have on learning or teaching?
- Participant positionings: How are participants positioned in relation to each other, to gay content, and to sexual identity?
- Interaction management: Who makes decisions about what is talked about, when, and by whom?
- Participant views: What issues, aspects, or moments are especially significant to participants, and why?

Due to variations between classes (and between interactions within the one class) as to which points were most salient, not all of these categories are addressed in each interaction that is examined.

Taking the view that interaction is one of the most important aspects of the curriculum (van Lier, 1996), I focus on classroom interactions. Moreover, since "teachers and students influence each other during the process of instruction" (van Lier, 1988, p. 47), I consider both teacher and student perspectives; in fact, each chapter considers the divergent perspectives of several students since students are understood to be active agents in the classroom experience and "what learners do in class effectively makes each lesson a different lesson for each learner" (Allwright & Bailey, 1991, p. 30). I make a point of quoting participants as much as practicable, rather than summarizing or paraphrasing their words. In so doing, I recognize that "the meanings transmitted by interactants come out of realities which are, in the moment of utterance, only rather cursorily experienced," which means that utterances "often convey more determinacy and fixity of meaning than the speaker could really, in all honesty, lay claim to" (Willing, 1992, p. 212). Even so, I take the view that attending to the specifics of what was said makes it possible to generate incisive analyses instead of overly broad generalizations.

Chapters 6–8 take a look inside three very different classrooms to find out how the topic of (homo)sexual identities emerged and how the teacher's approaches to that topic served to open up, or close down, opportunities for productive discussion.

CHAPTER 6

"Not Animal in the Zoo": Tony's Class

Tony was teaching a week-long unit of work on 'lesbian/gay culture', a topic that had been selected by his ESL students. At the start of the unit, Tony was enthusiastic about the subject matter, but by the third day he was finding it quite challenging. In an attempt to illuminate the challenges, this chapter critically analyzes two class discussions: the first discussion initiated the unit on lesbian/gay culture, and the second followed the class viewing of a television program with a lesbian character. I take into account the perspectives of the teacher and five of his students—two women from Japan, two men from Korea, and a woman from Taiwan. The analysis suggests that gay and lesbian material offers abundant opportunities for learning— but that rather than focusing on what gay and lesbian people are like, it may be more effective pedagogically to focus how gay and lesbian people are represented.

The Class

Part of a university-affiliated Intensive English Program (IEP), Tony's 'speaking/ listening' class met for 12 hours each week. During my observation period, 14 international students (11 women and 3 men) attended the class: Eight women and one man from Japan, three women from Taiwan, and two men from Korea. All of the students were in their 20s, except for one Japanese woman in her 50s (for the gender, country of origin, and approximate age of each student quoted or mentioned in Chapters 6–8, see Appendix C). At the time that I observed the class most of the students had been living in the United States for 2 or 3 months, with American host families. Approximately half of the class intended to eventually study 'regular' (non-ESL) classes at a U.S. university or college, while the other half would be returning to tertiary study or work in their own countries within the next 3–6 months. When interviewed, nearly all the students volunteered that Tony was a great person and a good teacher—especially appreciated was the warm interest he took in the day-to-day events of their lives.

Tony, in his 50s, was from the United States and had 20 years' experience teaching ESL/EFL there and in Asia. He wanted his classes to be lively, interesting, and enjoyable—he dreaded silence and boredom.

6.1 Tony: An ESL teacher's greatest reward is to have this buzz of excited noise.

In his view, successful class discussions were ones in which students felt free to 'jump in,' interrupt, express their views, disagree, and make jokes. In the classroom, Tony's style was enthusiastic and highly animated. He discouraged serious, bookish attitudes toward language learning, and encouraged students to see their time in the United States as an opportunity to experiment with new activities, meet new people, and get involved in local social and cultural events.

There was no class textbook, and Tony was free to determine what and how he would teach. His approach, like that of his colleagues in the program, was both 'theme-based' (Brinton, Snow, & Wesche, 1989) and 'communicative,' in the sense that choices about thematic content preceded, and essentially determined, choices about language study (Edelhoff, 1981). During the first week of class, Tony had given the students a handout with two dozen topics that had proved popular in previous classes, inviting students to nominate any additional topics that interested them and then to vote on their preferred topics. In this class, the topic 'lesbian/gay culture' (from the handout) had received the second-highest number of student votes (other popular topics were 'travel,' 'food,' and 'wine and beer').

Tony was excited that this class had voted for a lesbian/gay unit because in previous classes it had been a positive experience for the students and for him.

> 6.2 Tony: Because there is so much reticence going into it [a lesbian/gay unit], that allows for the possibility of really a great … inspiration, great learning … It really almost always is a positive experience … I mean, coming from that initial … this is something we laugh about and it's so distant from us … So it almost always has great room for all kinds of progress and … communication. […] And … personal growth … just learning to deal with what's different. And I think as human beings that's something that we all work on … pushing that boundary farther to accept things that, uh, are different. To be able to talk about things that are really disgusting to us. And we all have things that are disgusting to us but … it should be OK to talk about anything, almost anything.

Discussing Experiences of Gay and Lesbian People

For Day 1 of the lesbian/gay unit, Tony passed out a handout he had written with discussion questions about the students' experiences of gay and lesbian people and issues. Small-group discussions were followed by a whole-class discussion, with Tony reading out the questions (in bold below) and eliciting students' answers. Though many fascinating teaching issues arose during the 45-minute class discussion, I have had to select just a few to highlight here. (Please note: In Chapters 6–8, classroom transcripts are in italics so as to distinguish them from interview transcripts, and discussion turns are numbered.)

Tony's first question for the class to discuss was definitional:

> 1 Tony: *… I'll read the question. If a classmate from another country said they didn't know the meaning of gay or lesbian and asked you to explain, what would you say?*

2 Sharon:	Man love man. (laughter)
3 Student:	This is gay.
4 Sharon:	Yeah, woman love woman. [...]
11 Hae-Woo:	How about men want to become woman. [...]
13 Tony:	I don't know, I want- you tell me. (laughter) I don't know, I don't know.
14 Hae-Woo:	It's not you?
15 Tony:	I don't know. Ask them, ask them, don't ask me. (laughter)

As shown below, another student rephrased Hae-Woo's question (turn 11 above) as a vocabulary question and put it to Tony, who answered with much hedging and uncertainty before changing the subject.

28 Jun-Kyu:	Uh, Tony, what do you say a person who exchange gender?
29 Tony:	Um, tran- I think- I'm not sure, I think the word is transgender.
30 Jun-Kyu:	Yeah.
31 Tony:	Uh, who actually has a sex change operation. I think they say transgender. I'm not- I mean I've heard that word before. That MIGHT be the word. Trans, change, to go across from one to another.

Several points that become more evident as this chapter progresses are worth foreshadowing here. First, throughout this discussion and the entire unit, Tony did not readily provide information or answers to students but sought to elicit their own understandings and experiences (see turns 13 and 15). Tony almost always took the role of facilitator, encouraging, and in fact requiring, each student—especially those who seemed shy, hesitant, or less proficient in English than the others—to speak and share their perspectives with the group. He sometimes called on students by name, and his verbal and nonverbal responses to their comments were warm, welcoming, and nearly always uncritical.

Second, Tony consistently highlighted his own lack of knowledge or certainty about gay-related matters (see turns 29 and 31). And third, throughout the unit Tony spoke of 'gay and lesbian' people (and straight people) without ever acknowledging a broader range of sexual identities; when, on several occasions, the students brought up transgenderalism or bisexuality, Tony either said nothing and changed the subject or responded in a way that seemed disinterested or dismissive.

The second question on Tony's handout elicited the students' personal experiences of gay/lesbian people.

35 Tony:	... Uh, let's go to number 2. Uh, and again this is your own personal experience. **Do you have friends, know people, or know about people who are gay? If yes- if yes, tell the group about them, what kind of people are they, uh, how are they different from you?** Comments on that?
36 Students:	(talking to each other, some laughter)
37 Miyuki:	My- My- My (laughter) host- host family (much laughter) host family's son is gay.

38 Tony:	*Huh.*	
39 Miyuki:	*Yes. But*	
40 Jun-Kyu:	*You're safety.* (much laughter)	
41 Miyuki:	*Yes!* (laughter) *But is not different from- different- hm. Um, he is same, same, same.* (Miyuki makes circular gestures to indicate everyone in the room)	
42 Student:	*How old is he?*	
43 Miyuki:	*21.*	
44 Lynn:	*Does he look like women?*	
45 Miyuki:	*No, no, no, no.* […]	
50 Lynn:	*… But he look uh- move* […] *little like woman?*	
53 Miyuki:	*No. Just- Just- Just man.* […]	
61 Sharon:	*Yeah I saw, I saw him before. I think is the same. I cannot find out something strange or something different from the man. I don't think so.*	

With his first and second questions to the class, Tony was drawing on a common educational approach to a given topic, along the lines of "What does x mean and what are your own experiences of x?" Since he was referring to a category of people, his second question set up a clear straight/gay, us/them opposition. In asking what "kind of people" gays are and how they are "different from you," he was constructing the entire class as not gay, and gay people as a uniform, homogeneous type.

Tony's framing of lesbian/gay people as 'different from you' was countered, to some extent, by the students. Miyuki insisted that her gay host-brother was 'same,' apparently meaning that in appearance he was not readily identifiable as gay, and possibly also that as a person he was not fundamentally different.

By the time the class discussion came to a close nearly every student had, with Tony's prompting, described someone who either was gay, was thought to be gay, or knew someone else who was gay. In the vast majority of cases, these narratives were punctuated with much laughter, at times verging on hysteria, as in Miyuki's narrative above. However, a few comments had a more somber tone, as evident in the exchange below.

96 Hae-Woo:	*Korean people don't understand gay and lesbian.*
97 Jun-Kyu:	*Yeah.*
98 Tony:	*Uh-huh.*
99 Jun-Kyu:	*It's like- em. Hmm.* (pause)
100 Hae-Woo:	*Man is man, woman is woman. Man never think* (laughter) *never change woman. It's very strange.* […]
102 Jun-Kyu:	*… If a man or woman is homosexual, um, they are fired in their*
103 Tony:	*In their job. From their job?*
104 Jun-Kyu:	*Yeah. From their company.* (some students nod somberly)
105 Sharon:	*Uh, I will think maybe in Korea also have many people is gay or lesbian. But … if the boss know he or her- or she is a gay, and will be fired. So they just don't want to talk out. Yeah.* (she smiles) […]

111 Tony:	*... I think in fact maybe in every country this kind of attitude exists to a certain degree. And it's just- it's a different degree. Uh, I'm not even sure myself but, uh. OK. Um, let's look at number 3 ...*

Again, several aspects are worth pointing out here. First, when students made comments that could be seen as negative about gay people, they tended to attribute these points of view to a country rather than to themselves ("Korean people don't understand ..." not "I don't understand ...") (see Nguyen & Kellogg, 2005).

Second, Hae-Woo's comments above suggests that, for some students, 'gay' and 'transgender' may have taken on more similar meanings than typically ascribed to these terms in Euro/American understandings. Definitional questions about sexual identities were never discussed again during my 2-week observation period, so it is possible that in this discussion, and throughout the gay/lesbian unit, some students were associating 'gay' with a man who changes to a woman (turn 100), not a man who loves a man.

The third point is Tony's repeated emphasis on his own lack of familiarity with the subject matter. When Sharon notes that gay people exist in Korea but are not necessarily out due to social discrimination, Tony makes the point that this phenomenon exists everywhere, though to varying degrees. He then immediately casts doubt on his own knowledge—"I'm not even sure myself" (turn 111). As foreshadowed earlier, throughout the discussion (and indeed the unit), Tony seemed to be making a point of positioning himself as someone who is decidedly not an 'expert' on gay/lesbian themes.

Tony's third discussion question asked what students had already heard about the topic at hand, within different arenas.

111 Tony:	*... **What if anything do you hear about gays and lesbians in the newspapers, at school- maybe nothing, do you hear anything at school? Or in church?** [...]*
146 Vivian:	*... Last year, uh, Taiwan [...] a writer and a foreigner get married ... Gay. [...]*
167 Tony:	*They married?!*
168 Vivian:	*Yeah. In Taiwan.*
169 Tony:	*Is it legal to get married in Taiwan?*
170 Sharon:	*Yeah, now is legal. (she looks at Lynn, who nods)*
171 Tony:	*REALLY?*
172 Students:	*Yeah. Uh-huh.*
173 Tony:	*REALLY?*
174 Vivian:	*They have a wendy- wendy [wedding] party. Yeah.*
175 Sharon:	*So. Because now, uh, they have- sometime they have a movement in the park.*
176 Tony:	*Uh-huh.*
177 Sharon:	*So they not so serious, so secret. Yeah, they just say I'm a gay, yeah. So we- we will accept.*

An opposition emerged about perceived attitudes toward gay people in two of the students' countries: Korea, where they are reportedly considered 'strange' (turn 100), versus Taiwan, where they are reportedly 'accepted' (turn 177). Worth noting here is Tony's incredulity and disbelief whenever positive comments were made about the status of gay people in countries other than the United States.

Tony's fourth question moves from the public sphere of the media and school environments to the more private sphere of friends and family.

204 Tony:	*… Number 4. Let's look at that.* **Has the word gay or lesbian ever come up in a conversation with friends or family?** *What was the situation? What was said?* […]
214–222 Hae-Woo:	*When I was young, uh, our family saw TV.* […] *Investigation program. And they speak gay and lesbian. So … My father just say crazy.* (laughter, including Tony's) *We don't to talk about gay and lesbian.* (H laughs) […]
224 Vivian:	*I have a girlfriend, she … told me, uh, she afraid she is lesbian.*
225 Tony:	*Uh-huh.*
226 Vivian:	*Because she always, uh, always interesting in woman.*
227 Tony:	*Uh-huh.*
228 Vivian:	*She will- she never interest in boy. So she afraid she is lesbian. But she's not sure.* (everyone is extremely quiet)

Vivian's narrative was unusual in two respects: while most of the narratives drew peals of laughter and giggling, hers was met with dead silence; while most of the narratives characterized gays as 'crazy,' 'scary,' or sexual predators of straight people, Vivian's relayed a potentially gay vantage point. Even though Vivian's choice of words—"afraid she is lesbian"—has a negative framing, she was the first to seriously introduce the possibility that someone in the room could be close to someone gay.

Vivian's story seemed to bring about a more serious, self-reflective mood. After a brief pause, Tony's response was to invite others to contribute to the discussion, which raises another important issue. The discussion questions were often highly personalized and framed in a confessional mode—as in the above example, the students were asked to relay conversations with their family and friends about gay people. Yet, at the same time, the approach seemed oddly impersonal; as with Vivian above, when emotional issues did arise—which to me seemed inevitable given the types of questions being addressed—there was rarely any sort of follow up; usually, Tony simply changed the subject. This personal/impersonal paradox continued throughout the discussion and the unit.

The fifth question was about humor.

348 Tony:	*… Uh, number 5 …* **Has the word gay or lesbian ever come up in relation to humor or a joke?** *For any of you?* […]
352 Lynn:	*I will say Oooh you are gay!* (she laughs, others murmur affirmatively)

353 Tony:	OK. And why is that funny, I'm just curious. What- What is it that makes that funny? Just because gays are- we don't know about them, do you think?
354–356 Lynn:	Because in, um, we will think they- they didn't like the, uh, woman. So- so they sometimes … they will [act] […] like a girl … Is not normal.
357 Tony:	OK.
358 Lynn:	Yeah, so we will say if the- the boy he's [acting]… a little strange. And we will say "Ooh you are a gay!" (a student laughs) Yeah. (almost everyone is nodding)
359 Tony:	OK, everyone similar kind of, uh? (pause, a few murmurs) OK. Number 6 …

Tony's question—"why is that funny?" (turn 353)—is unique in this 45-minute class discussion in that it asks for reflection or analysis of underlying motivations. He questions the taken-for-granted nature of the 'joke' Lynn has relayed but immediately attributes his query to his own curiosity, thereby making his response seem more inquisitive and musing than challenging. Tony next offers a possible answer to his own question, by proposing that lack of knowledge about gay people is what leads to teasing.

When he says "*we* don't know about *them*," his choice of pronouns aligns him with those who lack knowledge of gays (and perhaps by implication, those who would use the word 'gay' to taunt or tease). In fact, following Tony's question/answer above, Lynn shifts from "*I* will say 'Oh you are gay'" to "*we* will say …" The effect is that such 'jokes' are made to appear less personal to Lynn and more a generic, common occurrence—perhaps an expected, even understandable occurrence.

Tony's apparent intention was to deepen the discussion by focusing on the underlying meaning of 'jokingly' calling someone gay, but Lynn's response was to elaborate on the descriptive, surface-level explanation rather than more critical, deeper-level explanation of the phenomenon. In other words, instead of explaining why people engage in name-calling behavior, which is what the teacher was getting at, the student explained why boys would be called 'gay'—because they didn't like women and they acted 'like a girl' or 'strange.' Tony did not pursue the question further. This pattern—posing a critical question, getting a descriptive answer, and then dropping the question—was one that occurred repeatedly (as we shall see next in the Day 3 discussion).

The sixth and final question explicitly invited students to discuss experiences in their country or this one.

| 359 Tony: | … *Have you ever visited a gay restaurant, coffee shop, or bar in your own country or in the United States?* |

Sharon told a lengthy story about a straight male friend of hers (in Taiwan) who would only go to a gay bar if accompanied by his girlfriend.

| 389 Sharon: | … *Because if the boy, he is not a gay. And if … he went to the gay bar, maybe the gay will- will think he is a gay. Maybe will touch him.* |

> So he say if the boy went to the gay bar you should, uh, uh, go together
> with your girlfriend. Yeah. So.
>
> 390 Tony: Safety?
> 391 Sharon: Yeah. (laughter)
> 392 Student: Maybe he is bisexual? (laughter, then a pause)
> 393 Tony: Anyone else? (pause) Been to a gay restaurant? Or a gay coffee shop
>   or a bar? In your country or? [...]
> 401 Reiko: Uh. One- one bakery shop [in the United States]. Maybe he's gay,
>   I think. He, uh, when he looked at some guy, eye is different. (much
>   laughter)
> 402 Student: (pointing to Reiko) Yeah, yeah! She knows the gay!
> 403 Tony: (to Reiko) You were disappointed?
> 404 Students: (many talking and laughing at once)

In the above excerpt, we see some of the same patterns that have already been identified. First, there is Tony's reluctance to expand the lesbian/gay theme to encompass, or even just acknowledge, any additional non-heterosexual identities. When a student suggested that Sharon's friend might be bisexual, which was the first time that word came up in the whole-class discussion, Tony did not respond at all, not even on a lexical level, for instance, to check that the class knew the meaning of the word.

Second, Tony's question about whether anyone had been to a gay venue seemed, once again, to construct the entire class as straight. This was reinforced by jokingly asking Reiko if she was 'disappointed' that the bakery worker seemed gay; the humor depended upon the presumption that she herself was straight.

Last, the characterization of gay people as hypersexualized, and possibly predatory, which was a constant theme throughout the discussion, was never explicitly acknowledged, addressed, or analyzed in any way—neither in this discussion nor in any of the subsequent ones.

The Teacher's Perspective

Overall, Tony was quite pleased with the first day of the gay/lesbian unit. For him, the salient points were that the students were, as he put it, "warm" and their "attitudes" about lesbian/gay people were mostly positive. He was particularly pleased that he had managed to keep his own views to himself.

> 6.3 Tony: I can sit back and listen to a lot of stuff that I don't agree with,
>   uh, much better than I used to be able to do ... There were times
>   when I used to jump in and say "No! What are you saying!"
>   (T laughs) ... [Now] I'm better at listening to students and
>   listening to things that may sound disgusting or abhorrent to me
>   personally, that I disagree with, or ... hateful things.

Tony clearly placed a high value on encouraging students to speak their minds, which, to him, meant not questioning or challenging their stated viewpoints.

I asked Tony if he ever thought about the possibility that some of his students could be gay or lesbian.

6.4 Tony: I rarely get the feeling, uh, that my students are gay. Uh. So ... I don't approach the [lesbian/gay] topic, um, with the sense ... that someone might be gay and I wanna help them along ... I don't ... [take] that care into my group of cares that I have when I'm teaching.

For Tony, the assumption was that students were straight unless there were clear indications otherwise. There also seems to be a view that gay students would need some sort of special support to be 'helped along' (a view that was discussed in Chapter 2).

What did concern Tony was the lack of learning materials on lesbian/gay issues. It had been easier to find "authentic" materials for his previous classes because they had been at a higher English-language proficiency level than the current class.

6.5 Tony: But one thing that goes against the gay and lesbian unit ... is the [students' English-language proficiency] level ... It makes it in some ways a little more demanding for me, I think, in choosing the materials that are readily accessible or comprehensible to them.

Tony had to create materials for each class session, which underscores one of the acknowledged limitations of "theme-based ESL courses"—namely, "the burden of materials and curriculum development" (Brinton et al., 1989, p. 29). This ongoing task is made more challenging in the case of gay/lesbian subject matter, which is already underrepresented in commercially produced teaching resources (see Chapter 3).

In developing materials for theme-based programs, "the key to success," according to Brinton et al. (1989), is being able to "'unlock' the interests of students, and to choose themes, text types, and activities which are relevant to [their] particular language needs" (p. 40). As Candlin (1987) puts it, there is a need to choose texts and text-types "whose messages are of striking and immediate personal relevance" to the learners (p. 17). Even though in Tony's class the gay/lesbian unit was selected through a majority vote, not all learners were enthralled by the topic or by Tony's way of approaching the topic, as we shall see below.

Students' Perspectives

On Day 2 during the lunch break, after Tony and most of the students had left the classroom, one student (Sharon, from Taiwan) began telling me her views on the lesbian/gay unit thus far, and two students (Jun-Kyu and Hae-Woo, from Korea) who were sitting nearby joined in.

6.6 Sharon: In our group different age, and different country ... I think even the same country ... the thought is different ... I think is normal ... Sometimes ... we will make joke in discuss, I think it's OK, it's very good. [...] We ... discuss the topic. I feel is very good.

	Because I find almost student there are very interesting and … speak out.
Jun-Kyu:	(joining the conversation) Do you like this topic? […]
Sharon:	Um. I'm interesting.
Jun-Kyu:	Why? (as if incredulous) The thing that I dislike and hate is
Sharon:	You hate? Why?
Jun-Kyu:	Yeah, yeah, yeah. The thing, only one reason that I dislike and hate is, hm, discuss- discussing about and seeing them on the other view, having curiosity … They are same people, uh, like us. And they are not animal in the zoo. Why, why, why do we discuss about this topic … I cannot understand.
Sharon:	But I- I feel if you use the hate to describe this topic, the person, the lesbian and gay, I will feel it's so serious, too serious … Because … they are human too … I interesting about the gay and lesbian because I just interesting what did they think in their mind. I just interesting I want to understand they say. Yeah.
Hae-Woo:	Why, why do you want to [?]
Sharon:	Because I have many many question. So I feel is OK, this topic can help me to more understand. Because in my coun- usually if we talking about gay and lesbian, just- sometime just like joke … Not very deep, so I cannot understand … Why you will say hate?
Jun-Kyu:	I dislike them.

The lesbian/gay topic was extremely interesting to Sharon and, in her view, to most other students too, whereas to Jun-Kyu, it was disturbing. This next section speculates about possible reasons for this disturbance, beyond the relatively straightforward matter of Jun-Kyu's stated dislike of gay and lesbian people. The point here is not to analyze Jun-Kyu's state of mind but to explore the pedagogic issues that his criticisms raise.

Framing Gay People as 'Different from You'

Education practices have a socially regulative function, defining not only what counts as knowledge and what knowledge will be taught but also what 'a student' is understood to be (Bernstein, 1996). Students are routinely coded as straight—or as having no sexual identity, which effectively amounts to the same thing (Britzman, 1997). This presumption of heterosexuality was repeatedly reinforced in Tony's teaching practices, as evident in the Day 1 discussion (see turns 35 and 353). Asking students to talk 'about' gay and lesbian people may not strictly preclude the possibility of students talking 'as' gay or lesbian, but it certainly constrains it. In other utterances, Tony's construction of the student cohort as straight was slightly more implicit (see turns 204 and 403), but the cumulative effect would serve to inhibit, rather than invite, the participation of students who do themselves identify as gay, lesbian, bisexual, or queer, or who are questioning their sexual identity.

But it is not just these students that Tony overlooks. Straight students who have gay acquaintances, coworkers, and loved ones may also find themselves excluded by comments like "we don't know about them," which presume ignorance, or affronted by questions like "what kind of people are they?," which 'dehumanize' gay people by constructing them as "a uniform type" (Watney, 1991, p. 394) and which presume that students will be willing to speak about 'them' within the public forum of the classroom.

Also, from the Day 1 class discussion onwards, Tony talked about gays and lesbians in ways that foregrounded only their gayness; there was never any acknowledgment that people have multiple identities and social roles, either in addition to (homo)sexual identity or within that identity category.

Tony repeatedly framed gay and lesbian people as 'not us,' as 'different from us.' Another way of discussing gay people and difference is evident in an ESL reading task (developed by Becky Boon-Mills and adapted by Clarke et al., 1996) that features several narratives about children and their families. One child, Eliot, has two gay fathers. The students are asked to list three ways in which Eliot's daily life is different from that of the other children (whose parents are straight) and three ways in which it is similar. Identifying points of difference and points of similarity conveys a much different message than identifying only points of difference.

Yet another approach would be to identify points of affinity—that is, common goals or aims across differences (see Phelan, 1994). Ó'Móchain (2006) did something similar in an EFL class at a women's college in Japan. He deliberately juxtaposed the life narratives of two young women—one lesbian (a university student) and one straight (a soccer player)—to encourage his students to draw parallels between the two; for example, "both had to negotiate the consequences of being identified as lesbian, rightly or wrongly, in social contexts" (p. 59). Ó'Móchain observes that analyzing the two life stories in tandem made it possible to explore "concerns common to young women, whether they identify as, or are identified as, heterosexual or homosexual. It may have also provided a sense of affirmation for any students who themselves had experienced same-sex desire" (p. 59).

Positioning All Students as 'Voyeurs'

Jun-Kyu's discomfort with gay and lesbian people *as a topic* (see 6.6) raises additional issues about how the teacher was positioning the students in the class—not just as straight but also as voyeurs. Similar concerns are discussed in relation to a university 'lesbian studies' class in Canada (Bryson & de Castell, 1997): "We [as instructors] said that, in the class, there could be 'no consumers and no voyeurs'"; instead, "each of us would have to develop a clear 'ethics of consumption' and a 'reflexive gaze'" (p. 275). In other words, the pedagogic aim was to develop self-reflexivity so that the students (and teachers) would consider the ways in which their own lives were implicated in the subject matter and the ways in which studying this subject matter might affect their own lives. However, this reportedly proved impossible for some 'white heterosexual women' in the class who, according to the authors, approached the study of 'lesbians' with "a sense of automatic entitlement" and "unquestioned privilege vis-à-vis Others, [whose] lives, stories, words, and traces represented … objects of consumption assimilated for purposes of self-advancement and little more" (p. 286).

The authors call these students' approach "a colonizing kind of 'intellectual tourism'" (Bryson & de Castell, 1997, p. 286, citing Anzaldua, 1987, and others). In other words, the straight students took from, or used, lesbian themes only for their own amusement or edification but without critically examining their own behavior or ways of thinking in relation to the topic.

In the lesbian studies class, it was the teachers who were dissatisfied with the subject positions taken up by some of the students, whereas in Tony's class it was a student who was dissatisfied with the subject position he was placed in by the teacher. Framing 'lesbian and gay people,' or any peoples, as subject matter positions the students (and, for that matter, the teacher) as onlookers, spectators—whether happily so, like Sharon, or unhappily, like Jun-Kyu—and it positions the studied as 'animals in a zoo.' These fixed positionings could be problematic for a student of any sexual identity.

A Weak Pedagogic Frame

Taking the view that education can be a form of social control, Bernstein (1971) observes that students learn what sorts of "experiential, community-based non-school knowledge" can, and cannot, "be brought into the pedagogical frame" (p. 58). In those classroom contexts in which little everyday knowledge is allowed, the framing is said to be 'strong.' He makes the case that when there are

> strong frames between the uncommonsense knowledge of the school and the everyday community-based knowledge of teacher and taught, ... such insulation creates areas of privacy. For, inasmuch as community-based experience is irrelevant to the pedagogic frame, these aspects of the self informed by such experiences are also irrelevant. These areas of privacy reduce the penetration of the socializing process, for it is possible to distance oneself from it.
>
> (Bernstein, 1971, p. 64)

This means that, when students are not asked, or are not permitted, to bring their nonschool experiences into the classroom, they are able to insulate themselves, at least to some degree, from the shaping effects of education.

However, in some classrooms the pedagogic frame is "relaxed" or "weakened" to allow for greater inclusion of everyday realities (p. 58), thereby "[blurring] the boundary between what may or may not be taught" (p. 61) and affording students (and teachers) less privacy:

> [W]eakened ... framing will encourage more of the pupil/student to be made public—more of his [sic] thoughts, feelings, and values. In this way more of the pupil is available for control. As a result the socialization could be more intensive and perhaps more penetrating.
>
> (Bernstein, 1971, p. 66)

To counter this, students (like Jun-Kyu, perhaps?) "may produce new defences against the potential intrusiveness" of this sort of teaching (p. 66).

Eliciting students' own experiences of gay or lesbian people, as Tony did, could be seen as a weakening of the pedagogic frame on two counts—because of the focus on personal experience and because of the subject matter (which, in North America and many other places, does not have a long history of being allowed into the pedagogic frame). Indeed, some ESL students might perceive Tony's framing as *extremely* weak compared with their prior educational experiences in their countries (in relation to either personal experience or gay content as subject matter, or both).

On the surface, this weak framing might seem to create a more relaxed, open, friendly atmosphere, which seemed to be Tony's goal, but it can also be seen as potentially more threatening for students—perhaps especially if there is any sense that it may involve being socialized into a foreign and undesirable set of values or way of thinking. In ESL, given the legacies of colonialism, concerns about socialization, or cultural indoctrination, need to be taken into account (see Canagarajah, 1993; Schenke, 1991). These concerns may become even more prominent in relation to lesbian/gay themes, given the prevalent heteronormative discourses that characterize gay people as sexual deviants and predators. For all of these reasons, students may feel disconcerted by a loss of control or a loss of privacy when expected to discuss with their peers and their teacher their own personal experiences of gay friends or acquaintances.

Discussing Whether Gays and Lesbians Are 'Normal'

On Day 3 of the lesbian/gay unit, the class viewed a videotaped episode of 'Ellen,' an American television sitcom that had received much media attention because in this particular episode, the lead character comes out as a lesbian, as mentioned in Chapter 3 (see 3.12). After watching the show, the students formed small groups to discuss questions on a handout Tony had written that began with "What do you think about Ellen? Do you like her as a person?"

From his desk, Tony could partially overhear some of the small-group discussions, and some of the comments concerned him.

6.7 Tony: I heard [Jun-Kyu] say … I hate gays and lesbians. But … I'm still not sure what he was saying because he then said … They are the same as all of us. And then I heard a girl Miyuki say … If they're the same then why do you hate them? … But then [Jun-Kyu] also went on to say … Since they're the same as everyone else I don't see why we're … studying this … One of my concerns always is how he's gonna affect the rest of the class … Then … Hae-Woo … in a very friendly nice manner … [said] I can't stand them, … if he was my best friend, uh, I would tell him to leave. (T laughs) So those are things that are kind of testing my limits. Because … all my experiences [teaching lesbian/gay content] have been, um, always so positive … They're respectful students in general … so that kind of harshness … I really wasn't prepared for … I hope I wasn't visibly upset.

Surprised and disturbed by students' anti-gay comments, yet determined to hide his own distress, Tony was finding it fairly stressful to work out how to proceed.

When the class reconvened for a whole-group discussion, the class was unusually quiet, and the mood seemed a bit somber. Tony had some difficulty getting a discussion going, so he began calling on students by name.

Just before the class transcript shown below, Tony had been saying that, for Ellen, to live with someone who loves her and who she loves—"for her, that's normal."

45 Tony:	So ... is that possible, that a- a gay person could be normal also? Or not?	
46 Student:	I don't think so, is normal.	
47 Vivian:	... Gay and lesbian have normal life, yeah. (rotating an eraser with both hands) Someone loves he, and he loves someone. Just the someone is same gender. Is normal life. [...]	
50 Tony:	... Other comments, uh. Gays and lesbians. Not normal, not natural? Norie, what do you think?	
51 Norie:	(scratching her head) Not natural, not normal. We. (pause) Hmm. (pause) We must have a baby.	
52 Reiko:	(laughs softly)	
53 Tony:	Uh-huh, uh-huh.	
54 Norie:	So not natural.	
55 Tony:	Really?	
56 Norie:	Yeah.	
57 Tony:	Really.	
58 Norie:	I can't understand [gays and lesbians].	
59 Tony:	OK. (T laughs) OK. So you think having a baby is, uh, part of what is natural.	
60 Norie:	Hm.	
61 Tony:	Gosh, I don't have any babies! (much laughter) Maybe I'm not natural. (using a funny, exaggerated tone and facial expression) Gosh, I never thought about that. (laughter)	

The focus in this Day 3 discussion on normalcy can be seen as a logical extension from the Day 1 focus on difference. This is because framing gay people as 'different from you' could be seen as paving the way for the question of whether or not gay people are 'normal' or 'natural.'

After calling on Norie, who answered that gays are not normal because of the imperative to reproduce, Tony reacted to her (quiet, pause-filled) answer with cheerful disbelief, using humor to gently contest her answer. He personalized the implications of Norie's stated view by using himself as an example, expressing mock surprise at his own unthinkingness, and his antics elicited the first strong laughter in this discussion. His demonstrative self-mockery implied that he was secure enough about his own childless state to make a public joke of it and that he rejected the proposition that 'natural' necessarily involved having babies (see Goffman, 1971, on 'body gloss').

Immediately following Tony's 'no babies' comment, another student took the floor.

62–72 Sharon: *... I think it depends on what did they think in their mind. [...]*
Yeah, I think that's very important. And if, uh, they want to choose
the, uh, gay or lesbian, uh, that's their, uh, freedom. And their
right. I think is OK. Yeah, because I think you love, uh, uh,
anyone, not just only the reason is for the [genital?]. [...] So I
think that ... can be, uh, normal or not normal, just depends on
what- what do you think in your mind. [...] WHY you will do
that, what's the reason ... Are you HONEST, ah, yourself. Yeah I
think that's what is very important.

Here Sharon challenges the narrow normal/abnormal frame that Tony has set up by reformulating the debate in a way that allows for either possibility—that gay people can be either normal or not normal. Sharon changes the focus from socially defined normalcy to personal integrity—the degree of alignment between an individual's thoughts and their actions. She thereby challenges the notion that it is possible or desirable to generalize about gay people as if they were a homogeneous group or to assess normalcy from an external vantage point rather than subjectively.

In shifting the focus from normalcy to integrity, Sharon—and earlier, Vivian (turn 47)—effectively broaden the focus from homosexuality to any sexuality. Thus, the two women are downplaying the importance of the 'gender of object choice' and a fixed association with gay identity in Foucault's (1990) sense of a 'species' and instead highlighting an individual's degree of self-honesty. This could be seen as opening up the classroom discussion so that it is relevant to anyone making relationship or partnering choices.

Tony responded to Sharon's comments about self-honesty as follows:

73 Tony: *Interesting comment. Uh, one last thing ... Are- are gays and*
lesbians, do you think they're born gay and lesbian or is this
something they choose to become?

Tony's response is to formulate a debate about causality, asking the class whether they think gayness is innate or chosen. This move of Tony's highlights (and perhaps subtly contests) the emphasis on choice and the de-emphasis on gender in Sharon's (and Vivian's) comments.

On Debating the Causes of Gayness

Why some people are gay seems to be a common question within public debates about gay issues (Phelan, 1994). However, according to poststructuralist theorizations of identity, questions of causality are problematic.

Just as the question of what 'causes' heterosexuality makes no sense for vast and contradictory reasons, an examination of the causes of homosexuality ... makes no sense. *No* sexual identity, even the most normative, is automatic, authentic, easily assumed, or without negotiation and construction. It is not that there is some stable heterosexual identity out there waiting to be assumed and some unstable homosexual identity best left to its own. Rather, every sexual identity is an unstable, shifting, and volatile construction, a contradictory and unfinalized *social relation*.

(Britzman, 1997, p. 186)

In this view, asking whether gay people are born gay or choose to be gay makes little sense because 'being gay,' like 'being straight,' is an ongoing negotiation.

The pedagogic focus can be shifted away from the causes of gayness and onto the causes of discrimination against gay people, by asking questions such as the following:

Why does homophobia exist? Why is heterosexism so central to Western thought, and why is there so little tolerance for diversity? Why should it be important that we all develop heterosexual attachments and desires? What are the stakes here? Why is homophobia virulent in some societies and mild or nonexistent in others?

(Phelan, 1994, pp. 48–49)

This international perspective could be useful in language classes.

Also, it may be useful pedagogically to focus not on the causes of identifications but instead on their consequences:

The real problem does not lie in whether homosexuality is inborn or learnt. It lies instead in the question: what are the meanings this particular culture gives to homosexual behavior, however it may be caused, and what are the effects of those meanings on the ways in which individuals organize their sexual lives.

(Weeks, 1991, p. 154)

Of course, in language teaching contexts the interest is not in the sexual aspects but the communicative aspects of people's lives. So the question becomes "What are the meanings this particular culture gives to sexual identity in general (or gay identity in particular) and what are the effects of these meanings on how people communicate and interact?"

Participants' Perspectives

The perspectives of the teacher and four of his students further illuminate some important considerations in negotiating lesbian/gay subject matter.

The Teacher's Perspective

After the Day 3 discussion, Tony felt quite frustrated about how the unit was going. In our interview he explained why.

6.8 Tony: When I was in front of the class … I addressed this issue … about … normal, not normal. Well, normal is … having babies … And I said Gosh I don't have any babies! Which of course also implies that I'm straight, right, that … I'm normal in every other way except for I don't have babies. (C laughs) … If someone asked me at this point I think I'd tell them. [But] I would like to come out … on a positive note. And I didn't feel a lot of positive feeling … I do want certain kinds of answers, I guess. Or at least I want some balance and I wasn't getting the balance.

With students expressing few gay-positive views, Tony felt reluctant to come out to this class, which disappointed him because for quite some time he had been longing to be able to teach as an openly gay man.

It is interesting that Tony did not interpret Vivian's and Sharon's comments (turns 47, 62–72 above) as gay positive; this may have been because their comments associated gayness with choice and downplayed gender, neither of which matched Tony's own views of gay identity. It was clear from numerous things Tony said (in class and in our interviews) that he understood gay identity to be a stable, innate essence, who a person *is*, whereas Vivian and Sharon seemed to focus more on what a person *does*. Furthermore, in Tony's view, gender was a defining feature of lesbian/gay identity, but Vivian and Sharon minimized the significance of gender in relationships. It is possible that these theoretical disjunctures caused Tony to feel that the discussion was not 'balanced' and lacked 'positive feeling.'

It is also interesting that Tony felt that his comment about not having babies (turn 61) implied that he was straight, whereas I thought it was more likely to imply that he was gay. Students may have also had divergent interpretations of that comment. But in any case Tony's choices regarding his sexual-identity representations in class were clearly shaping his teaching practices.

6.9 Tony: [In class] I definitely, I guess, present myself as a straight person … Maybe especially now because we're doing this gay topic … One of the reasons that I'm not out to them is they're pretty much fresh off the boat, they've just gotten here and the one thing they don't need (T laughs) is to have a- a gay teacher on their hands and deal with him, culturally. I mean they have enough culture shock as it is … I'm gonna be kind of the normal American guy … Because I am gay I am cautious to a certain degree … I want the class to be a good class. I want them to leave with a good experience. I don't wanna tell them I'm gay … if I think that's gonna … upset their- their whole experience abroad.

Given Tony's fear that having to 'deal with' a gay teacher would dampen his students' enjoyment of international education, he deliberately crafted a straight persona for the classroom, which helps to account for his positioning of himself as a nonexpert on gay matters, as evident in the Day 1 discussion. It may also explain the personal/ impersonal paradox that seemed evident throughout the unit: on the one hand, Tony had a very personalized style of relating to students and an interest in eliciting personal experiences as subject matter, but on the other hand, he felt he had to approach gay themes in an impersonal way so that the students would not suspect that he himself was gay. Perhaps his desire to construct a straight persona in the classroom was linked to his construction of his student cohorts as straight too.

Students' Perspectives

When interviewed after the gay/lesbian unit had come to a close, most of Tony's students said they had enjoyed the unit, but two points of contention arose. The first concerned the question of whether or not it was appropriate to study a group of people.

Opposite opinions on this question were expressed by Hae-Woo and Jun-Kyu, who chose to be interviewed together. (By way of reminder, in the Day 1 discussion Hae-Woo had said that Koreans did not understand gays and lesbians [turn 96], and in a Day 2 class break Jun-Kyu had objected to gays and lesbians as a topic [see 6.6].)

6.10 Jun-Kyu:	What I dislike [is] … to make some … difference, like a kind of person, a material of topic … I think it is wrong. […] Is not only … gay and lesbian … Any kind [of person] […] Homeless, junker (meaning 'junkies') … They have … a right to live happily. And they are equal under law- law. They are same person as us. But why we discuss about them … only different from us. […]
Hae-Woo:	I don't think so. (H laughs) […] I want to learn English, and I want to learn American culture … [Good topics would be] Native American. (H laughs) … or Black people … or homeless … They live in America and they have a lot of problem.

To Jun-Kyu, studying any group of people was morally objectionable, whereas to Hae-Woo (and nearly all of the other students in the class) this represented an opportunity to learn about 'American culture.' The fact that various identity-based groups had 'problems' was, for Hae-Woo, exactly what made them interesting and worth studying.

A second point of contention between the students had to do with positive versus negative characterizations of gay people. Most of the students (especially the women) had had lengthy conversations with members of their American host families about the gay/lesbian themes they were studying in class. In these interactions, the students encountered divergent reactions to the subject matter.

Miyuki's experience was extremely positive. (On Day 1, Miyuki had told the class that her host family's gay son was not "different" [turn 41].)

6.11 Miyuki:	I feel [studying] gay or lesbian is pretty good experience for me … Because of this topic … I could speak to my host mother … She gave me, um, a lot of information about gay or lesbian … And so she … taught me about love. (wiping tears

from her eyes) […] She has gay son … And gay sister also. And she has two best friends, so they are gay.

Amazed and deeply moved by the intimacy of conversations with her host mother, Miyuki (from Japan) was grateful for the gay/lesbian unit because it had opened up opportunities for such meaningful conversations at home.

Norie (also from Japan) had also spoken at length with her host mother about the gay unit, but her experience was quite different than Miyuki's. (Norie was the student who, on Day 3, had said that gays were 'not normal' because "We must have a baby" [turn 51]. Also, below she refers to the gay and lesbian guest speakers who Tony had brought into class on the last day of the unit.)

6.12 Norie: I think we didn't study about gay life … We talked to them. But … they have job. And … they have a same partner always. And they have house and pet. But my host mother said is different. […]She said … Gay and lesbian has a lot of problem, for example, drug, alcohol, and AIDS … My host mother … has a before husband. Her husband died because of AIDS. He is gay … She talked about him … […] I was sad. She was sad … We talked for 3 hours.

Like Miyuki, Norie felt that studying this topic had opened up possibilities for conversations at home that had not existed previously. But after talking with her host mother, who reported overwhelmingly negative experiences of gay people, Norie felt a degree of disbelief or suspicion about how lesbians and gay men had been represented in the class.

Taken together, the gay/lesbian representations that featured in Tony's class—including the television character of 'Ellen' as well as the guest speakers' oral narratives and other materials beyond the scope of this chapter—had all highlighted the socially functioning, 'positive,' or 'normalized' aspects of the lives of gay people, such as having a home, a job, one long-term partner, a pet. These representations contrasted sharply with those offered by Norie's host mother, who, drawing on her own experience, represented gay people as socially dysfunctional, and riddled with problems related to drugs, alcohol, and AIDS.

Tony's Approach

'Lesbian/gay culture' generated so much interest among Tony's students that it was voted in as a class topic, yet studying the topic turned into a fairly fraught experience for some students and for Tony himself. Tony attributed the difficulties to some students' negative views of gay people, but I think there were problems with the teaching practices themselves. In taking a critical look at the teaching featured in this chapter (and throughout this book), I should emphasize that my aim is not to discourage teachers from experimenting with lesbian/bisexual/gay themes in class; on the contrary, I seek to increase the likely effectiveness of such experiments by mapping out potential pitfalls to watch out for as well as effective strategies to build on.

Analyzing Representation Practices

One of the tensions that emerged in this class was Norie's feeling that they had not 'really' studied gay and lesbian people—apparently because gay identity and gay people had not been framed as (or linked to) 'social problems.' According to Misson (1996), writing of education at the high school level, one challenge of dealing with lesbian/gay themes involves a "tension between asserting that lesbian and gay people are 'normal,' while acknowledging that they have special problems and difficulties because of the heterosexist beliefs and practices of mainstream culture" (p. 124). Misson (1996) elaborates on these negative/positive polarities:

> One wants to assert that homosexuals are inherently just as well-balanced and strong mentally as heterosexuals, while acknowledging that they are more likely to suffer mental disturbance or commit suicide because of the pressures on them. One wants to assert that homosexual people are just as capable of sustaining deep and lasting relationships, while at the same time acknowledging that the pressures on their relationships are such that they do tend statistically to last a considerably shorter time.
>
> (p. 124)

A way to avoid being locked into a positive/negative characterization, which is itself potentially contentious, is to consider the case put forward by Britzman et al. (1993). They explain why a multicultural model of education that seeks to promote tolerance toward previously underrepresented cultural groups is problematic:

> Generally ... mainstream orientations to the field of multicultural education have been preoccupied with supplying students with 'accurate' and 'authentic' representations of particular cultures in the hope that such corrective gestures will automatize tolerant attitudes. These newly represented cultures appear on the stage of curriculum either as a seamless parade of stable and unitary customs and traditions or in the individuated form of particular heroes modeling roles. The knowledge that scaffolds this view shuts out the controversies of how any knowledge—including multicultural—is constructed, mediated, governed, and implicated in forms of social regulation and normalization. The problem is that knowledge of a culture is presented as if unencumbered by the politics and poetics of representation.
>
> (Britzman et al., 1993, pp. 188–189)

Britzman et al. (1993) propose that subjecting representations to critical scrutiny has more pedagogic potential than simply 'parading' representations in the hope of changing student attitudes. Thus, the emphasis is less on real-world phenomena and more on how these phenomena are represented, interpreted, and negotiated.

Applying this approach to Tony's class might look something like this. Instead of having the class discuss whether or not they liked Ellen "as a person," the teacher might have posed questions that highlighted the constructedness of 'Ellen' by asking about aspects such as the following: how this particular representation of 'a lesbian' was similar and different to other mediated representations of lesbian characters that students had encountered on television or the Internet, or in movies, books, or newspapers (perhaps especially in other countries); what sorts of audience might consider the character appealing or unappealing; what the social consequences of this TV show might be in terms of changing attitudes about gay people; or, drawing on Misson (1996), how humor was created in the show by deliberately juxtaposing clashing perceptions associated with lesbian/gay themes.

Examining the complex practices of representing lesbian and gay people may have been a way to diffuse some of the underlying tensions that teacher and students alike were experiencing by depersonalizing the discussion somewhat. Looking at gay/lesbian representations instead of gay/lesbian people could also prove more do-able for teachers who, like Tony, identify as gay but are not out in the classroom.

Questioning Lived Experience

As in Tony's class, it is common for language classes to involve some form of 'autobiographical work' in which students are asked to speak or write from their own experience (Schenke, 1991; see also Duff & Uchida, 1997). But events are "culturally signified and defined" (Hall, 1993, p. 87), which means that experience is "open to contradictory interpretations" that are shaped by broader sociopolitical interests rather than by an individual's "objective truth" (Weedon, 1987, p. 80). Critical pedagogues have argued that the experiences of students need to be not just elicited but interrogated: "How can we acknowledge previous experience as legitimate content and challenge it at the same time? How do we encourage student 'voices' while simultaneously encouraging the interrogation of such voices?" (Simon, 1992, p. 62). There is a need to examine "the multiple discourses that have shaped 'personal experience'" (Malinowitz, 1995, p. 74), or similarly, how "the subject [is] multiple and formed within different discourses" (Pennycook, 1990, p. 26; see also Norton Peirce, 1995).

Tony's emphasis on eliciting students' experiences was not followed by any sort of analysis or querying of those experiences, such as discussion of how one's viewpoints shape the ways in which events are experienced or how one's experiences shape one's viewpoints. This meant that students expressed, and heard, pejorative comments about gay people but without there being any sort of follow up, which could alienate some students—especially gay ones, as the following incident suggests.

Kappra (1998/1999) recounts the experiences of a gay student from Japan in an IEP in the San Francisco area. The student, Yuji, found his "encounters with homophobia" on campus and in the classroom to be "new and frightening experiences" (p. 19). One incident that the student found disturbing was "a class discussion on homosexuality, [in which] the teacher allowed students to make negative comments about gays and lesbians and, according to Yuji, 'accepted all opinions equally'" (p. 19). This suggests that teachers need to find ways of not merely eliciting experiences or opinions (in this case, about gay/lesbian people) but doing something educationally constructive with these views, as discussed in Chapters 3 and 4.

Sharing Pedagogic Decision Making

Candlin (1984) suggests that a syllabus should be "dynamic and negotiated" rather than "static and imposed," which means that it needs to be renegotiated on an ongoing basis in order to have continuing relevance for the learners (p. 33). Even though Tony's course began with the learners voting on the topics they wanted to study during the term, during the period I was observing the class, decisions about what was studied, in what manner, and for how long were made exclusively by Tony without any consultation or negotiation with students. In my view, there were a number of aspects where teacher control could have been "usefully relaxed to allow more [student] initiative" (van Lier, 1988, p. 178).

For example, at the close of the Day 1 discussion Tony explained the types of activities he was planning for the unit. An alternative would have been for the class to brainstorm, discuss, and negotiate aspects of the topic that interested them or the types of activities they would like to pursue. Including the students in more of the pedagogic decision making would be a way of customizing the learning to better fit the students' particular interests in the topic of 'gay/lesbian culture,' while fostering language learning in the process. As Breen (1985) explains it, "the teaching-learning process requires decisions to be made, and decision making has high communicative potential. The sharing of decision making in a language class will generate communication which has authentic roots in getting things done here and now" (p. 152).

Another example was that, on Day 3, Tony decided that a second viewing of 'Ellen' was warranted without attempting to find out whether the students agreed. The students then discussed assigned questions about the show but were not encouraged to generate their own. Also, in forming small groups for discussion it was Tony who regularly determined their configuration. Even when having the class interview passersby and friends/host families about lesbian/gay issues, Tony would write the interview questions with no input from the students who were going to be asking them. Throughout the lesbian/gay unit Tony took it upon himself to determine which thematic and linguistic aspects to focus on and what activities to use in doing so; without the benefit of student input on these decisions, it is not surprising that he found this somewhat burdensome and stressful.

Turn taking was another aspect where students lacked control since Tony often called on students who had not yet spoken. While there may be pedagogically valid reasons for doing this, especially in a class where some students are much more vocal than others, it has been argued that "[a] significant source of motivation and attention is lost when turn taking is predetermined rather than interactionally managed by the participants" (van Lier, 1988, p. 133). In this case, given the highly personalized approach that Tony was taking to the content (which was itself potentially emotionally charged), students who were called on may have felt 'put on the spot.'

Also, during the term, there were no opportunities for learners to provide feedback to the teacher about the class. Legutke and Thomas (1991) suggest that, when learners are "unclear as to the purpose or value of an activity," it may be useful to implement a 'process-evaluation activity,' which asks learners to evaluate the class activities and their learning from an affective as well as a cognitive perspective (pp. 142–143). Eliciting learner feedback is also a way to involve learners in making decisions about the learning/teaching process:

> Learners must have an opportunity to criticize both teacher and materials and to learn how to express themselves when the teaching and the tasks are not effective. They not only have a right to reasons why particular teaching strategies are being adopted, they must share the responsibility with the teacher for the choice of teaching and learning strategy.
>
> (Piepho, 1981, p. 12)

In Tony's class, if there had been a means for Jun-Kyu, for example, to express his concern about studying specific groups of people or for Norie to express her concern that the gay and lesbian characterizations presented in class reflected an overly positive bias, then opportunities to examine the links between language, culture, and identity may have been enriched in interesting ways.

Learning from the Challenges

Framing sexual diversity as subject matter can clearly foster conversations, both in and out of class, that students find eye opening, thought provoking, and even inspiring. The experiences of Tony's class provide some insights that can help teachers to make the most of gay/lesbian material. In terms of broaching gay/lesbian topics, some students may feel hesitant or uncertain about how their peers or their teacher might react if they were to show an interest in this subject matter; therefore, to make it clear that queer conversations are indeed welcome in the classroom, teachers may need to take the initiative—as Tony did by including 'lesbian/gay culture' on the list of possible class topics offered to the students. Tony's class also underscores the importance of providing opportunities for students to voice their own ideas or concerns about what they are studying and how they are going about it, as doing so may uncover divergent understandings that have the potential to enrich class discussions. Moreover, in approaching gay/lesbian material it is important not to characterize the students and the studied in fixed, straight/gay, us/them positionings, and not to merely elicit personal experiences of gay/lesbian people without at least subjecting these narratives to some form of critical analysis or reflection.

In closing, I would like to note that Tony's teaching practices were constrained by two factors that must be addressed in the profession at large. First, the general dearth of commercially produced learning materials that engage with sexual diversity means that it is left to teachers to create level-appropriate materials for their own classes. Though language teachers often create their own materials, whether by choice or necessity, creating materials for intercultural discussions of lesbian/gay topics can be especially complex, given the likelihood of divergent experiences, viewpoints, and knowledge levels and the risks involved in broaching potentially contentious subject matter. Even teachers who are very enthusiastic about engaging these topics, as Tony was, may find it daunting to have to generate suitable materials on a daily basis—especially if their extra efforts are likely to be devalued (by students, colleagues, or administrators) or dismissed as inappropriate, as we have seen examples of in previous chapters. Second, given the broader social forces that devalue non-heterosexualities, it can seem impossible to teach gay/lesbian themes as an openly gay man or woman. In Tony's case, he felt he had to routinely disguise not only his life experiences but also the distress that he felt when his students spoke disparagingly about gay people.

Despite the difficulties of creating gay/lesbian curricula for his students and, at the same time, a straight persona for himself, Tony was dedicated to tackling issues of difference in his classroom. His efforts highlight both the complexity and the necessity of finding effective ways to talk in language classes about sexual diversity.

CHAPTER 7

Invisible Outings: Gina's Class

In Gina's academic ESL class, gay and lesbian themes arose in several interactions during a unit of work on 'community.' In the first of these interactions, a student seemed to be insinuating that a classmate was gay; in a subsequent discussion of online communities, the gay community was included as an example; and later, in answering a vocabulary question, the teacher used a lesbian example. In analyzing the teaching practices in terms of which aspects worked well and which did not, I take into account the perspectives of the teacher and five of her students—a woman from China, a woman from El Salvador, a man from Laos, and two women from Vietnam. It becomes clear that lesbian/gay subject matter can arise in unplanned ways through student innuendos and that teachers may need to follow up such instances by communicating quite explicitly about lesbian/gay meanings rather than presuming familiarity and shared understandings.

The Class

Gina taught the ESL version of an academic English class at a university. The class met for nearly 4 hours per week. The 22 students hailed from eight different countries (China, El Salvador, Japan, Korea, Laos, Norway, Singapore, and Vietnam); half of the students were women, half men; and they were all in their 20s or 30s (for more details, see Appendix C). A few were international students, but most were refugees or immigrants, some of whom had arrived in the United States as children or teenagers while others had arrived as adults. All the students I interviewed enjoyed the class; they considered Gina a demanding teacher but a very good one, and they believed their writing was improving as a result of her feedback and suggestions.

Gina, who was in her 30s, had been teaching ESL/EFL for about 12 years, first in Europe, where she was from (English was her second language), and then in the United States. For this class there was no set textbook, and Gina was free to decide what and how to teach. The course had been organized into units of work based on themes. Class time was usually spent either in small-group or whole-class discussions of the readings or in individual student–teacher consultations about the written assignments.

Gina was passionate about teaching academic language and literacy in a way that would engage students:

> 7.1 Gina: They can be great computer programmers, great engineers, [but] if their English is not good this is gonna be extremely limiting … I see my role as somebody who needs to find ways to turn them on to language … I'm trying to show them that I'm interested in what they have to say. [...] They're not gonna be good writers … if they can't think about ideas critically, discuss ideas, look at other people's points of view … I think it's also my role to provide a forum in the ESL class where they can do that in a fairly safe environment. So that maybe in their philosophy class or their history class or their human sexuality class they can … pipe up, they can talk, they can … share their ideas.

Above all, Gina wanted to challenge students to think critically, to question, and to express themselves so that they could overcome the social discrimination she felt they were likely to face, as second language speakers of English, on campus and in the workplace.

Discussing Earrings on a Man as a 'Lifestyle'

A gay subtext emerged during a brief activity introducing the unit of work on 'community.' The students had formed small groups and each group was instructed to identify two things that all their members had in common. The students then wrote that information on the board, which resulted in the following list:

all Asian + all single
play the piano + like to watch comedy movies
second year + swimming
wear earrings + speak Mandarin
like shopping + like pink color

Gina next asked the class to think of categories to describe the words on the board. As an example, she proposed 'marital status,' and the students came up with 'identity,' 'ethnicity,' 'hobbies,' and 'language.' The lively 3-minute discussion shown below (with key utterances to be discussed further on featured in bold) begins with Gina eliciting additional categories.

> 7 Gina: *… What about … like pink or wear earrings or love the beach or. Any other category?* [...]
> 13 Peter: *Interests?*
> 14 Gina: *Interests?* (as if doubtful) *Like pink*
> 15 Peter: *Nah.*
> 16 Gina: *Is an interest?* (laughter) (writes "interest" near "like pink color") *OK. Wear earrings is an interest?*
> 17 Peter: *No.* (Peter and others laugh)
> 18 *Many students talking at once [?]*

19 Ping:	*I think it can be. It can be.*
20 Student:	*Fashion.*
21 Gina:	*Fashion, OK.* (Peter laughs, Gina writes "fashion") *So earrings as a fashion statement?*
22 Student:	*Hm-hm.*
23 Gina:	*OK, well wearing earrings, like. Well, let's talk a little bit about this.* (laughter) *Um.* **What is that all about? Liking pink or wearing earrings or. Why do we do things like that?**
24 Ping:	**I think it's lifestyle.** (Ping laughs)
25 Gina:	**Lifestyle? Why- Why so, Ping?**
26 Ping:	**Um. You know, wear earring just for woman. But for man lifestyle.**
27 Gina:	**Aaah!** (laughter) (G smiles) **Is THAT what you think?** (much laughter)
28 Many students talking at once [?]	
29 Gina:	(writes "lifestyle") **So- So what is that telling us, this kind of comment? From Ping.**
30 Lucy:	**Not only girls, not only women wear earrings. Even male does the same thing.**
31 Gina:	**OK but see for Ping, an earring on a man means something else.**
32 Lucy:	*Uh-huh.*
33 Gina:	*Right?* (laughter)
34 Student:	*Right.* [...]
36 Gina:	*Well yeah, we do certain things and people look at us in certain ways from, you know, the way we dress or*
37 Rita:	(as if to challenge) *So that means if you don't wear earrings we're a tomboy? Is that it?* (laughter)
38 Student:	[?]
39 Gina:	*What? I don't know. What do you think?*
40 Eva:	*Well it just depends on the person, I guess. If they like wearing it, they wear it. If they don't like it* [?]
41 Peter:	*I think it's*
42 Lucy:	*Personality.*
43 Peter:	*Personality.*
44 Ping:	*Personal character. Personal character. Personal character.*
45 Gina:	*Personal character, yeah. I was thinking of personal choice ... Yeah, and there's what- what we choose and also how people perceive us because of what we choose. Like, if I take off my earrings* (taking hers off) *or if I put my earrings back on, you know. Somebody- If a man wears earrings or*
46 Peter:	*Also ... second year. I, um, meant to- to put, like, second-year college student. So ... status.*
47 Gina:	*OK. So ... who are the people who are in second year in college?* (students raise hands) *... What are some of the things that all second-year people have in common?*

The discussion of second-year students led to a discussion of why people like finding others with similar backgrounds and interests and then to defining 'community' and naming examples of communities.

The Teacher's Perspective

Gina thought this discussion had gone quite well. She had decided to respond to Ping's comment that men wearing earrings indicated a 'lifestyle' (turn 26) because she believed that Ping was deliberately implying that a classmate, Ben, was gay (he was in the small group of students who had in common that they all wore earrings). Gina decided to intervene because she felt that Ping's insinuation that Ben was gay was meant to be derogatory and that Ping was about to make an anti-gay remark.

> 7.2 Gina: I knew exactly what I was getting into and so [did] they ... which was boy[s] who wear earrings may be gay. I mean that was ... the underlying thing that was never said. But that was understood I think by most people ... I mean, I knew that Ben was the person with an earring. I knew that Ping knew that Ben was the guy with an earring. She looked right at him when she said that (turn 26) ... When she said Well I think it can be an interest (turn 19), I kind of predicted what she was getting into ... I wanted to address it ... I looked at [Ben] and he kind of looked at Ping and I thought this is a potential for this kind of really nasty stuff to come up. And I wanted to address it because I think by addressing it then I'm saying Well then you're gonna have in some ways to discuss it ... You can't ... just ... make these kinds of comments ... You're making assumptions about somebody's sexual orientation because of the way they look. And we never got that far into the discussion but then we got to say Well that's a personal choice.

Gina wanted to get the message across to Ping and the rest of the class that it was not appropriate or acceptable to insinuate that a classmate was gay or to make anti-gay remarks. Gina felt that, if she had not addressed Ping's comments, an uncomfortable confrontation may have ensued.

> 7.3 Gina: When something like that comes up ... I usually deal with it ... Not all students are happy discussing and arguing in the classroom.

Gina explained why, when Ping said that men wearing earrings indicated a 'lifestyle,' she responded with "Aaah! Is THAT what you think?" (turn 27).

> 7.4 Gina: It's a way to say Ah, oh really ... Which implies ... there is more to what you said than what you say there is. (G laughs)

Thus, Gina meant to cast Ping's comment in a dubious light but without directly criticizing it.

Throughout the earrings discussion words such as "sexual orientation," as Gina put it, or "gay" were never actually uttered, yet Gina thought the gay subtext had been understood by most students nonetheless.

7.5 Gina: It was all very much underground. It was not very obvious ... But ...
            I don't think ... many people were left out of it.

Students' Perspectives

Students who had spoken during the earrings discussion had varied understandings of it. At least one student, Lucy (from Vietnam), showed no awareness whatsoever of the gay subtext. Lucy interpreted Ping's comment that earrings on men indicated a 'lifestyle' as having to do with cultural identity, not sexual identity (both Ping and Ben were of Chinese heritage).

7.6 Lucy: In Chinese tradition, if a guy have ear pierced that means that their
            parents is afraid that [he] would never grow to be a man ... So
            they pierce the ears ... hoping that ... will make the kid understand
            how to respect people and be a good boy and grow up to be a good
            man ... So it's not amazed to me that Ping said that.

Peter (from Laos) did become aware of the gay subtext in the earrings discussion, but he decided not to say anything about it.

7.7 Peter: When the subject of- of wearing earrings came up, and ... [Rita]
            said, like, if the girls don't wear earrings other people might see them
            as the, um, tomboy (turn 37), and all that stuff. That's when ... gay
            subject, it just popped on my head. But I didn't wanna say it.
            (P laughs)

I asked him why not.

7.8 Peter: [Because] it might offend someone. Or it might hurt their feeling. Or
            they might take it in wrong way. Um, 'cause I might not use the
            correct word or the right word. 'Cause ... in high school [in the US]
            especially when someone's gay or lesbian seems like the students
            always makes fun of them. And I kinda feel bad because I did too. But
            when I came here [to university] I looked at things differently ... Even
            though they're gay or they're lesbian they still have feelings. So we
            should not put ... them down ... So we should respect them. At the
            same way as, um, um, heterosexual people ... 'Cause I have a few gay-
            gay friends and a few lesbian friends. And they seem pretty normal.

Peter was concerned not to hurt or offend gay or lesbian students by inadvertently saying something homophobic, which may explain why he interrupted the teacher to change the subject from wearing earrings to second-year students (turn 46).

Ping herself had yet a different experience of the earrings discussion. Ping, who was from China and whose English-speaking proficiency level was lower than that of many of her classmates, explained to me that, when the topic of earrings came up in the class discussion, she noticed for the first time that Ben was wearing an earring and she wanted to let the class know that this meant he was gay.

7.9 Ping:	I saw some mans (P is laughing) wearing earring too! (P laughs) … I look up … one guy here … [Ben], see that's a gay … Do you know homosex? Is two men love together.
Cynthia:	So you saw a guy wearing … one earring …?
Ping:	Yeah. It's a sign. Sign means it's, uh, two men love together…
Cynthia:	So when you saw this you thought He's gay.
Ping:	Yeah (P laughs) yeah. […]
Cynthia:	So when [Gina] says OK but for Ping, an earring on a man means something else (turn 31) … what do you think is something else?
Ping:	(P laughs) I think he's a gay. Gay man … If you're gay, this one [wearing one earring] is S-I-G-N, is sign … So … I tried explain for people.
Cynthia:	That a gay man would wear one earring?
Ping:	Yeah, yeah
Cynthia:	Do you think everybody listening understood that?
Ping:	I don't think so … Different people have different background.

In the earrings discussion Ping saw herself as a sort of cultural informant for her peers, teaching classmates with 'different backgrounds' that within the local social/cultural context an earring worn by a man (in this case, Ben) serves as a gay signifier. Ping did not seem to think the word 'gay' was widely known; in fact, she set about explaining its meaning to me, someone she knew to be an ESL teacher. It did not seem that in class Ping had intended to communicate anything negative about gay people, as Gina had suspected.

Ping understood Gina's interjections as being primarily about vocabulary. Ping believed that she had used the wrong word when she said 'lifestyle' and that was why Gina had queried her comment (see turns 24–27).

7.10 Ping:	I never get this correct … word … Because (P laughs) my language is Chinese … I tell 'lifestyle.' But, hm, this one is too wide […] I just try [to explain] what kind is wearing earring. But I never get it good words … I tell this, [Gina] said Why? … [Then she] gave this one … 'personal choice' (turn 45). It's good. […] I think 'personal character' (turn 44) is good here. If you choose man, woman, is … no clear. You know, good word, 'personal,' you can get woman and man, it doesn't separate … female and male, just a person … This words is really good.

Ping saw herself as someone who was searching for the right vocabulary to get her ideas across, and she saw the teacher as someone helping in that endeavor by explaining that instead of using 'lifestyle' she should use 'personal choice' (a term that was preferable, in Ping's erroneous understanding, because the 'person' in 'personal' made it gender-neutral).

Ping did not seem to understand that Gina had meant to challenge Ping's point that earrings on a man signified gayness and to discourage Ping from insinuating that another student was gay. Instead, she thought Gina was helping her to make her point more clearly—and that 'personal choice' was simply a better term to use than 'lifestyle.'

Responding to a Student's Insinuation that a Classmate is Gay

In light of the students' perspectives, it seems that in this instance Gina's teaching practices had mixed success. I want to first analyze the aspects that I think were impressive before turning to those that were somewhat problematic.

First, Gina chose to focus on the gay innuendo rather than avoid or overlook it, even though gay themes had not been a planned part of the activities for that day (nor for that unit of work). Some teachers—on finding themselves in a similar situation, with a student suddenly insinuating a classmate was gay—might simply ignore the comment, feeling unprepared or uncertain about how to proceed. Yet Gina was open to exploring the topic, in what could be characterized as an 'in-flight' interaction (Cazden, 1988, p. 90).

> It is likely that every language teacher has had the experience of having something unexpected occur during a lesson. Whether it leads to a derailment of the lesson or a contribution to learning is often largely a matter of how the teacher reacts to the unexpected, and the extent to which the co-production is encouraged or stifled.
>
> (Allwright & Bailey, 1991, p. 25)

In this case, Gina encouraged 'co-production' by opening the floor. She could have simply expressed the disapproval that she felt at Ping's comment and then quickly moved the discussion along (as some teachers did in a similar situation; see 4.25 and 4.26), but instead she made it the focus and invited other students to voice their views on the issue at hand. So the second positive point is that Gina attempted to fashion a learning opportunity from Ping's spontaneous remark that earrings on a man indicated a 'lifestyle' by *opening the comment for discussion*.

Third, Gina did not invite just any sort of response to Ping's comment, but she guided the discussion in a certain direction. The teaching aim was not to "deliver a verdict of right or wrong but to induct the learner into a new way of thinking about, categorizing, reconceptualizing, even recontextualizing whatever phenomena … are under discussion" (Cazden, 1988, p. 111). In this case, Gina managed to steer the discussion away from *the sexuality of men who wear earrings*— or of Ben, or of any other men in the class who happened to be wearing an earring that day—and onto *the practice of making assumptions about sexuality based on appearance, while at the same time calling this practice into question*. By steering the discussion away from the identification of a student as gay, Gina averted the homophobic remarks that she feared would follow this public 'outing.' She also managed to reposition men who wear earrings (including those in the classroom at that moment) from passive objects of study whose behavior is interpreted by others to active agents making choices of their own (turn 45).

Querying the assumption that earrings on a man necessarily signify gayness reinforced two notions that Gina wanted her students to learn: in the context of learning the local social conventions, the notion that it is not desirable to out someone else as gay, and in the context of learning academic English, the notion that generalizations, claims, and, assumptions need to be questioned. For the reasons outlined above, I think Gina's improvised response to the unexpected 'lifestyle' comment can be considered quite masterful. However, the limitations of her approach are also worth considering.

Unfortunately, the gay subtext was so subtle and indirect as to be inaccessible for at least some of the students. At no point during the earrings discussion did Gina (or any of the students) make explicit the gay meaning of Ping's 'lifestyle' comment and thus of the subsequent discussion. This meant that some students, like Lucy (7.6), missed the gay subtext of the conversation altogether, while others, like Ping (7.10), missed the underlying message that Gina was trying to convey. Those who did pick up on the gay subtext, like Peter (7.7 and 7.8), may have been reluctant to use the word 'gay' because the teacher did not use it. Some students may have even inferred that the teacher considered gay/lesbian themes to be inappropriate or unwelcome in the classroom context; that is, if a gay innuendo arises but the teacher does not name it and address it directly, students may formulate their own reasons for the teacher's indirectness.

Of course, indirect communication has its benefits. It can allow discussions to progress: "Ambiguity does not impede talk. On the contrary … it can allow talk to proceed without the interminable wrangling that would ensue if every nuance had to be clarified" (Edwards & Westgate, 1994, p. 137). In the classroom context, it is not always feasible to take time to clarify every nuance since doing so can detract from the planned focus of the lesson at hand. Moreover, in the language classroom in particular, indirection communication can serve as a teaching tool to help students learn how to make sense of and negotiate meanings that are not necessarily fixed or unequivocal (Candlin, 1981). Communicating indirectly can also be a way for teachers to avoid being prescriptive about students' beliefs and values, and that is what I suspect Gina was trying to do—to steer Ping away from calling someone gay and taunting them for it but without telling Ping in so many words what to believe or say.

Thomas (1983) makes the case that language teachers are supposed to facilitate learners' ability to communicate, not determine what they are to say.

[I]t is the [language] teacher's job to equip the student to express her/himself in exactly the way s/he chooses to do so—rudely, tactfully, or in an elaborately polite manner. What we want to prevent is her/his being *unintentionally* rude or subservient. It may, of course, behoove the teacher to point out the likely consequences of certain types of linguistic behaviour.

(p. 96)

Of course, learners' intentions are not always clear, but this is exactly the point. When a language teacher finds a learner's speech (or text) offensive, rather than criticize the learner or move off the topic it may be more effective to clarify the learner's intended meaning and discuss the likely effects or consequences of their speech (or text) on their interlocutors, as discussed in Chapter 4.

The latter approach may be especially useful with lesbian/gay themes, given the likelihood that many students will have had little or no experience discussing these in a classroom context. In fact, of the 28 students I interviewed across the three classes (Chapters 6–8), Peter was the only one who had talked about lesbian/gay content in a previous class (a human sexuality class); the other students said they had never before talked about this subject matter in any ESL class nor any other class. Also, some second-language students may have a limited familiarity with local terms and concepts associated with sexual diversity and local social rules associated with talking about them.

Furthermore, as De Vincenti et al. (2007) point out, sexuality-related meanings and innuendo are often communicated indirectly or even nonverbally, so language learners may need explicit instruction in interpreting subtext, cues, and nuances of language and gesture pertaining to this identity domain. They give the example that, for Japanese speakers, "The right hand held at an angle against the left cheek … indicates that a male is effeminate or perhaps gay" (p. 68). The authors argue that "not recognizing, or unintentionally misusing, these cues can inadvertently indicate a different meaning or cause confusion," so second- and foreign-language learners need to be made aware of nonverbal signals to do with sexual identities (p. 68).

In the earrings discussion, Ping and Gina each misread the other's messages, but without either of them realizing it. Gina responded to Ping's 'lifestyle' comment (turn 26) by strongly implying that Ping's view was neither the prevailing viewpoint in the class, nor a desired one ("Is THAT what you think," turn 27; "So what is that telling *us*, this kind of comment? *From Ping*," turn 29; "OK but see *for Ping* …," turn 31). Yet Ping's intentions were not necessarily hostile, as Gina took them to be. Ping seemed to think that men wearing earrings have chosen to be 'out' as gay and that out gay men are considered acceptable in that city; accordingly, she had no qualms about drawing attention to this public sign in order to inform those classmates who did not realize what it meant.

If Gina had assumed innocent description on Ping's part, rather than something potentially 'nasty,' she might have responded along the lines of "What do you mean by 'lifestyle'?" or perhaps "Do you mean a gay lifestyle? Yeah, in some cases when men wear earrings it's because they want to show that they're gay. What are some other reasons why men might wear earrings?" This would also have made it possible for students like Lucy to mention the culture-based meanings of earrings. It may also have modeled a way of talking about gay people that would neither insult them nor ignore them, which could have been helpful to students like Peter, who seemed to think it was safer to say nothing on the subject than to risk saying the 'wrong' thing (see 7.8).

Discussing the Online Gay Community

After putting some careful thought into how to follow up the earrings discussion, Gina managed to integrate gay issues into the next class session. She did so without framing these issues as a debate or a controversy (see Chapter 4) and without eliciting students' personal experiences of gay/lesbian people (see Chapter 6).

For homework for Day 2, in preparation for an upcoming essay on the theme of community, the class was assigned three readings, including an article on 'cyberhood' that briefly mentioned the gay community (alongside the Hispanic community and the medical community). Linked to the readings were compare/contrast questions about 'computer communities' versus 'traditional communities.' In class on Day 2, the students discussed their answers in small groups and wrote them on the board, before having a whole-class discussion with Gina adding to their answers. For example, under the heading "E-community," students listed things like "don't know people appearance" and "no body language," to which Gina added "less prejudiced," "accessible all the time," and "support."

Below I show how gay themes arose during the whole-class discussion of this question set: "What functions do these electronic communities serve? Why do people use them?" Immediately preceding the transcript below, the class had been discussing homeless people and why they were not taken seriously until they formed an online community to advocate for their rights.

1 Rita:	*… [W]e have been hearing like stereotypes about [homeless people]. So we- we see only the physical. We don't see like what they think, … how bright they are, how smart.* (Gina is writing "stereotype" on the board)
2 Gina:	**OK, can't stereotype. You remember, uh, what happened last time when we talked about earrings?**
3 Rita:	*Uh-huh.*
4 Vince:	*Stereotype.*
5 Gina:	*Right. OK, we started having a- you know, talking about that was an example of a stereotype, or at least how our- our OWN views-* **we look at people and oops! We pass judgment right away. OK, so in this case we can't, um, stereotype. In the … reading 'Cyberhood … Versus Neighborhood,' they listed a bunch of communities and they mentioned the gay community. What would be- why would it be an advantage for gay people maybe to start a community online?**
6 Student:	*So that they know about them, and they can express themself- express themself.*
7 Gina:	*OK. What else?* (short pause) *If we look at the things that we put on the board.*
8 Sara:	*[I think?] can fight some stereotypes. Overcome [?]*
9 Gina:	*How so, Sara?*
10 Sara:	*Like, uh, some people still don't get used to it, with the fact that there are gay or lesbian people. Still have some bad talk about it. So on someone computer I think is, uh [?].*
11 Gina:	*Do you mean*
12 Sara:	*Like, well I understand some gay or lesbian people still get attacked, like people still violent.*

13 Gina:	*Violent.*
14 Sara:	*But on the computer they don't- they don't get it.*
15 Gina:	*OK. So is it- it would be a safe place? To meet and talk? (Rita raises her hand) Rita?*
16 Rita:	*It might encourage others to say like that, like don't be afraid to say that they are lesbian or gay.*
17 Gina:	*OK. So what do you think, do you see that as an advantage? Why?*
18 Rita:	*Why? (as if surprised) 'Cause they are humans too. They have rights.*

Next the discussion turned to a disabled man described in a class reading and how he was not able to walk or talk. The transcript below begins with Gina summing up the benefits of online communities to the disabled man and the homeless people described in the reading, before returning to the topic of the gay community.

34 Gina:	*So for him [the disabled man], it [being part of an online community] was a question of accessibility, right?*
35 Student:	*Uh-hm.*
36 Gina:	*For the homeless it was a question of not being stereotyped. And both people got some support.* ***How about for gay people? For the gay community?***
37 Eva:	*(quietly) They have more power when they get together [?]*
38 Gina:	*How so?*
39 Eva:	*(quietly) Well more chance of getting heard- heard. Getting their, uh, I don't know how to say it.*
40 Gina:	*So it enables people to get together?* ***Is there a question of access to the gay community?*** *See we [have] Gaytown (a gay neighborhood in the same city). Right?*
41 Students:	*Uh-huh. (some students are nodding)*
42 Gina:	***So it's really easy for people who are gay, or, you know, people who are friends with people who are gay, or people who are gay-friendly, or people who question whether they are gay, to just go to Gaytown.***
43 Student:	*Uh-huh.*
44 Gina:	*Or go anywhere in [this city] because you're bound to run into somebody who is gay, right? But is that as accessible to everybody in the country, or the world?*
45 Many students:	*No. No. (many are shaking their heads)*
46 Gina:	*No, right. So, uh, what purpose then, what function would an electronic community serve?*
47 Student:	*For those people.*
48 Ping:	*(quietly) [Group can support together each other?]*
49 Students:	*(several students speaking softly at the same time)*
50 Gina:	***Right, so even if you're- if you're here*** *(drawing on the board small circles far apart from each other)* ***and I'm here and***

> *somebody else is here and somebody else [is] here, and we're*
> *hundreds of miles apart from one another, then you can ... still get*
> *support. So ... that adds also to the definition of community that*
> *we were talking about before, right? ... [P]eople ... who get*
> *together, people who have something in common.*

Gina wrapped up this discussion by adding 'sexual preference' to the list that the class had co-constructed of things pertaining to communities (including 'ethnicity,' 'interests,' 'job'), before proceeding to the next question.

The Teacher's Perspective

Gina felt pleased that she had managed to integrate the topic of the gay community into the unit on communities. She thought this was useful subject matter because all the students, in the course of their day-to-day interactions, were bound to encounter sexual diversity among their interlocutors.

7.11 Gina: [Students] work with gays ... their dentist is gay, their teacher is gay. And ... we're here to educate people to be critical thinkers so that they can, you know, make choices that affect their world. But we let them go around the world like this (covering her eyes with her hands) and say 'No you don't have really to look at anybody being different from you.' And so ... that's why I think it's important to- to have gays being visible.

She was also aware of sexual diversity as a facet of life among the students themselves and also their families.

7.12 Gina: They don't always come out to me right when they're taking the classes, but every semester I have several queer students. Or I have people whose mothers are queer, whose sisters are queer, whose uncles are queer, and it always comes up.

With these things in mind, Gina had carefully considered how to follow up on the gay subtext that had arisen in the Day 1 earrings discussion.

7.13 Gina: I ... didn't want to ... ask people to write their OPINION about being GAY ... But I also want to bring up the issue ... I can work on making gays and lesbians more visible and connecting them to ... important issues such as community ... I think there is a way for me to bring up the topic for discussion ... without asking [for] a black and white condemn or condone type of response.

Though Gina thought the discussion had gone well, she was concerned that she may have talked too much.

7.14 Gina: I remember that vividly as being pretty much [an] ... I'm standing on my soapbox kind of thing [...] But ... it was beyond the stereotypes and the earring, [which] ... you can laugh about ... Violence ... accessibility ... safety. I mean some deeper stuff had come up at that point ... I think maybe that's ... why ... they were not so, um, external in their responses.

I asked her what she meant by being on a soapbox.

7.15 Gina: Being on the soapbox is ... me feeling exposed ... I am treading ... dangerous waters. Because ... I'm getting to become very personal. And I think there's always an element of being self-conscious. [...] Sometimes I feel that I take over too much ... directing ... bringing up issues ... But it's also my role to facilitate and ... help them see different sides.

Gina's comments raise the question of how teachers can strike an effective balance between bringing up multiple perspectives and vantage points but without either being too controlling of the discussion or revealing too much of themselves.

Students' Perspectives

Once again, the students' divergent experiences highlight some interesting teaching issues with regard to lesbian/gay themes.

In Ping's view, the gay-community discussion had been very difficult to follow and the students had not said much because the teacher was jumping from topic to topic. Ping understood that Gina meant to use the gay community as an example to help the class understand the concept of community but did not think this example was well chosen.

Ping thought it would have been better if the teacher had taken time to elicit students' understanding of the notion of 'gay community' before proceeding to discuss it.

7.16 Ping: Maybe [Gina] write down the gay [community] in the blackboard, and ... said Tell me this one. Use the several sentences connected, then people can keep going.

In addition, Ping objected to the thematic content of the discussion.

7.17 Ping: I don't think ... this is a good [topic]. [...] Because lots of people doesn't understand. [...] Doesn't know what this mean ... Because we from a different country. [...] And ... gay and just for [this city] and the USA. [...] [If the teacher used labor union] I think it's clear. [...] Lots of people know this one [labor union]. Because ... lots of students take the [public transport]. [...] Lots of students ask ... after class ... Oh what's this community? [...] If she [Gina] maybe

> use the labor union, [then] understand, Oooh is a group of people make the same goal. [...] But is gay. (whispering) *Gay! What are you doing?* All these people think Gay, aaaaaah! Is, uh, men love men. But we don't know is community, this men. [...] But ... hers goal want you understand community. Don't (P laughs) understand men love the men ... Lots of people confused, Oooooh what's this!

Ironically, even though Ping was the one who had initially brought up the topic of gay men and their 'lifestyle' (in the earrings discussion), she felt that the gay community was not a good example to demonstrate the meaning of 'community.' To Ping, the labor union would have been a better example because it would have been more familiar to students and because for her it conveyed the meaning of 'community,' whereas 'men loving men' did not.

Sara's perspective was quite different than Ping's. (Sara was the one who, during the Day 2 discussion, had said "some gay and lesbian people still get attacked" [turn 12].) I asked Sara (from Vietnam) if she had felt comfortable speaking up in that class discussion.

7.18 Sara: Hmmm. Uh, yes but- but no. Yes because, uh, this subject ... I'm familiar at- in some part of it. But I don't feel comfortable because I'm not sure that I should bring that subject into the class. Especially ESL class. [...] Because ... ESL is most Asian people. And to me, Asians still cannot accept that fact. [...] Because I remember when I came back to my country ... [I wanted] to tell people in my country ... [about] the gay community [here] ... And my sisters object me- I- I shouldn't tell them. [...] Because ... people in my country ... do not accept the fact that people are gay or lesbian ... I am not sure that I accept it or not but ... just like wearing earring, ... you see that ... happen, in your eyes ... I just comfortable in some way because that is happen in here. But it's uncomfortable because I'm not sure, uh, other student will familiar with that. Or they want to talk about it, or that subject too strange for them, or they can't accept it. So it just yes and no, same time.

In class Sara was negotiating conflicting desires—feeling comfortable with the gay community as a fact of local life yet unsure of her own level of acceptance; wanting to inform people in her home country about the gay community in her new country yet unsure of their level of familiarity, comfort, or acceptance.

Given Sara's mixed feelings on speaking about the gay community in this international class, I asked her what she thought of the teacher mentioning it.

7.19 Sara: If I was Gina I would mention it ... Because ... it's in one of the reading too. Because that is really happen in the world. I think every people should know it ... Especially if you living here, you should know it ... Because at first ... I didn't know anything about it ... I can hear from the TV ... Or ... some article I pick up when I reading in the doctor office ... Because you're living here and that things happen. It's not ... hidden away. It just happen in front of your eyes. You should know it ... the gay community, the gay people ... When you walking ... you see the gay people they holding the hand. I even see them kissing each other ... If you don't know those gay people exist, you would question. But if you know they are gay ... you understand.

Sara stressed that openly lesbian and gay people were part of the local social fabric and featured in local media, and as such ought to be part of classroom discourse—especially since ESL students, as newcomers, needed to understand things they were witnessing.

For Rita, talking about a gay topic in a classroom was a very welcome experience. (Rita was the one who, in the discussion, had said that going online "might encourage others [not to] ... be afraid to say that they are lesbian or gay" [turn 16].) In class when Gina raised the question of whether it was easy to meet gay people everywhere in the world (turn 44), Rita's thoughts turned to how, in her native country of El Salvador, lesbians and gays are discriminated against, and she was remembering how, her first night in the United States, she had felt inspired by a gay rights demonstration on the television news. She went on to explain how she felt about gay people.

7.20 Rita: I really like them. To me like I feel proud of them. [...] 'Cause like, well, I clean house and ... [a client] he's gay [...] I go clean his house. And he has his boyfriend there too ... I know that he's gay. He knows that I know too. But we don't treat each others that way [disrespectfully]. [...] Also I see that they are more organized. And respect more other people ... So ... when people like talking bad about them, I will defend them ... I don't think the negative way, like that they're bad or they shouldn't be gay ... I think only the positive. That they have the right to be who they are.

When I asked Rita why she felt proud of gay people, she explained:

7.21 Rita: They keeps going no matter what the people say ... 'Cause I think like before they were kind of hiding themselves, you know. They aren't afraid [now].

Rita strongly related to the experience of being discriminated against, and she admired the strength and dignity that made it possible to triumph over these day-to-day struggles.

Rita said that this was the first time the subject of gay people had come up in any of her classes. I asked if she had any advice for teachers when dealing with gay topics.

7.22 Rita: I think like the best they [teachers] can do is, like, keep it positive. What the people say. Instead of negative ... But everybody has opinions and sometimes ... we don't really think [about what] we're gonna say. So we might hurt someone else feelings ... [Gay students in the class] might feel proud that someone is there, like, defending themselves or talking good about them. BUT sometimes no one might say, like, positive things about them and then they might feel hurt. [...] It might end up good, it might not. So it's kinda a risk that you're taking, or that they are taking too, professors.

In Rita's view, given the potential for strong opinions and insensitive speech, there was a risk for students and teachers alike in talking about gay themes.

Given this sense of risk, I asked Rita how she felt when she spoke up during the gay community discussion (turns 16 and 18). (By this point in our interview, Rita had already volunteered—with no prompting from me—that she was not a lesbian and felt upset whenever people asked her if she was; this occurred often, she said, because she did not have a boyfriend.)

7.23 Rita: Even though they might think that I am lesbian ... I know who I am. So it doesn't bother me ... If I think about that ... I wouldn't speak, because I would be afraid. But- And I said it but nothing [bad] happened.

Even though Rita felt that saying something pro-gay in class could make it more likely for others to think she might be a lesbian, she did not let this inhibit her from speaking.

Rita's account indicates that the sorts of dilemmas and anxieties that teachers reported about their sexual identity negotiations in class, as discussed in Chapter 5, are also relevant for students. Whether or not they themselves identify as gay, students may be weighing up the possible consequences of being categorized by their peers or their teacher as gay, perhaps especially when discussing gay themes; and these deliberations may in part determine what people are and are not willing to say in class.

Integrating Gay Themes and Adopting a Gay Vantage Point

In several respects, Gina's teaching strategies in the gay-community discussion demonstrate a skillful integration of gay/lesbian themes into the curriculum. This is evident in two main ways: how she introduced the subject matter and how she framed the discussion and positioned the students.

As to introducing the subject matter, she initiated the topic of the online gay community by linking it to the previous discussion of men in earrings. By 'retroactively recontextualizing' the earrings discussion, Gina enriched its meaning and at the same time signaled the existence of a thematic system (following Cazden 1988, citing Lemke, 1982). The notion of stereotyping was first raised by Rita in relation to homeless people (turn 1), and Gina then used it to remind the class of the earrings discussion, which was recontextualized as "an example of a stereotype" (turn 5). In this way, the meaning of the earrings discussion was reframed as an instance of judging people based on limited information. A parallel was drawn between stereotyping homeless people as not smart and stereotyping men with earrings as gay; in this way, a thematic link was established between the two class sessions. As Mercer (1995) explains it, when teachers "*reconstructively recap* what has been said and done" in class, they "help learners perceive continuity in what they are doing" (p. 33).

Gina then called forth a discourse of mutual respect. When she said "we look at people and oops! We pass judgment right away" (turn 5), her use of 'we' positioned the students (and herself) not as the objects of stereotyping (as in the earrings discussion) but as the agents—as those with the potential to stereotype other people. She made the very strong statement that "we can't stereotype," apparently meaning we should not stereotype. Significantly, it was only *after* Gina stated unequivocally that stereotyping is undesirable that she raised the topic of the gay community.

Next she made a reference to the one and only phrase in all the class readings to mention the gay community, and she used that very brief mention to focus the online communities discussion onto the gay community in particular. This is noteworthy because, in the classroom context, information is not simply relevant (or irrelevant) but must be constructed as relevant *through pedagogical efforts* (following Britzman, 2000). Interestingly, Sara, like a number of Gina's students, considered gay themes relevant to the class at least in part because they were mentioned in a class reading (see 7.19), which underscores the authority of class resources in terms of constructing legitimate themes for class discussion. Interestingly, the students seemed to have no awareness that it was Gina who had chosen the reading, and Gina who had chosen to bring up for discussion the reading's sole mention of the gay community.

How Gina framed the gay-community discussion and positioned the students is also noteworthy, as it was very different in one important way from all the other teaching practices analyzed throughout this book. She asked the class to think about online communities from a gay vantage point: "Why would it be an advantage for gay people maybe to start a community online?" (turn 5). Thus, the class was not asked to debate the existence of gay communities online (see Chapter 4), nor to share their own experiences of the topic (see Chapter 6), but to consider what functions those communities serve *from the point of view of their members.*

Not formulating gay issues as a matter for either debate or self-disclosure made it possible for students like Sara, who felt unsure of their own opinion on the issue, to actively participate in the discussion. In Sara's case, she was able to speak openly about her knowledge of gay people and the negative reactions ("bad talk") they sometimes face (turn 10). An important consideration for Sara in speaking up in class about this topic was the comfort level of those students who, because they too hailed from Asia, would be unused to talking about gay/lesbian matters in the public arena of a classroom. Her concern highlights the likelihood that students may feel a sense of uncertainty about whether or how to discuss gay/lesbian themes with their peers in class. In Sara's case, she decided to speak up despite that concern because at the same time she also felt strongly that students from other countries needed to be able to become conversant with gay themes given their ubiquitous presence locally.

While Sara's concern was for Asian students who might find the subject matter uncomfortable (see 7.18), Rita's concern was for lesbian and gay students who might feel hurt by what was (or was not) said about them in class (see 7.22). For Rita, the sense of risk in speaking up about this topic was heightened by the possibility that doing so would make it even more likely that her peers would think she was a lesbian. Yet this caution was outweighed for Rita by the admiration she felt for gay people due to their strength in the face of adversity and respect for others. Gina's framing of the questions to the class made it possible for students with concerns like Rita's to participate in the discussion because they could put forward ideas about the benefits to gay people of going online without having to disclose their own sexual identity.

Also interesting is Gina's own contribution to the gay-community discussion. Using a technique called 'cued elicitation' (Edwards & Mercer, 1987), Gina offered clues and prompts to the answer she hoped to receive, but these did not seem to elicit quite the answer that she was after; eventually, Gina explained that in this city people (of any sexual identity) can readily meet gay people, but in other places this is not the case (turns 42, 44, and 50). The answers students did give—fighting stereotypes, safety from violence, encouraging more people to come out, gaining power, getting heard—could, I think, all be considered 'advantages' for gay people going online. But there is a subtle distinction between the students' answers and Gina's that is worth noting.

In most of the students' answers, gay people were understood to be connecting with each other online as a way of resisting and transcending the controversy, discrimination, hostility, and violence to which they are subjected by the wider straight world. For example, "fighting stereotypes" (turn 8) implies gay people contesting narrow stereotypes inflicted upon them by the powerful straight world; "getting heard" (turn 39) implies gay people wresting the attention of the otherwise uncaring straight world. Thus, the students' answers positioned gay people as banding together in order to 'fight back,' or at least 'talk back,' to the straight world that oppresses them.

In contrast, the advantages that Gina proposed associated gay people with 'building community' in a more positive and less embattled sense, positioning gay people primarily in relation to each other. In this construction, the aim of gay people is not to change how they're seen or treated by straight people but to find other gay people. Furthermore, Gina's comments construct the gay neighborhood in that city as a place that welcomes not only gay people but also those who think they might be gay, or those who are not gay but who have gay friends or who simply enjoy socializing around gay people (turn 42). Thus, in relation to the wider straight world, the gay community is constructed by Gina as more of a 'friendly host' than an oppressed minority.

This is interesting pedagogically because it serves to reframe the students' emphasis on the difficulties that gay people experience to a more joyful, ordinary, friendly construction of gay people. Similarly, whereas the students used 'they' and 'them' when referring to gay people, Gina's pronoun choices effectively positioned herself and the rest of the class as members of the imagined gay community that she was enacting: "if *you're* here and *I'm* here and … *we're* hundreds of miles apart … then *you* can … still get support"(turn 50). These positionings reinforced Gina's efforts to encourage the students to think about community from a gay vantage point.

Given the predominance of straight perspectives within the vast majority of language teaching materials and research, asking students to 'think gay,' if only for a few minutes, can be considered a bold move—and a welcome contrast to approaches that ask students not just to 'think straight' but in fact to 'think heteronormatively,' as Tony did in asking his students how gay people were different from them (see Chapter 6).

These positive aspects of Gina's teaching notwithstanding, Ping's criticisms of the gay-community discussion echo the problems with implicit communication that were evident in the earrings discussion. It seems that more explicit scaffolding could, once again, have helped students with relatively lower levels of English to better follow the discussion and understand its key terms. Even when Gina alluded to the earrings discussion (just before broaching the topic of the gay community), she still did not make its gay subtext explicit; so opening the gay-community discussion with a quick reference back to the earrings discussion may have established a thematic link for some students but not for those who had missed the gay subtext of the earrings discussion (as Lucy had) or its underlying message (as Ping had). Furthermore, Ping's puzzlement that 'men love men' would have any link whatsoever with 'community' underscores the fact that the concept of a gay community is not necessarily going to be familiar across an international mix of students and so may need some unpacking.

Ping's criticism that the gay community was a topic that was foreign and irrelevant to the students (see 7.17) raises questions about how 'community' was being conceptualized. Throughout the class readings and discussions, communities (whether homeless, gay, or disabled) were characterized as discrete rather than overlapping and as entirely positive rather than encompassing a mix of positive and negative attributes. Yet, to poststructuralists, the notion that communities offer a sense of "home," of "full and uncomplicated belonging," is problematic (Phelan, 1994, p. 82); a community is actually "not a place of refuge, of sameness, but … its opposite" (p. 84). This is because those who form a community are alike in the one way that brings them together, but they are not alike in many other ways (Bourdieu, 1991). Though a community is often associated with sameness, it is in fact marked by experiences of difference.

Pedagogically, then, it may be useful to examine communities as overlapping and intersecting—for example, by considering the perspectives of individuals connected to disabled *and* gay communities or gay *and* Asian communities. Acknowledging the multiplicity of community identifications and relationships might pave the way for discussing not just the positive functions of communities—the affirmation and support they offer members—but also their constraints and challenges.

Explaining the Meaning of a 'Nontraditional' Family

The issue of the teacher's sexual-identity negotiations in the classroom (see Chapters 5 and 6) arose on Day 3 of my observation period. The students were discussing the class readings in small groups and Gina was circulating among them when I overheard her tell one group that she was a single parent. In our after-class interview, I asked her about the interaction.

The Teacher's Perspective

In an attempt to explain a vocabulary word, Gina used her own life as an example.

> 7.24 Gina: I told them I was ... a dyke ... They were trying to understand the concept of traditional and nontraditional family ... I said Well how about a single parent, and I said How about ... same-sex parents ... and I used myself as an example. I said I was a single parent, but I was a single parent and the other parent ... was another woman. So my family ... was nontraditional in many ways. [...] It did not hinder the discussion in any way. I think on the contrary they were like OK so that's nontraditional and this is traditional, and then we kept going ... I do use a lot of examples. And I try often to find something that is really tangible to them ... I knew they were gonna listen to that ... Because it's about me.

Gina felt that using her own life as an example had been an effective way to illustrate the meaning of an abstract concept. She felt that coming out as a lesbian to this group of students had gone over well, with no uncomfortable or hostile reactions from students. To Gina, who had come out in previous classes, this event was ordinary and unremarkable, so much so that she did not even think to mention it to me until I questioned her about it.

A Student's Perspective

Lucy was one of the students in that small group, so I asked her what had transpired when Gina was speaking with their group.

> 7.25 Lucy: [Gina] said something like For example my family. I'm- I'm thinking, uhhh, What about your family? There must be something that I don't know– we don't know. And it's a personal thing. [...] And then she said something about two mother. And I was thinking Two mother, hmm. Really interesting ... [Later] I said (to classmate Bill) Do you understand what she's saying, like two mother, or something like that? And [Bill] said No I don't know. I was like I don't know either ...

Cynthia: … I thought I overheard her saying something about she was in a nontraditional family, or something. Did-

Lucy: Hmm. I don't remember … nontraditional family. She just [?] say that two mothers live in two different houses, something like that. […] [In class she] never mention her husband or anything else. And then she mentioned her daughter once, or her son, I don't remember … And … she mention herself Miss. So I just kind of Oh, probably, you know, something happened. And then … on that group day … we was confused about- about the [reading] … And then she kind of explain I think by giving herself as an example. But I'm not sure what example was she pointing it out. So we were kind of confused by that. But I didn't want to ask. Because it's … really not my business … Probably she want to keep this the privacy of her own.

Cynthia: Because she's the teacher?

Lucy: Yeah, of course. If you're a friend, probably I ask you … So I'm not sure what I was listening to. (L laughs)

The Ambiguities of Coming Out

Gina thought the students were unfazed by her coming out, but Lucy did not realize that she had. Whereas Gina thought that using her life as an example would make the abstract notion of a 'nontraditional family' more concrete and familiar to students, Lucy did not understand what Gina meant by 'two mothers' (or, for that matter, how it came to be that she had a child yet called herself 'Miss'). Gina thought the students would be especially attentive if she talked about herself because she was the teacher, but Lucy felt less inclined to ask Gina about her 'personal' life precisely because she was the teacher.

In order to decode Gina's coming-out narrative—in which she alluded to her current status as a single parent as well as her coparenting arrangements with her female ex-partner—her students would have had to make a series of culture-based inferences about same-sex partners, ex-partners, lesbian parenting, and multihousehold families. Though these relationship configurations were common locally, they were apparently not sufficiently familiar to Lucy, a young refugee from Vietnam, that she could follow what Gina was saying.

Gina's Approach

Due in large part to Gina's willingness to acknowledge and discuss sexual diversity in class, gay subject matter emerged on several occasions as her academic English class studied 'community,' with quite a few students contributing to the gay-themed discussions. However, students' after-class responses were varied—some were positive, others perplexed. This mixed success underscores two important points with regard to teaching lesbian/gay issues.

Taking up Opportunities to Engage with Sexual Diversity Issues

The first point is that teaching is an opportunistic process (Jackson, 1968). As Gina's case shows, students' spontaneous or offhand remarks about sexual diversity or (homo)sexual identities can be used to configure learning opportunities that link to the thematic focus and learning objectives of a particular task or unit of work. Moreover, questions or tasks can be framed in ways that neither elicit personal experiences of gay people, nor ask students to debate gay rights. Gina asked her students to consider the functions of electronic communities from a gay vantage point, which allowed students with little, if any, experience discussing such matters in a classroom to contribute to the discussion—whether drawing on their firsthand knowledge, their secondhand knowledge, or their imagination.

Since a number of teachers in this study decried the dearth of lesbian/gay/bisexual content in language learning materials, it is worth noting that teachers may be able to integrate these themes into the curricula—and to do so in ways that students find relevant—simply by selecting readings or other class resources that include even a brief mention of sexual diversity and then using that material to illuminate the broader issue or subject matter at hand, as Gina managed to do.

Also worth noting is that, when discomfort or potential conflict associated with sexual identities/inequities arises (or is anticipated), instead of seeking to circumvent such moments, it may be more effective for teachers to allow students to speak, help them to clarify what they mean, and encourage others to respond. Guiding students through the sometimes challenging process of negotiating what can and cannot be said within a given group, rather than shielding them from this process, could strengthen their competence at managing potentially fraught or uncomfortable interactions in their second or foreign language.

Making Implicit Sexual Meanings More Transparent

Taken together, the divergent teacher/student accounts of the earrings discussion, the gay-community discussion, and Gina's coming out all serve to underscore an important point made by Luhmann (1998):

> The queer pedagogy that I imagine engages students in a conversation about how textual positions are being taken up or refused, for example when reading lesbian and gay texts or when listening to somebody speaking gay … *What does the student actually hear* [italics added] and how does he or she respond to the text?
>
> (p. 153)

The need to attend closely to students' actual understandings of gay/lesbian themes or perspectives is crucial in language classes, where building students' linguistic and cultural fluencies is the core business.

Learning, as Lave and Wenger (1991) explain it, requires transparency; thus, teaching involves making knowledge visible or explicit so that learners can learn how to integrate this knowledge into their activities until eventually it becomes tacit or invisible. Intercultural interactions in particular often require a high degree of explicit communication (R. Scollon & S. W. Scollon, 1995; Willing, 1992). In addition, meanings pertaining to sexual identity/diversity are often spoken about through innuendo, subtext, and nuance, as we have seen in this chapter. For all these reasons, in the language classroom discussions of sexuality-related matters may need to be more explicit and transparent than they would otherwise be, as Gina's class so aptly illustrates.

Because students, like Gina's, do encounter sexual diversity at work, in the classroom, in friendship networks, in the media, and on the street, they need to be able to recognize, decode, contribute to, and critique conversations that address sexual diversity directly or allude to it indirectly. This includes conversations that take place between not only straight/straight interlocutors (who are already well represented in language learning materials) but also between gay/straight, gay/gay, and other such combinations. Therefore, when a student seems to be outing a classmate or putting forward negative views of gay people, such instances can be considered useful opportunities for exploring the implicit meanings, and likely consequences, of particular utterances between interlocutors in particular contexts. In some cases, it is possible to explore sexual diversity issues on the spot as they arise spontaneously, but in any case it can be useful to revisit these issues in a more considered way and even to integrate them into the official curriculum, as we saw Gina do.

CHAPTER 8
Foreign Meanings: Roxanne's Class

In Roxanne's ESL class, lesbian/gay themes emerged during a grammar lesson, when a task on the use of modal verbs for speculation led to a class discussion of same-sex affection and its local and international meanings. In examining the six stages of this discussion and its key teaching issues, I draw on the perspectives of the teacher and four students, a woman from Korea and three men from Mexico, Morocco, and Thailand. The analysis shows that teaching practices that explore sexual diversity in tandem with cultural diversity can resonate with students' lived experiences in significant and varied ways and, furthermore, that productive discussions of sexual-identity practices can take place throughout the curriculum, even in a grammar lesson.

The Class

Roxanne's grammar-based class met 10 hours each week at a community college. The class was part of a government-funded ESL program for refugees and immigrants, some of whom had had to wait months to get into the program. The classroom was crowded, with 26 students seated at long tables all facing the front. The student cohort was notably diverse linguistically and culturally, comprising immigrants and refugees from 13 countries: Brazil, Cambodia, Ethiopia, Gambia, Hong Kong, Japan, Korea, Mexico, Morocco, the Philippines, Somalia, Thailand, and Vietnam. Half the students were women and half men, and their ages ranged from early 20s to early 70s (for more details, see Appendix C). They had been living in the United States anywhere from a few months to a few years, and while many were currently working and several were retired, most intended to go on to further study. In my interviews with the students, nearly all volunteered that they were pleased with the class and that they considered Roxanne a very good teacher—kind, patient, and enthusiastic about their learning.

Roxanne, who was in her 40s, was from the United States and had 20 years of experience teaching ESL/EFL in that country and in Asia. In this class, Roxanne had a fair degree of flexibility in terms of choosing topics and designing tasks to meet the set curriculum objectives. A grammar textbook had been assigned to the class, but Roxanne used it only every few days; more often, the students worked with materials that she had created, in conjunction with local newspaper articles and other everyday texts.

A central concern for Roxanne was that students be treated with respect and dignity in her class. She was keenly aware that some were the primary caregivers for young, sick, or elderly family members; some were currently working night shifts in low-status jobs; and some had experienced the traumas of extreme poverty, war, and torture. Given the competing demands on her students' time, Roxanne's goal was to make the class as meaningful as possible in relation to their day-to-day lives.

> 8.1 Roxanne: I feel accountable for covering certain grammar structures. At the same time I want- really want each class to be relevant … and useful. I mean right now in their life useful … And make sense to them. And not seem as contrived and from a book as it actually is in terms of what I'm accountable for.

She approached the study of grammar by embedding it, whenever possible, within themes that students were writing about in their homework or talking about in class.

The community college was located on Oxford Street, which was the main street of what was typically referred to as a gay neighborhood. Same-sex couples could be seen strolling down that street on a daily basis. I also noticed fliers about a local lesbian/gay rights event posted near the door of Roxanne's classroom and elsewhere on campus.

Discussing Same-Sex Affection

I was observing the class during a unit of work on modal verbs. On Day 5 of my observation period, the class was given a worksheet that Roxanne had written on the use of modals to speculate or draw conclusions. The worksheet listed a number of scenarios and asked students to "think of 3 or 4 different possibilities to explain what is occurring." The third scenario was "Those two women are walking arm in arm." I asked Roxanne why she had included that scenario.

> 8.2 Roxanne: It's a GREAT example for students to use in speculating because it's not necessarily clear one way or the other. […] [And it's] a beautiful example because people see [same-sex affection], especially on Oxford Street … Almost across the board if a person's from this country they're gonna visit the conclusion or speculation that the women are lesbians. And I think in other countries you could talk for a long time before that particular thing could come up for people.

In class on Day 5, Roxanne first had students form small groups and share their written answers to the worksheet, which they had prepared for homework. She instructed them to discuss not only their speculations but the reasons for them: "Share your examples, but discuss them also … Why do you think so?" As Roxanne circulated among the groups, she addressed the grammatical problems in student answers, not (as she told me later) "how they felt about the situation." She noticed that, with the two-women-walking scenario, many of the students had answers with 'love' but these were "awkward" grammatically.

When the class reconvened as a whole group, a lively discussion of the two-women scenario ensued. In this part of the chapter, I illustrate the six key stages of that discussion, with an emphasis on how the teacher managed to gradually shift the focus from language onto content. (Once again, the utterances in bold are of particular interest to the subsequent analysis.)

Stage 1: Beginning with Grammar

After addressing grammar questions that students raised about other scenarios on the worksheet, and with just 15 minutes of class time remaining, Roxanne brought up the two-women scenario.

1 Fabiola:	So does that mean when you see, um, present tense like 'always' in that sentence (number 6) we- we must use i-n-g? Or we CAN use past?
2 Roxanne:	OK. If you see a sentence in the present tense you must use i-n-g? Well, sometimes not. For example, I talked with a few of you about number 3? **Those women are walking arm in arm. So is that past, present, or future?**
3 Students:	Present. Present. [...]
7–14 Roxanne:	OK so a lot of people wanted to write something about this (writes on board "love"). And a lot of people were thinking about continuous. [...] Because it says [...] walking. What would be an example? **Some people have an example with love?** (Tran raises his hand) You got one, Tran? What is it?
15 Tran:	She could be loving.
16–18 Roxanne:	(writing his sentence on the board) [...] How many people?
19 Tran and others:	Two.
20 Roxanne:	So what's?
21 Many students:	They.
22 Roxanne:	(changing the sentence to read "They could be loving") They could be loving ...?
23 Pablo:	Friends. [...]
27 Neuriden:	Each other.
28 Roxanne:	Let's say "each other" because that makes this a- a verb here. (adding "each other" to the end of the sentence) **They could be loving each other. Most of the time we keep this one** (pointing to "loving") **in base form. Like and love and hate. Did you know that? In English?**
29 Student:	Uh-huh.
30 Roxanne:	There's some verbs that we don't make continuous.
31 Students:	Action. Action verbs.

32–45 Roxanne:	*So how can we say this again?* [...] *OK, I heard a couple examples. They could love* [...] *each other. They could be lovers.* (writing these sentences) [...] **This is actually the same grammar structure.**
46 Student:	*They could be lovers.*
47 Roxanne:	**Modal plus ...?**
48 Student:	*Modal plus base form.*

The opening stage of this class discussion followed a pattern of interaction that was already well established in this class. Through a structured sequence of questions, Roxanne first elicited student answers—in this case, on 'love'—and wrote them on the board and then engaged the class in a process of identifying and correcting any lexico-grammatical problems. In this stage, which was distinctly 'teacher centered,' the students' comments (and eye contact) were consistently directed at the teacher, who took the role of regulating the discussion (see Cazden, 1988). Roxanne's teaching practices were 'visible' in the sense that the "rules of organization," such as gesture and pace, were made explicit and as such were known to the students (in contrast to 'invisible' teaching practices, in which such rules are implicit and therefore not known to students) (Bernstein, 1996, p. 112).

Though visible practices like Roxanne's are generally seen as conservative (while invisible practices, like Tony's, are seen as progressive), another way of looking at this is that the teacher's authority in the classroom was not hidden but explicit and the rules of interaction were clear (Bernstein, 1996; see also van Lier, 1996). Such consistency has certain benefits. As Cazden (1988) points out, "a clear and consistent event structure ... allows participants to attend to content rather than procedure" (p. 47). In this case, following a familiar pattern of classroom interaction while introducing same-sex subject matter could be seen as a way to legitimate that subject matter.

Stage 2: Transitioning from Issues of Language to Issues of Culture

When Ebou, a man from Gambia, answered that the two women could be lesbians, Roxanne attempted to shift the focus first to vocabulary and then to cultural variations, but this shift was not smooth or linear; the discussion zigzagged back and forth between issues of language and of culture, as evident below.

54 Ebou:	**I said They could be lesbians.**
55 Students:	(laughter)
56 Roxanne:	**They could be lesbians.** [...]
58–78 Roxanne:	(writing 'They could be lesbians') **Does everybody know that word?** [...] **Lesbian means ...?**
79 Fabiola:	*Same sex.* [...]
82 Student:	*Loving each other.*
83 Roxanne:	*Loving each other. Yeah. They could be lesbians. They could love each other. They could be lovers.*
84 Neuriden:	*They could be involved.*

85 Roxanne:	*Is this true in your country too?*
86 Student:	Yes.
87 Roxanne:	*If you see two women arm in arm?*
88 Many students:	(talking at once) Yes. No. [...]
91 Roxanne:	*Tell me about that.* [...]
93 Irma:	They can be very friendly.
94 Fabiola:	Yeah, they don't see each other for long time. [...]
96 Roxanne:	*Speculation like They could ...?* [...]
109 Raúl:	They could be lesbians. (turning his hands palm upwards as if to say 'no big deal')
110 Roxanne:	*They could be lesbians.* (cheerfully) *Sure!! Or they could be ...?*
111 Student:	Best friends. [...]
119 Irma:	Mother and daughter.
120 Roxanne:	*Give me a sentence.*
121 Irma:	They could be mother and daughter.

Of interest here is how Roxanne validated the legitimacy of the 'lesbians' answer in several different ways. She did not join in the class laughter but instead immediately repeated the sentence ('They could be lesbians') in a tone that was at once authoritative, matter-of-fact, and positive, thereby suggesting that the women being lesbians was indeed a possibility and that this was not in any way negative. She also elicited the meaning of 'lesbian,' thereby legitimating it as a word worth knowing but without presuming students would be unfamiliar with it (i.e., not asking "Does anybody know that word?"), and she wrote the 'lesbians' sentence on the board before reading it out along with the other student answers.

She then pursued the topic with follow-up questions about how same-sex affection would be interpreted in students' countries of origin, which could also be seen as an attempt to 'naturalize' lesbian subject matter since students' countries of origin are a typical topic in ESL classes (see Holliday, 1999; Norton Peirce, 1995). But the shift from grammar to content was not linear; Roxanne returned to the grammar focus by asking students to rephrase their remarks using the (modal-plus-base-form) sentence structure they had been studying for speculations (turns 96 and 120). Later, Roxanne explained that at this point she was deciding whether or how to proceed with the discussion, and returning to grammar gave her "something to hang onto," as she put it, while contemplating her next move. (In fact, Roxanne felt quite anxious about broaching lesbian/gay subject matter in class, which I discuss in Nelson [2004a].)

Stage 3: Shifting the Focus toward Learning Cultural Meanings

Roxanne next attempted to shift the focus onto how the students learned the local gay meanings associated with same-sex affection in public.

| 124–128 Roxanne: | *But I have- I have learned over the years that in some countries* [...] *two ... men can hold hands. Women hold hands.* [...] *Sometimes it's not about loving each other, right?* |
| 129 Students: | Yeah, no. |

130 Student:	Just best friends. […]
133 Roxanne:	**Do you remember when you discovered in the United States it was different?** […]
137 Students:	(talking at once) Yes. Yeah. Yes. [?]
138 Mary:	(quietly to herself) Lesbins. Lesbians. Lesbians. (to Roxanne) What- How do you spell that? Lesbins? […]

After addressing Mary's questions, Roxanne reformulated the question she had put to the class about learning cultural meanings.

155–159 Roxanne:	**So I wanna know, how did you find out it was different in this country? Or, it could be different?** […] **How about two men, 30 years old, walking down Oxford Street, they're brothers. Holding hands, yes or no?**
160 Students:	No, no, no.
161 Roxanne:	**How did you learn that?** […]
163 Pablo:	(barely discernible) I knew before I came.
164 Roxanne:	**A volleyball game? Whadju say?**
165 Pablo:	Oh no.
166 Roxanne, Pablo and students:	(laughter)
167 Pablo:	I said I knew before I came to America.
168 Roxanne:	**You knew before you came.** […]
171 Neuriden:	What's the question, please?
172 Roxanne:	**The question. Two men are walking down the street, and they are brothers. In [this city]. Do they hold hands?**
173 Student:	Yeah.
174 Many students:	No. No. No.
175 Roxanne:	**How did you know that? How did you learn that?**

This series of questions from Roxanne was noteworthy in several respects. First, her persistence: in attempting to shift the focus from grammar to interpreting same-sex affection, Roxanne had to repeatedly rephrase her question. Second, she sought to engage students' local and international knowledge and to situate this discussion of lesbians within broader objectives that are typical of ESL classes—namely, how to make sense of unfamiliar sociocultural practices (see Chapter 3). Third, Roxanne's reformulations are noteworthy because of the nature of her questions. In the main, they were open-ended—she did not know the answers, any student could answer, and their answers could be personal or impersonal (although the question would have been less personal if it had been phrased as "How do people learn that?" rather than "How did you learn that?"). At the same time, Roxanne's questions were not vague (e.g., "Any responses to that?") but quite directive and specific.

Importantly, she did not ask students to evaluate or judge the situation. Instead, she asked how they would interpret the same situation in their countries versus in the United States. Once Roxanne established that for most students these two interpretations were different, she asked how they learned to interpret it in the new country in a different way. The focus was on the process of meaning making rather than on the meanings per se. This underscored that cultural norms or 'rules' of behavior are not inherent or 'natural' but socially constructed and therefore must be learned.

Stage 4: Students Raise Various Issues Related to Same-Sex Affection

In the next stage of the discussion, which turned out to be the lengthiest, the focus turned away from language and onto content. Nearly half of the students in the class spoke up in what proved to be a very high-interest discussion. Roxanne took more of a background role with regard to driving the content and also managing the interaction pattern (though the students continued to direct their comments to her and not to each other). The students discussed a range of issues related to same-sex affection, such as their dilemmas about how to negotiate same-sex affection when returning to their home countries, given their experiences in the United States, and about how affectionate to be with children in the United States, given the tendency in that country for affection to be interpreted in a sexual way (see Nelson [2004a]). Also discussed were the varied norms and expectations regarding same-sex affection in public according to age, gender, and, as shown in the excerpt below, locality.

196–200 Mi-Young:	*... On the street people ... same sex ... hold hand each other, we never thought they are gay or they're lesbian. In our country (Korea) ... not many people ... watch and find out gay or lesbian. [...] Really difficult. Very small.*
201 Roxanne:	*It's a secret kind of? You mean?*
202 Mi-Young:	*Yes. [...]*
206 Raúl:	*It's not that open.*
207 Student:	*No. [...]*
209 Raúl:	***It's like, uh, if were in my hometown (in Mexico) we see two people walk, two mens, holding hands. Afraid they're gonna get shot.*** (little laugh)
210 Students:	(laughter)
211 Roxanne:	***Really?!***
212 Students:	(laughter)
213 Roxanne:	***Wow.*** (said with seriousness and concern, as if hearing bad news)
214 Raúl:	***Bad down there too.***
215 Roxanne:	***Wow!*** (with even more seriousness and concern)
216 Raúl:	*Usually ... they're kinda open, but they're not like—not this open you know like*
217 Roxanne:	*Uh-hm.*
218 Raúl:	*So normal here to see couples holding*
219 Roxanne:	*Yeah.*
220 Raúl:	*Same sex together.*

Roxanne's serious, concerned response to Raúl's account of anti-gay violence contrasted sharply with the laughter from the class. Participants' perspectives on the above interaction are discussed further on in this chapter.

Stage 5: Eliciting Participants' Own Experiences of Same-Sex Affection

By this point in the class discussion it was established that, in many of the students' countries, same-sex affection would generally indicate that those involved were friends or relatives, whereas in the United States it would generally indicate that they were lovers; and also that in Mexico same-sex affection between men was dangerous due to the threat of anti-gay violence. Roxanne then initiated a new line of questioning, about students' own experiences of same-sex affection.

242 Roxanne:	*Do you miss it [same-sex affection]?*	
243 Pablo:	*In my country (Mexico) in every state is different.*	
244 Roxanne:	*Every state.*	
245 Pablo:	*Yeah.*	
246 Fabiola:	*It's so funny how this working because I used to walk … like that with my brother […]*	
291 Roxanne:	*So do you miss, I mean*	
292 Student:	*I think it's true.*	
293 Roxanne:	*Do you still hold hands in this country?*	
294 Student:	*No.*	
295 Fabiola:	*Oh yes I do.*	
296 Student:	*Not here.* (He laughs)	
297 Mi-Young:	*I do.*	
298 Neuriden:	*Here? No.*	
299 Roxanne:	*With your friends or your best friends or sisters or […]*	
328 Roxanne:	*I can't remember when I stopped. I used to hold hands with my sisters. And I must- I must have been very young, like four or five when we stopped doing that, I think. I can't even remember!* (Mary chuckles) *I think I held hands with my mother.*	

With Roxanne's question "Do you miss it?" (turn 242), the assumption seemed to be that in the United States none of the students hold hands with another of the same gender; given the thematic content of the discussion to this point, the implication was that students would refrain from same-sex hand holding for fear of being seen to be gay or lesbian. However, Roxanne quickly rephrased her own question so that, instead of assuming that students no longer hold hands, she asks whether they 'still' do (turn 293). Nonetheless, the emphasis remained on what students lost in the move to the United States (a point that will be taken up in the next section of this chapter). Shortly thereafter, Roxanne spoke about her own experiences with same-sex hand holding as a child; interestingly, during my 2 weeks in her classroom, this was the only reference that Roxanne made to her life outside it.

Stage 6: Acknowledging Some Discomfort and Closing the Discussion

With the class time nearly over, Roxanne brought the 15-minute discussion to a close.

352 Roxanne:	*I'm just curious about this. Number 3, **if you had the same situation in your country, it would be a different situation, is that what you're saying?***
353 Raúl:	*Well they could be friends, or they could be relatives, or they could be*
354 Mi-Young:	*Or they could be lesbians.*
355–359 Raúl:	*Why not, they could be lesbians.* [...] *No big deal.* [...]
362 Roxanne:	**Some people are uncomfortable.** (Roxanne laughs)
363 Students:	(laughter)
364 Roxanne:	**In this class. Goin' like** (Roxanne smiles, wiggles her arms and hips in an exaggerated squirm, and uses a funny high-pitched voice) **Oh God, I wanna go home!**
365 Many students:	(laughter)
366 Roxanne:	**I don't wanna talk about this anymore!**
367 Many students:	(laughter)
368 Roxanne:	(she smiles) **OK then, I'll give you some homework!**
369 Raúl:	*Oh, homework!*
370–372 Roxanne:	**Thank you though, I appreciated that conversation because I still, you know, I've been teaching ESL for a looong time, I still appreciate learning different cultures, different experiences. It's a big deal. I'm passing out some homework, it's a worksheet** [...] **on past modals.**

In bringing the discussion to a close Roxanne acknowledged that some students appeared uncomfortable with the topic, and, as if providing a rationale for having discussed it anyway, she framed the topic as something of personal interest to her—"I'm just curious about this" (turn 352). She stressed that *she* was learning from *them* (turns 370–372) and expressed her gratitude to them for being willing to educate her, despite any discomfort of their own. In closing off the open-ended discussion, she returned once again to the established curriculum goals—in this case, the grammar-based objectives—by passing out another worksheet on modals.

Participants' Perspectives

Here I interweave the perspectives of the teacher with those of four students.

The Teacher's Perspective

Roxanne felt the class discussion had gone well, which might encourage future discussions on this topic.

8.3 Roxanne:	It's possible now that ... the whole thing about, um, two men or two women could come up more freely now in the classroom. As it might go through someone's head and not be said out loud.

Making spaces for lesbian/gay topics in the classroom could also open up spaces for other potentially contentious topics.

8.4 Roxanne: I think the message is we can talk about issues that are often considered taboo or inappropriate.

An issue that concerned Roxanne during the class discussion was what to do if her students seemed uncomfortable talking about lesbian/gay themes. She noted that some students did become uncomfortable with the discussion, but she was pleased that she had not reacted to this by changing the topic.

8.5 Roxanne: I was surprised how many people seemed comfortable talking about two women walking arm in arm. And then ... 10 minutes into it ... there were people ... gettin' squirmy. Which ... could mean anything. And I didn't feel like we needed to stop the conversation but I was aware ... as the teacher- of squirming bodies. [...] [I think] everyone in the room was listening and was getting a heck of a lot ... I don't think they were spacing out even if they had a book in front of them ... Even if they had to protect themselves by ... looking down, ... doing student stuff with the worksheet ... I just think that, um, *I* was probably squirming. You know, I don't think that means anything.

In wrapping up the discussion, she made a point of acknowledging the discomfort that she had sensed in the room, but she did so by acting it out in a humorous way (turns 362–366).

8.6 Roxanne: It was sort of comic relief for me, like I notice that there's some discomfort and we can still talk about this.

A number of other teachers in this study spoke of discomfort—their own and/or their students'—when dealing with gay subject matter, but Roxanne was the only teacher other than Tess (see 4.14) to openly acknowledge this emotion in the classroom. A key role for teachers, as Mercer (1995) explains it, is "to help students make an education out of their experience" (p. 51), and one way that teachers accomplish this is by "*describ[ing] the classroom experiences that they share with students* in such a way that the educational significance of those joint experiences is revealed and emphasised" (p. 26). Through her comical enactment, Roxanne managed to acknowledge the discomfort some students seemed to be feeling with lesbian/gay content, but without suggesting that such content was problematic.

I asked Roxanne who had appeared uncomfortable in the class.

8.7 Roxanne: I would stereotype that the Muslim people are sitting there ... praying to Allah: Sorry about this ... I'm stuck here, I'm not the one that started this conversation! But [then] Hassan's the one (R laughs) that was writing in his journal about ... [the]

persecution of gay and lesbian people and [how] that's not a good thing. I think he's Muslim.

Roxanne was referring to an assignment from that week in which Hassan (from Ethiopia) had written that gay and lesbian people are seen as harmful to society, but this conclusion is made without finding out what motivates them to, as he put it, "chose the life style they live in." So Roxanne was gauging her students' comfort levels with lesbian subject matter, but at the same time she was questioning her own generalizations and stereotyping about which students would be most likely to feel discomfort.

Students' Perspectives

Neuriden, a man from Morocco, spoke in detail about his experience of the class discussion. He reported that in his small group the number 3 scenario had generated the most discussion. Neuriden and a male classmate had speculated that the women walking arm-in-arm were lesbians, while his female classmates had said they were friends. In Neuriden's view, this scenario was "the most sensitive" one on the worksheet, which was why it had prompted the most laughter.

8.8 Neuriden: There was joking, especially when we talked about number 3 ... Joking is like maybe we give the situation ... something not serious. We try and maybe to escape it ... make it funny.

Neuriden said that, in many of the students' home countries, expressing gayness was forbidden.

8.9 Neuriden: In my country or the other countries the Third World, the- the secrets it's IN ... We have gays in Morocco ... If they express themself they're gonna be reject ... from the family. From the society ... Imagine me in Morocco I am gay. In my neighborhood nobody gonna talk to me. Maybe ... they're gonna do something bad to me ... Maybe I'm go to the stalls they're gonna not sold to me things ... But here in the United States ... people unusual can express themself. Lesbian, homosexual.

He explained that the prohibitions, in some countries, against being gay would extend to discussing this subject in a classroom context.

8.10 Neuriden: Our education system, in the class we don't talk about that ... in Morocco ... ALL the society is prohib to talk about that ... [Students in this class] ... don't feel comfortable because they ... [think] they should not talk about that ... Or if they talk, they talk with joke ... and laughing ... It's a kind of style ... that makes more easy to talk about it.

Neuriden's comments show that class laughter at gay topics does not necessarily mean the intention is to insult or denigrate gay people, or to change the topic, but can in fact serve as a sort of warm-up or lead-in to the topic.

For Neuriden, Roxanne's question to the class brought to mind a very memorable occurrence.

8.11 Neuriden: Do you remember when you discovered in the States that it was different? (turn 133) … I answered yes (turn 137) … Yeah, the first time I moved [to this city] I stayed in [this same neighborhood of the college]. And there was a lot of lesbian here. Not only lesbian but homosexual too. It was new for me … [Two] girls … were sitting in the same hostel and while I was watching the TV show … [they were] caressing. So after when I go the street I [see other women with similar] clothes and how they cut their hair and how they walk … [In class] I was thinking when I comes here (N laughs) I was imagining all the things how it comes to my mind they are lesbian … That's like … flashback.

He went on to explain why he had decided not to share this flashback with the class.

8.12 Neuriden: Maybe something I want to check with myself. Yeah, that's something I don't like to say it … Because … it's something new for me … to say that people are the lesbian. It's just– Because it's just 1 year now I came here … So when [Roxanne] talked me about that, it's still something foreign. I need to judge it and I need to review it … Maybe in the future it's gonna be familiar for me and common in my conscious, in my unconscious … [But] now it's not … in my deep mind. It's kind of surface … It's like a movie, it's like a film. You see all the film and then you are ready … From the beginning to the end. And then you can talk about it … [But] I never talk about this before … Maybe in 2 years, 3 years, it's gonna be OK. Talk like Aaaaah! (We laugh) … [So I was] checking with myself, yes. It's like another personality in me. He told me OK, you cannot talk now. (N laughs)

Cynthia: Another personality?

Neuriden: Something like that, yes … We have two personality … You have yours, and you have another one represent the society and all kind of education we receive … [and sometimes] there's conflicts in our inside.

Neuriden did not feel ready to articulate, within the public domain of the classroom, his first social encounter with out lesbians, as he had not yet come to terms with the experience for himself. The struggles that anyone might experience between an inner sense of self and the rules and teachings of society can be heightened for new immigrants, who are having to adjust to, assimilate, resist, appropriate, and negotiate competing cultural knowledges and practices.

The class discussion of same-sex affection seemed to be quite a moving experience for Neuriden.

8.13 Neuriden: I think it was different from the other discussion we have in class ... Everybody was- was talking about something he means, a part of him ... I think that's very good ... that's very helpful, ... when you say what you want ... With this kind of discussion you feel you- you express yourself, you feel very comfortable, you feel happy after that.

Neuriden's enjoyment of the discussion suggests that it is precisely because sociosexual subject matter can be somewhat fraught and unfamiliar that it has the potential to provide rich and meaningful material for those grappling with a new language and culture.

Just a few hours after the class discussion recounted in this chapter, I was waiting for a bus near the college when another of Roxanne's students—Alak, a man from Thailand—suddenly emerged from a lesbian/gay bookstore that was adjacent to my bus stop. We spoke only briefly, as he appeared to be very distressed that I had seen him leaving the store.

When we met the next day for our (previously scheduled) interview, Alak was especially anxious to account for his visit to the bookstore.

8.14 Alak: My uncle came here from Thailand because he had some trouble with his job. Yesterday I went to a gay and lesbian bookstore. I buy a book for him.

With much emotion, he explained why his uncle, with whom he lived, had immigrated from Thailand to the United States.

8.15 Alak: Because my uncle ... he was in Thailand, he's gay. He can work, ... he get money, he help people. He's nice. He feel comfortable being gay. But people in Thailand say Why you be like that? So he say What's your problem if I do this? I didn't hurt the people. That's why he came to this country. Some people don't understand. But I have uncle, I understand him. I don't care who's gay, who's lesbian, who's straight. Just be nice. I think a lot of people just think they are nasty. Nasty! Why they be that way! They don't understand they are same as you. Same as me.

According to Alak, the United States was a much more welcoming environment for openly gay people than Thailand.

8.16 Alak: In this country, they're open. In my country, no. People do it, but they say No. They don't talk about it.

He was distressed about the unfair treatment to which his uncle had been subjected, and he emphasized that he did not hold anti-gay views himself.

8.17 Alak: People will call you bad word. We have to think about that, you know, what to do. They don't want to be gay, I think it come from the inside. They cannot change it. It just come from inside you. Nothing wrong with that.

During Roxanne's class discussion, Alak had not spoken at all. In our interview, he did not talk specifically about the class discussion, and I did not pursue the issue because I did not wish to prolong his obvious discomfort.

Nonetheless, his account of his gay uncle underscores the fact that, for some language learners, gay/lesbian themes, rather than being unfamiliar, are integral to their own day-to-day lives.

More on the Teacher's Perspective

The central question Roxanne posed to the class was how they had learned that, in the United States, same-sex affection in public usually meant the pair were lovers rather than friends or family, as it would in many other countries. This question sparked a lively discussion on the meanings and consequences of same-sex affection, with about half of the students in the class managing to get the floor and make a contribution. Nonetheless, Roxanne observed that nobody had specifically addressed her question.

8.18 Roxanne: I wanted people to talk more about "When did you discover that it was different here?" (turn 155) ... I think people would have been willing to visit that question if I had asked it differently, or asked them to write about it, or asked them to talk with me privately even, which would be very difficult with [26] people. But I think people had stories ... I saw body language ... but nothing came out really ... The factors there, I could speculate. I don't wanna offend my teacher. I don't know enough about this ... since it was a shock to me that I couldn't hold hands with my friend—I'm speculating, Mi-Young, Korea ... It's so different here, it's so sexual here, I don't know how to talk about this appropriately in a classroom, a coed classroom ... And ... I haven't ever talked about it before in English maybe, or ever.

Roxanne surmised that for some students, like Mi-Young, lesbian/gay topics were probably too novel and unfamiliar to be discussed in the public zone of the classroom.

A Student's Perspective

In the class discussion, Mi-Young was the one who had explained that in her home country, Korea, there are few openly gay and lesbian people (turns 196–200). When I interviewed Mi-Young, she told me she had never before talked about gay subject matter in a class, apart from joking with classmates that another classmate was gay. She spoke very animatedly about why she had found Roxanne's question impossible to answer.

8.19 Mi-Young: [Roxanne] asked you how did you learn that (turn 161). But this one is nobody tell. Nobody teach us. When you walk down the street [in the U.S.] … you can see two womens or two mens holding each other, they are gay. Nobody tell … but you can see … Western culture we learnt from movie (she mentions *Philadelphia*, a movie about a gay man). [In Korea] we don't teach … at school … So I think nobody TEACHING us that word but … most of the student know that word and what that means … I think maybe long time ago … I read it in magazine or TV.

Mi-Young could not answer the question because the topic was so familiar, not, as Roxanne suspected, because it was so unfamiliar. Through extensive exposure to (Western) media, Mi-Young had long been familiar with the lovers interpretation of same-sex affection and also the meaning of the word 'gay,' so it was not feasible to pinpoint a learning moment. Mi-Young said she had felt comfortable during the discussion and she thought her classmates had too, with the possible exception of "older people" or "very religion people."

Over the course of several interviews with Mi-Young, it became clear that she was grappling with her own mixed feelings about the lesbian topic. Her initial answer to the two-women scenario was "They must be gay," but in her small-group discussion of the worksheet, a classmate (Ebou, from Gambia) answered "They must be lesbian."

8.20 Mi-Young: Ebou explained to me … this woman woman. I said I heard these days, gay is … man and man, [or] woman and woman. Gay just … that kind of people. So he said … lesbians two woman, gay is two mans … We discuss about that a little bit. (M laughs)

Later, in the whole-group discussion when Pablo answered "They could be loving friends" (turns 22–23), Mi-Young felt embarrassed and self-conscious about her own answer, "They must be gay." Apparently, she felt that 'gay' was too stark or too precise, whereas 'loving friends' was preferable because it was softer and less specific.

8.21 Mi-Young: Loving is good word, … beautiful word compared [to] gay … Kind of negative things I wrote in my conclusion. But some students … positive, like mother and daughter or sister … Same sentence we study together. (M laughs) I said gay, they said like this. So … this kind of surprise for me … It's not good word, gay.

Throughout the whole-group discussion the word 'gay' was never uttered by the teacher (or the students), nor written on the board, which may have led some students, like Mi-Young, to think that 'gay' is a bad word. The fact that 'gay' was never uttered also meant that Mi-Young and Ebou's debate over its use to describe women never become part of the whole-class discussion.

In fact, Mi-Young had many questions about what exactly identifying as gay actually meant, how someone could suddenly 'decide' they were gay, and what gay people were like. Just a few weeks previously, her father-in-law had informed Mi-Young and her American husband that he and his wife were separating because she (Mi-Young's mother-in-law) was gay. The mother-in-law denied this was the reason for the breakup, explaining that years ago she had been gay, but that she was no longer gay. (Below Mi-Young refers to her American mother-in-law as 'mom.')

> 8.22 Mi-Young: Actually I'm still to understand my mom's was gay or what ... She's really nice woman. Just normal woman ... really good mother.

This situation was a subject of debate within the family and a source of consternation for Mi-Young.

> 8.23 Mi-Young: [In Korea] people doesn't like the gay people. This kind of some disease. AVOID them ... Maybe my mind is I'm still Korean ... I keep asking my- my husband ... Could you explain, you know, definition, REAL definition about gay? (M laughs) So maybe my mind is maybe doesn't want to hear that like- like same as Korean people think. Like maybe ... I don't want to believe that.

In part because of finding out that a member of her own family was (or had been) gay, Mi-Young felt she should not say things that could hurt or offend gay people.

> 8.24 Mi-Young: When I say something I must careful like what I said. I don't want to hurt [gay people]. And ... if I know they are gay, I really must careful ... But most ... people ... I don't know who they are. So ... if I say something I thinking about what I said is correct word or not ... I didn't want to tell like mean word. [...] Actually ... gay people just looks normal ... [If] they didn't tell me I'm gay I can't realize they are gay or not.

Mi-Young felt anxious that, as a second language speaker of English, she might inadvertently offend someone whom she had not realized was gay.

Mi-Young spoke very positively about the affection discussion in Roxanne's class, which she felt had prompted her to critically reflect on her own discomfort with gay people and to reconsider her views on the subject.

8.25 Mi-Young: If I ... discrimination for them [gay and lesbian people], maybe people, and I say white people, they may also discrimination about Asians. It's same situation. People didn't like me, it's not good. (M laughs) Someone don't like me it feels not happy. So [it's not] OK with gay people.

Expressing empathy for gay people subjected to heterosexist discrimination, she drew parallels between that experience and being subjected to racist discrimination. Another reason she did not want to discriminate against gay people was that doing so seemed socially unacceptable in her new country.

8.26 Mi-Young: Someday [when] I find a job, my boss, my coworker [could be gay], who knows ... Maybe I loss job because I've discrimination. People can tell, I think, if I do that ... This country is, uh, most people open ... So maybe Roxanne ... had a good idea to use that. We study grammar and she use this sentence. And then we can change a little bit, you know, like we can talk a little bit about that.

Mi-Young's comments confirm that some students are eager to develop what teachers in this study referred to as either 'cultural fluency' or 'political correctness' with regard to the sociolinguistic norms associated with sexual diversity (see Chapter 3). Her comments also show that even students who say relatively little in a gay-themed discussion, as Mi-Young did, may find such discussions meaningful and thought provoking, in ways that remain unknown to the teacher.

More on the Teacher's Perspective

As the class discussion was unfolding, an issue that Roxanne was finding even more challenging than whether the students were comfortable with lesbian/gay topics was how she would respond if someone said something homophobic.

8.27 Roxanne: I was in the hot seat [because] ... I don't know ... if I'm gonna get a homophobic comment ... I think people look at me like What's she gonna do or say? ... How's she gonna react?

She was aware that her reactions could have a shaping effect on what students were willing to say.

8.28 Roxanne: Racism, homophobia, certain topics ... are very important to me that they come up. And I feel like everything I say or do is on the line ... I wanna be able to affirm wherever that person's coming from and also not have that be a stopping place for them.

For Roxanne, a significant moment was when Raúl said that, in his hometown (in Mexico), men holding hands could be shot (turn 209). (Below she refers to the process of 'behavior modification.')

8.29 Roxanne: I think that [Raúl] picked up my judgments here. Raúl is starting to talk about getting shot. And whatever I do at that point could change what he says next. And I feel like I was behavior modding him with WOW, like That's NOT cool, that they might get shot … I felt like then he was almost defending Mexico … Like he was like tracing his steps again, feeling a little bit judged by me.

With her 'Wow' response, Roxanne was signaling the seriousness of the matter, as if to discourage Raúl from proceeding to condone, or perhaps mock, anti-gay violence. In retrospect, Roxanne was concerned that her disapproving response could have been interpreted as a criticism of Mexico, which underscores the complexities of discussing homophobia or heterosexism cross-culturally.

A Student's Perspective

Pablo (also from Mexico) vividly recalled Raúl's 'get shot' comment but what captured his attention was Roxanne's response.

8.30 Pablo: I remember Raúl saying that you get shot down there if you- if you do that (turn 209). And that's true … Roxanne's answer ("Wow") is not really- really like she likes that … Like she can't, uh, believe that that happens in a very close country to, you know, to the one where she lives that it doesn't happen. She's like Wow, are they crazy.

Pablo's reading of Roxanne may help to explain why some teachers find it challenging to respond to students' homophobic comments in class, as discussed in Chapter 4: especially in second-language classes, teachers may feel that criticizing (or being seen to be criticizing) homophobic practices within a student's country of origin might be seen as criticizing the country or even the student.

During the class discussion Pablo followed up Raúl's 'get shot' comment with the statement that "In my country in every state is different" (turn 243), which Roxanne acknowledged by repeating, in a neutral tone, "Every state" (turn 244). However, another student immediately took the floor and altered the focus of the discussion, and neither Roxanne nor Pablo ever returned to his point.

8.31 Pablo: I was thinking about saying … there are some states [in Mexico] where gay people are accepted … more than in other [states] … I was trying to say that if somebody ask me. But nobody did.

I asked Pablo what he would have said in class had he been asked to elaborate.

8.32 Pablo: In the south … they are more open minded to gay people … [But] in the north they have laws that don't accept to have like, uh, gay places … it's not legal. If you go to a gay bar you can pick out (be picked up) by the police. (P laughs) … In the city where I am [from, in the north] is- gay people is killed ... There are like, uh, homophobia or something against gay people ... And gay people they's very quiet ... They're not kissing each other on the street and they're not holding hands on the street.

Pablo spoke at length about the violence and social discrimination against gay people in his hometown; when gay men were murdered, he said, their murders were not even investigated. In fact, Pablo had moved to the United States for this very reason—seeking safety from the constant threat of homophobic violence.

8.33 Pablo: What if [in Mexico] ... I meet ... the murder guy ... I think if somebody's murdered, for their families it's very hard ... If they don't know they're gay and then after the- the guy is murdered, they will public in the newspaper. He was gay. He was murdered because of that. I mean his family ... will be like crazy ... So finally I decided to come to this country because ... I want to ... be in a place where [being gay] is accepted, to- to see what I feel, how I change.

Pablo reported that, in Mexico, men holding hands was considered a gay signifier and as such was heavily regulated against in social interactions.

8.34 Pablo: [In Mexico] when you are walking down the street with your friends [if] you [accidentally] hit [their] hands or something. And they say Don't ... hold my hand because you're gay. (P laughs) They say that! ... You're gay! You are trying to hold my hand!

Living in the United States, however, was very different for Pablo.

8.35 Pablo: [In the United States] if I'm gay and I have my partner and I'm holding a hand anywhere. And- And I see a group of Mexican people or Latin people from any country, I know ... they will want ... to shoot me ... But ... I would say You are in America. And this, uh, this country it is permitted ... I'm sorry. Sorry, guys [that you are] so, uh, [closed-minded], so! (P laughs) ... Give me your hand, let's go! (We laugh)

It was not feasible for Pablo to even contemplate holding hands with a man until he moved to the United States. In light of this information, how might students like Pablo be expected to address a question such as "Do you miss [same-sex affection]?" (turn 242) or even "Do you still hold hands?" (turn 293). Roxanne's questions implicitly positioned the students as straight, which exemplifies the challenge for teachers in making space for the perspectives of students across a spectrum of sexual identities.

In fact, Pablo's homosexuality was a key factor in his desire to master English.

8.36 Pablo: Since I was a child, I felt I was gay ... I have never had a partner in my life. (P laughs) ... I have always dedicated my time to school. You know, to be better. To be prepared for the future ... Since I felt I was gay ... I thought I should continue with school and ... have good grades and ... make my parents ... feel proud of me ... I'm trying really hard to learn English because it's very important ... for gay people ... to be prepared ... I will meet [gay] people maybe from Iraq ... But he is not going talk with me in Spanish, in my language. And not even in his language. He's gonna talk with me in English. So I need to- to speak English well.

For Pablo, learning English, being gay, interacting with gay people, and being well positioned in life were all interrelated in significant ways. In Pablo's view, becoming more proficient in English was very important precisely because he was gay, with English functioning as a sort of lingua franca in the gay world (see King, 2008).

Yet ironically, the gay-themed discussion in Roxanne's class was the first that Pablo had ever experienced in any language class. He found the discussion to be a very positive experience overall—and a very amusing one.

8.37 Pablo: I enjoyed EVERYTHING in that class [discussion] ... every every word, you know. I couldn't record them all in my mind. But I remember being very comfortable in the class. (P laughs) ... I was like watching cartoons!

When Pablo first saw the worksheet, he immediately thought the two women walking arm in arm were lesbians.

8.38 Pablo: [In my small] group they are like afraid or embarrassed, they don't like to talk about that. But I do ... I mean, if we're talking about some example like that and we are giving opinions why they are walking arm in arm, why not? Then it's OK to think they were lesbian. So I say it. If somebody say But why you talking about lesbians, I say I'm not talking about them. That's a possibility, and we are doing that. So. Give yours! (P laughs)

To Pablo, number 3 on the worksheet provided a valid reason, even a welcome justification, for talking in class about lesbians. Pablo's sense of glee at this unprecedented opportunity to "think they were lesbian"—and to say it aloud—underscores the importance to sexual minority students that class materials encompass sexually diverse representations.

An issue very much on Pablo's mind was how to negotiate his own sexual identity in class. As we have seen, Roxanne felt disappointed that the class had not addressed her question about how they had learned that, in the United States, same-sex affection usually indicates lovers (8.18). But actually Pablo did attempt to answer it: he said "I knew before I came" (turns 163 and 167).

8.39 Pablo: When I said that, Roxanne was like You knew before you came! Oh, that's cool! (P laughs) ... I think she wasn't expecting me to say that ... [But] maybe because she's American she WAS expecting me to say that ... because you know in America being gay ... is not a prohibited thing. And if she would be a Mexican teacher, she would not be expecting me to say that ... If I would be in Mexico I would be worried to say it ... [But] here I can say it anywhere ... In my case this ... makes people think ... about you being gay ... I was not planning to say more. But ... if I was asked ... I would, you know, say something.

Pablo was very intently focused on the teacher's reactions to each contribution he made to the discussion. He was constantly gauging how much it was possible to say about his own perspective and experiences and what sort of reaction he was receiving when he did share these things. Choosing to reveal his prior knowledge of same-sex affection conventions in the United States felt to him like a subtle form of coming out.

Roxanne reacted to Pablo's "I knew before I came" in the same way as she had to his 'every state' answer: by mirroring his words and then allowing another student to take the floor, with no further follow-up to Pablo's point. Once again, Pablo was keenly aware of not being asked to elaborate. At the same time, he was very excited that it was possible to reveal that much about himself in a classroom without having to be anxious about possible negative repercussions.

Despite his pleasure and delight at Roxanne's willingness to broach lesbian/gay topics in class, he did express some frustration with his classmates' reactions.

8.40 Pablo: [The class] didn't get a very negative reaction. But ... there is still something weird to talk about this. WHY? ... That's the question that ... I ask myself always. [...] If there's, uh, gay liberation ... if there's freedom to be gay, why it's still- it's STILL ... something different? ... Because usually people who have their careers or people who have studied for a long time, they're really really polite ... And if they are doctors or ... teachers or ... something and they don't want to talk about it, they just avoid it. Nicely.

Despite the lack of overtly negative reactions to the lesbian/gay discussion, Pablo sensed some underlying tensions and polite avoidance.

This frustration notwithstanding, Pablo found the class discussion highly entertaining. He was especially delighted when Roxanne very cheerfully exclaimed "They could be lesbians. Sure!!" (turn 110).

8.41 Pablo: She's so open ... (using funny lilting voice) *What's the problem, I mean, they could be [lesbians]! ... And that's OK if they are!* (P grins)

In class when Roxanne spoke of her own experiences with same-sex affection as a young child (turn 328), Pablo found this very amusing.

8.42 Pablo: I was thinking ... You sure? ... You stopped doing a long time ago? (P laughs) Or you did it yesterday?

Pablo suspected that Roxanne was deliberately 'acting straight.'

8.43 Pablo: Since the beginning of the term I felt ... something that made me feel very comfortable with Roxanne as a teacher ... something special ... I would like to know if she is [a lesbian], you know? And I would not say anything. I- I just would be the same way I am. And. But I will never ask her ... I would like to know, but maybe I don't know ... HOW to ask her ... Maybe [if] I ask her, we will not get along anymore.

In fact, Pablo suspected that Roxanne had raised the two-women-walking scenario in order to gauge her students' attitudes about lesbians.

8.44 Pablo: [Roxanne wanted to find out if students had] any problems with the word lesbian ... She was trying to know if it was OK ... Like testing.

Pablo's yearning for confirmation that Roxanne was in fact a lesbian shows that some students have concerns about whether or how to ask their teachers about their sexual identity, just as some teachers have concerns about whether or how to disclose this information to their students (see Chapter 5).

More on the Teacher's Perspective

Whereas for Pablo, saying "I knew before I came" was a very significant moment because it constituted a subtle or tentative form of coming out, it was not taken that way by Roxanne (or, for that matter, anyone else I interviewed). In fact, she clearly did not expect anyone to come out in the public zone of the classroom.

8.45 Roxanne: I'd be shocked if someone came out in front of all of us suddenly and unexpectedly. But I wouldn't be shocked if someone came out in a journal or before or after class, or something like that.

Whereas Pablo was eager for Roxanne to come out to him, she told me that she did not identify with any sexual identity categories, which she considered 'labels' (though she stressed that she had no objection when others did use them). For her the topic of her own sexual identity was a sensitive one, as she felt both unable and unwilling to define herself.

8.46 Roxanne: I'm sensitive because most often I think people wanna know how you categorize yourself ... I'm afraid somebody's gonna, um, judge that part of me that doesn't yet know how to label myself ... I don't want to, even. So that if the issue came up in class ... I would already walk into it with sensitivity.

She dreaded being asked by students whether she was a lesbian, as this had occurred in a previous class and had made her extremely uncomfortable.

Roxanne was glad she had taken part in this study because it stimulated useful self-reflection about her teaching practices.

8.47 Roxanne: My brain's trying to figure the puzzle of how my teaching and things I do in class might influence a student in terms of sexual identity ... In my daily teaching what is it that I do in the classroom ... when I'm not aware of it even, that would contribute to a person's perception of identities in general and even sexual identity specifically. What messages do I give off, that they could perceive. This is what she thinks about me even though she's never told me. Or this is what she thinks about this, even though she's never said it. That kinda stuff. I'm thinking about that more.

Roxanne felt she was becoming more aware of unspoken messages about (sexual) identity that she communicated in the classroom on an ongoing basis—not just when dealing with lesbian/gay themes.

Roxanne's Approach

Even though within the set curricula and the class textbook, lesbian/gay themes received no mention whatsoever, Roxanne managed to incorporate these themes into a lesson on using modal verbs for speculation, thereby striking a balance between "offering ... opportunities for open-ended exploration ... and ... achieving established curriculum goals" (Mercer, 1995, p. 29).

Interpreting Sexual Meanings as Part of Cultural Learning

The success of this lesson can be traced in part to how the worksheet was written. By including the two-women scenario on the worksheet, Roxanne made it likely that students would raise the lesbian interpretation but did not require that they do so since there was no 'right' answer. Also, she wrote the task in such a way that it addressed students of any sexual identity since anybody could witness same-sex affection and speculate about its meaning. Furthermore, the scenario of seeing affection between women was presented as both ordinary *and* noteworthy—both within the realm of the everyday and involving a degree of ambiguity, uncertainty, or potential misunderstanding, particularly interculturally.

Importantly, the task asked students to speculate about what public affection between women might indicate, not debate whether or in what circumstances women should have the 'right' to walk arm in arm. Thus, it is not the women's behavior but one's interpretive processes that were framed as potentially problematic, thereby emphasizing "*ways* of knowing" rather than "*states* of knowledge" (Bernstein, 1971, p. 57). The pedagogic focus was not on discovering the meaning that resides *in* texts but on examining how meanings are made *of* texts—examining "how oral and written texts of all sorts mean in their social and cultural settings" (Gee, 1990, p. 174).

The success of this class discussion was also due in part to how it was facilitated. In their small groups, the students had shared their interpretations of the two-women scenario and questions had arisen about grammar and vocabulary, but when the class reconvened none of the students brought up that scenario. So Roxanne did, thereby communicating to the class that this was in fact legitimate subject matter. Once a student voiced the lesbian interpretation, Roxanne's persistent attempts to extend the discussion were noteworthy. As we have seen, after addressing some grammar points, she moved on to content, posing a question to the class that she had to repeat and rephrase quite a number of times before a fairly complex discussion finally got underway. During that stage of the discussion, Roxanne took a background role while at least half of the cohort of 26 spoke up, raising related issues of interest to them. Thus, her persistence with the general topic was complemented by her openness to the various issues and perspectives that her students raised on the topic; she was guiding the direction of the discussion but without controlling or censoring the views that could be put forward.

In terms of Roxanne's facilitation, also worth noting is the knowledge stance that she took with regard to gay-related matters. Whereas Tony deliberately highlighted his ignorance on these matters (Chapter 6) and Gina highlighted her knowledge (Chapter 7), Roxanne framed the discussion as one in which she was seeking information from students, thereby constructing herself as a learner on the subject and the students as informants—for example, "Tell me about that" (turn 91), 'But I have learned … that in some countries …' (turn 124), "So I wanna know, how did you …" (turn 155). The students were being asked to share with the teacher their own knowledge and knowledge-making processes with regard to interpreting sexual identities and relationships cross-culturally. Thus, there could be no 'wrong' answers, which may help to account for the fact that so many of the students attempted to get the floor and contribute to the discussion.

Engaging with Sexual Diversity as an Aspect of Social Interactions

In Mi-Young's case, it became clear during our interviews that she appreciated the opportunity to engage in class with a matter she was giving much thought to out of class. At the time of the lesson, having just learned that a close family member in her new country was (or had been) a lesbian, Mi-Young was grappling with linguistic and transcultural dilemmas, and her own mixed emotions, as an immigrant from a country in which gays are 'not that open.' After discussing and reflecting on the lesbian scenario, Mi-Young went from considering 'gay' to be not a good word and feeling embarrassed for even thinking it to considering how she might inadvertently insult potential interlocutors at work if she overlooked or mocked the existence of gay people. As a newcomer and a second-language speaker, Mi-Young was actively experimenting with new ways of thinking, living, and speaking with regard to sexual diversity.

In relation to pedagogy, Mi-Young's reflections illustrate an argument made by Kumashiro (2002) in advocating what he calls 'antioppressive pedagogy': namely, that the teaching/learning aim should not be to foster knowledge and understanding about others—in this case, queers—but about our own ways of reading others, and ourselves.

> [L]earning about how we are already implicated in the knowledge we produce and reproduce involves reflecting on the reading/learning/teaching practices themselves. Antioppressive reading/learning/teaching practices do not aim merely to change the way we read others. They also aim to change the ways we read ourselves. They aim to queer our very senses of self.
>
> (Kumashiro, 2002, p. 108)

In language education, it could be argued that, while the teaching aim is not to queer anyone's sense of self, developing linguistic and cultural fluency surely does require a nuanced understanding of one's own knowledge-making practices and interpretive processes. To this end, the processes of recognizing and interpreting sexual diversity can prove useful subject matter, as Roxanne's class demonstrates, especially given the cultural variations and potential ambiguities associated with sexual identities/relationships.

Allowing for Multiple Vantage Points and Degrees of Disclosure

My interviews with Neuriden and Alak highlight how difficult it can be for some students to discuss lesbian/gay themes in the public domain of a classroom—not necessarily because they themselves hold anti-gay attitudes, but because they may be from countries where it is rare to discuss such themes in a classroom context. Furthermore, their own experiences of these themes may be deeply personal, involve emotional anguish, or feel too new and raw to be shared with others.

Roxanne broached lesbian/gay themes in a way that allowed for multiple vantage points and multiple levels of self-disclosure. In designing the worksheet and formulating the follow-up question to the class, she did not specifically elicit personal experiences; moreover, as mentioned above, there were no right answers. Also, in facilitating the class discussion, Roxanne did not call on specific students but invited comments from anyone. Thus, nobody was put on the spot or pressured to speak.

Pablo's experience of Roxanne's class discussion also raises some important teaching points. For Pablo, becoming more adept in English was critically important because he considered his bilingualism to be a valuable tool or resource in preparing himself for the future and meeting potential partners. A similar point is made in Beebe's (2002) study of Raimundo, who attained fluency in English, German,

Japanese, Spanish, and Swedish and had a working knowledge of a number of other languages. In his home country of Argentina, Raimundo was tortured "for being suspected of being gay" (Beebe, 2002, p. 20), but as a multilingual man he was able to live, teach, and travel in a number of countries. Beebe (2002) observes that drawing on "multilinguality to resist or escape oppressive subject positions" (p. 18) can help gay people to deal with difficulties encountered as a result of anti-gay discrimination. As I pointed out in Chapter 2, providing gay and lesbian students with a supportive learning environment is especially important in language education contexts since some students may be learning a language in order to relocate to a less homophobic region and/or to communicate with a same-sex partner of a different language background (see Ellwood, 2006).

At the same time, Pablo's case highlights some of the contradictions that lesbian, bisexual, gay, transgender, or questioning students may experience in the classroom context. On the one hand, Pablo was overjoyed that Roxanne had provided a rationale for talking about lesbian/gay content in class as this had made it feasible for him to speak up on the subject despite the mocking or discomfort of his peers. Yet at the same time, he did not feel able to express himself in an open, carefree manner but seemed hyperattentive throughout the discussion, closely scrutinizing the reactions of his classmates and teacher on an ongoing, moment by moment basis in order to gauge how much it was possible for him to say on the subject.

It is interesting to note the gaps between what he did say and what he did not. During the class discussion, he said that before arriving in the United States he already knew that adults engaging in public displays of same-sex affection were more likely to be lovers than siblings or friends ("I knew before I came," turns 163 and 167), but he did not go on to explain how he learned that (which was what Roxanne was asking the class). When the class discussion turned to anti-gay violence, he mentioned that in Mexico "every state is different" (turn 243), but he did not go on to explain how they differed. In our interviews, he mentioned several times that he would have said more 'if asked' (see 8.31 and 8.39). On this point it is interesting to note that, during the discussion, Roxanne typically responded to Pablo's contributions by simply echoing his remarks in a nearly identical tone and intonation to his own, which came across as a sort of deliberate neutrality—in contrast to her enthusiastic responses to other students, which very overtly encouraged them to elaborate. It was as if she was leaving it up to Pablo how much to disclose about himself, without wanting to influence him one way or the other, while he was looking to her responses to help him determine how much he should say.

Pablo had, in fact, moved to the United States because he wanted the opportunity to seek a same-sex partner with whom he could enjoy ordinary activities such as walking down the street holding hands, without fearing a violent attack. Thus in a sense the issue of hand holding, with its cultural meanings and social consequences, was integral to Pablo's major life choices of moving to a new country and studiously pursuing fluency in English. It seems unfortunate that more of his out-of-class experiences were not able to be brought into the discussion since these experiences were highly relevant to it.

In terms of gauging how much he could say, Pablo seemed to be closely scrutinizing Roxanne's reactions to him and the reactions of his classmates. As

Bourdieu (1991) has pointed out, how people believe their speech or text is likely to be received in part determines what they say or write—or, as he puts it, how the 'conditions of reception' for one's discourse are envisaged in part determines the 'conditions of production' of that discourse (pp. 76–77).

> Since a discourse can only exist, in the form in which it exists, so long as it is not simply grammatically correct but also, and above all, socially acceptable, i.e. heard, believed, and therefore effective within a given state of relations of production and circulation, it follows that the … analysis of discourse must take into account … the social conditions of acceptability.
>
> (Bourdieu, 1991, p. 76)

In order to create classroom environments in which it becomes 'socially acceptable' for students to speak from sexually diverse perspectives—as gay people, as straight people with gay relatives, and so on—the integration of lesbian/gay themes and viewpoints would probably need to be sustained beyond just the one discussion in an entire class and beyond just the one class in an entire language program or degree.

Becoming Self-Reflexive About Sexual Diversity in the Classroom

An important insight of Roxanne's was that, through the daily goings-on in the classroom, subtle and perhaps unintended messages about sexual identity are being conveyed to students (see 8.47). As Redman (1994) puts it, "[s]chools are necessarily a significant place in which pupils learn about sexuality whether schools intend this or not" (p. 142) (see also Foucault, 1990). This raises important questions about the role of schooling in not merely reflecting sexual identities but shaping them. In other words, education may do more than ignore or acknowledge, condemn or affirm, sexual identities in their plurality. It may influence the ways in which people 'accomplish'—and evaluate—their own and others' sexual identities. Redman (1994) argues that an "emphasis on the ways in which sexuality is *constructed* within schooling (and other cultural) processes tends to disrupt the educational 'common sense' that existing relations of sexuality are 'natural,' 'normal,' or, at least, unchangeable" (p. 143). Such a shift of emphasis "forces us to look at what is going on inside schools, in particular in the hidden curriculum" (p. 143).

To enhance awareness of the hidden curriculum, there is a need for self-reflexivity on the part of teachers, and, as Roxanne noted, this would extend beyond those obvious instances when lesbian/gay content emerges. Teachers can practice self-reflexivity by becoming ethnographers of their teaching situations (Golombek, 1998); one way to do this is through systematic self-monitoring, which might involve:

> the teacher making a record of a lesson, either in the form of a written account or an audio or video recording of a lesson, and using the information obtained as a source of feedback on his or her teaching.
>
> (Richards, 1990, p. 18)

Roxanne (and Gina) found it illuminating to listen to the audiotapes of gay-themed discussions in their classes; where practicable, this technique may prove useful to teachers who are keen to rethink their own teaching practices in light of the issues discussed in this book.

Some language teachers hesitate to bring up gay, lesbian, or transgender issues or perspectives in class because they are of the opinion that students do not generally talk about these matters in their home countries. This chapter has shown that having a chance to talk (or just listen as others talk) in class about the gay/lesbian dimensions of their culture-crossing lives can indeed be a novel experience for many students, but that does not mean it is necessarily a negative one; on the contrary, the novelty of this subject matter as subject matter can make it all the more meaningful and memorable.

Furthermore, the fact that students may lack experience in talking about lesbian/gay issues in a classroom context does not mean that they lack day-to-day experience of these issues. On the streets, at work, or in their own families, students are negotiating the cultural and linguistic novelties of interacting with openly gay people—in some cases, *as* openly gay people. By doing something as simple as incorporating a same-sex scenario into an overwhelmingly heterosexual curriculum, as Roxanne did, teachers can provide relevant, effective discussion prompts for exploring the sociosexual dimensions of verbal and nonverbal communication. Moreover, framing these discussions in ways that anticipate and allow for multiple vantage points can help to engage groups of students who are diverse not only culturally and linguistically but also sexually.

PART IV
Conclusion

CHAPTER 9
Framing Sexual Diversity as a Pedagogic Resource

What are the implications of sexual plurality for language pedagogies? This study of over 100 English language teachers and students has shown that lesbian/gay themes and perspectives are, in fact, being raised in language classes—by learners, by teachers, and through materials used in class, in seriousness and in jest, as a brief sideline, and as the central focus of an activity or an entire unit of work. Sexual diversity is being discussed in relation to not only vocabulary and grammar but also broad themes such as cultural diversity, family, community, difference, and body language, to name a few. The topic of sexual diversity features in student writing and in discussions of current events, literature, popular culture, and classroom rules. In their day-to-day lives beyond the classroom, language learners are clearly encountering sexual plurality in the media and in a variety of social situations and settings—and, as such, need to be able to comprehend, negotiate, and produce often nuanced and culturally variable meanings pertaining to sexual identities.

While gay-themed class discussions can help learners to articulate and develop important linguistic/cultural knowledge, at the same time such discussions can prove complex and challenging for teachers and learners alike. The case I have made throughout the book is, in a nutshell, that *the challenges can be understood as pedagogic opportunities—if they are framed as such.* This concluding chapter synthesizes the key findings of my study by outlining five broad strategies that may help teachers to more fully exploit the pedagogic potential of queer themes and perspectives in fostering language learning. Though sexual diversity is my focus here, the discussion speaks to broader questions about how socially significant yet potentially contentious issues pertaining to identity, diversity, equity, and inequity can be shaped into useful educational experiences—especially in increasingly globalized classrooms, which are characterized by multiple perspectives and vantage points.

Of course, it would not be feasible or desirable to propose specific teaching strategies to be applied uniformly across language education, given the diversity that characterizes every dimension of the field—for example, students' proficiency levels, interests, and aims; teaching styles and priorities; course objectives and program curricula; and the particularities and politics of the institution, the cultural milieu, the region, and so on. In short, "each collection of students involves the teacher in a different set of decisions to make, which can only be made on the basis of local understanding combined with professional judgment" (Brumfit, 1985, p. 153). Accordingly, the 'macrostrategies' outlined in this chapter are intended to provide informed guidance that teachers can use "to generate their own situation-specific, need-based microstrategies or classroom techniques" (Kumaravadivelu, 2003, p. 38).

Based on the empirical evidence and theoretical research presented in this book, I recommend the following macrostrategies: teaching sexual literacy as part of teaching language/culture; in doing so, experimenting with a discourse inquiry approach rather than adopting only a counseling or a civil rights approach; deconstructing anti-gay discourses for teaching purposes; recognizing that student cohorts and teaching staff are not monosexual but multisexual, and that this diversity is intellectually enriching; and evaluating language-teaching resources and research in terms of whether heteronormative thinking is being upheld or challenged. Each of these is discussed in turn below.

Strategy I: Recognizing that Sexual Literacy Is Part of Linguistic/Cultural Fluency

Given the widespread circulation through the Internet, the media, and other arenas of discourses and images pertaining to global gay formations and local homo-sexualities, being able to communicate now means being able to communicate about sexual diversity matters, and with sexually diverse interlocutors. Because sexual identities tend to be construed, interpreted, and valued differently in different cultural settings and situations, language learners need to become familiar with the practices and norms of the new language and cultural milieu vis-à-vis sexual identity. For example, as we saw in Chapter 3, teachers in this study wanted their students to understand matters like the following: a male referring to a 'boyfriend' would have a gay connotation, whereas a female referring to a 'girlfriend' would not necessarily; the local bar where they and their classmates would hang out was actually a gay bar; and certain teasing and joking would probably offend gay people in the new locality.

Interestingly, similar learning goals were expressed by the students themselves, as shown in Chapters 6–8. Some sought a deeper understanding of what gays and lesbians 'think in their mind,' as opposed to just the superficial joking about gay people that was common in their home countries; some were interested in how gayness was signaled in the new country; and some hoped to learn how to interact in the new language and locality without inadvertently offending one's boss, for instance, who might turn out to be gay. In fact, many of the students in my study found that moving countries meant interacting for the first time with openly gay or lesbian people, including clients, friends, neighbors, and members of their host family. Students who were having this novel experience spoke about learning to identify and negotiate the intricacies of divergent cultural expectations associated with sexual identity. For other students, being able to interact as an openly gay person, and with other openly gay people, was actually the motivation for moving countries—but even in such cases there was still the need to learn how to communicate and manage sexual-identity negotiations within the more open environment.

These varied accounts about how sexual diversity manifests in learners' intercultural social interactions give credence to Britzman's (1997) critique of what she calls 'the privatization of sexuality' or the notion that "what one 'does' in private should be of little consequence in public" (p. 192).

> The insistence that sexuality is to be confined to the private sphere reduces sexuality to the literal and specific sexual practices one performs ... Such a myth makes it impossible to imagine sexuality as having anything to do with aesthetics, discourses, politics, cultural capital, civil rights, or cultural power.
>
> (Britzman, 1997, p. 192)

Britzman's argument is that matters of sexuality are in fact matters of knowledge and society and as such are manifest in the public domain and are relevant to anyone, not just gay people. Part of the problem, she argues, is that typically "knowledges about homosexuality and heterosexuality are positioned as if they have nothing to do with one another" (p. 191); in education contexts, heterosexuality is widely acknowledged, yet other sexualities are often hidden. Understanding categorizations of sexuality to be interrelated rather than separate (as discussed in Chapter 3) enables a focus on sexual identities rather than just sexual minorities.

Another useful concept is provided by Alexander and Banks (2004), who point out that teaching writing means, among other things, teaching about what they call 'sexual literacy.' Pedagogically, this involves not just "including queer voices" but addressing ways of "becoming literate about sexuality" in a more general sense (p. 287). They emphasize that a pedagogic focus on developing sexual literacy has the potential to benefit students of any sexual identification.

> Thinking about sexuality in terms of literacy opens the door to considering how our understanding of almost any aspect of sexuality in our culture is shaped by public discourse ... And given the vast number of personal, social, and political topics related to sexuality—topics such as who gets to define what marriage is, debates about who is and is not appropriate for military service ... it is imperative that students understand the complex connections between discourse, information, identity, and community represented by the term *sexuality*. Ignoring critical inquiry into these connections runs the risk of enabling, perhaps even furthering, students' ignorance about the strong connection in our culture between sexuality and identity.
>
> (Alexander & Banks, 2004, pp. 287–288)

Although Alexander and Banks are concerned with tertiary writing instruction in the United States, the findings of my study suggest that the concept of sexual literacy can be usefully applied to the international, intercultural arenas of language education. Language learners need to be able to decode the sexual dimensions of cultural and linguistic information and practices—and not only the explicit or overt meanings, but also those that are communicated more subtly through, for example, intonation and body language. This would be especially important in those geographic regions or settings where communications about homosexualities tend to be more covert than overt.

De Vincenti et al. (2007) observe that in Japan, for example, information about gay identities tends to be communicated indirectly. For example, "using the intonation of the other sex can signify sexual preference" (p. 69), so that a male who uses 'female' intonation or *wa* at the end of a sentence may be signaling that he is gay: "Yet unless students hear both intonations and learn the implications, they may not be aware of the message they are sending, or pick up these distinctions in the speech of others" (p. 69). The authors point out that, in Japan, gayness can also be signaled through gesture—for men, this might mean holding one's right hand at a certain angle against the left cheek. Thus, learning to communicate in a new language may involve learning how to interpret the particular cues and nuances through which sexual identities are communicated among speakers of that language.

For all of these reasons, then, developing sociosexual literacy can be considered an integral part of developing intercultural language proficiency.

Strategy II: Facilitating Queer Inquiry about the Workings of Language/Culture

As we have seen throughout the book, by and large the teachers in this study were eager to integrate lesbian/gay themes into their classes, yet at the same time some expressed concerns and hesitations about doing so. Some teachers were concerned not to impose their own viewpoints of lesbian/gay issues as this would constitute 'cultural imperialism.' Another common concern was not wanting students to feel uncomfortable or 'put on the spot'; in fact, some teachers felt that lesbian/gay themes should only be raised if there was sufficient class time to explore any strong feelings that these themes might engender among the students. At least one teacher did not consider it her role to 'play God' by trying to persuade students to adopt pro-gay attitudes (3.18). Other teachers reported that their colleagues were forbidden to disseminate information to students about local gay venues or even to discuss gay topics at all (despite the classroom being located across the street from a gay bar!) (3.7).

The learners in this study also expressed concerns and hesitations about lesbian/gay themes in the classroom, as shown in Chapters 6–8. Some students spoke of having to assess whether or not it would be acceptable to raise lesbian/gay content, how they might justify doing so to other students, and how their classmates might react. Sara, for instance, told me that classmates from her part of the world might find the subject "too strange" to accept (7.18), while Rita told me that her classmates might think she was a lesbian if she spoke up about the topic in class (7.23). Other students felt uncertain about how lesbian/gay content related to the learning point at hand; Ping saw no reason to be talking about "men [who] love men" during a lesson that was supposed to be about communities (7.17). In addition, some were concerned that partial or biased information was being presented in class about lesbian and gay people; Norie had heard that gays and lesbians did not have "a same partner always and ... house and pet," as represented in class, but problems with "drug, alcohol, and AIDS" (6.12). Still others thought that discussing lesbian and gay people as a homogeneous group was in itself problematic; Jun-Kyu protested that "they are not animal in the zoo" (6.6).

The concerns of teachers and students underscore the need to promote sexual literacy and cultural/linguistic knowledge about sexual diversity, *but to do so in ways that are not prescriptive, simplistic, or voyeuristic.* As I have tried to show throughout the book, the difficulties that students and teachers alike were having with sexual diversity as subject matter can, in many cases, be traced to the limitations of the teaching practices themselves (and the sexual-identity theories that underpin them).

Three main approaches to framing sexual diversity as subject matter were evident among the varied teaching practices analyzed in this book. I have called these the counseling approach, the controversies approach, and the discourse inquiry approach. Table 9.1 (see below) outlines the key features of each approach, together with a few illustrative examples from this book.

I should explain that these three approaches are not mutually exclusive; some teachers moved back and forth between them. But by and large, I found that most teachers in my study would adopt either a counseling or a controversies approach to sexual diversity, rather than a discourse inquiry approach. *In other words, most teachers would focus on individual homosexuals or gays and lesbians as a social category, rather than on the linguistic/cultural acts associated with sexual identities; most teachers sought to either elicit—or conversely, to avoid—their students' feelings about gay people or opinions about gay rights, rather than analyzing the sociosexual dimensions of communication much as they would any other dimensions; and in incorporating gay and lesbian content, most teachers sought to enhance students' personal growth or stimulate their interest in social justice, rather than improve their ability to comprehend, critique and contribute to discourse practices.*

Overall, the approach that seemed most effective—within the international, intercultural, multilingual contexts of language classes—was the discourse inquiry approach. Informed by queer and poststructuralist theories, queer inquiry means getting beyond condemn-or-condone debates about gay and lesbian people, to paraphrase Gina (7.13). It means turning our attention to sexual matters (identities, norms, relationships) within everyday patterns of thinking, speaking, learning, and working, with a view to understanding the complex sociosexual dimensions and meanings that are part of day-to-day interactions, cultural practices, and social structures. Questions that might be considered include how sexual identities are accomplished discursively, what purposes these identities serve, how they are valued or devalued, what they mean or signify, and how people come to know, or learn, these meanings.

In other words, facilitating queer inquiry involves unpacking the language acts through which sexual identities are constituted and enacted and made to seem normal or not normal—or, as Britzman (2000) puts it, "attending to the conditions that allow normalcy its hold" (p. 54). It means seeking out not just straight but also lesbian, bisexual, gay, and other perspectives, while at the same time recognizing the limitations of producing such categorizations in the first place.

TABLE 9.1 Three Approaches to Framing Sexual Diversity as Subject Matter

A Counseling Approach	A Controversies Approach	A Discourse Inquiry Approach
The personal, the interpersonal	The social, the societal	The textual, the discursive
Individual homosexuals	Gays and lesbians as a group	Linguistic and cultural practices
Sexual identities as inner essences—suppressed or expressed	Sexual identities as sociohistorical constructs—vary by time/place	Sexual identities as performative—instantiated through everyday interactions
Exploring feelings, attitudes	Promoting civil rights, debating controversial social issues	Analyzing acts of language/culture/identity
Focus on homophobia—fear/hatred of gay people	Focus on heterosexism—institutionalized discrimination	Focus on heteronormativity—the making of 'normal'
Personal growth, tolerance	Social justice, minority rights	Textual/discursive analysis—how texts mean
Including positive/ mainstream representations of gays and lesbians in curricula (see Chapter 3); othering gay people, us versus them (see Chapter 6)	Debating 'both sides' of sociosexual issues and controversies; forbidding homophobic speech or discussions of what constitutes this (see Chapter 4)	Analyzing how language and culture work regarding all sexual identities; questioning the presumption of heterosexuality (see Chapter 3); reflecting on sociosexual meanings and how these are learned (see Chapter 8)

Inquiry involves not only curiosity but also skepticism and innovation (Foucault, 1988). Applying those concepts here, practicing queer inquiry in the classroom means not just learning to understand and decode the sociosexual dimensions of linguistic and cultural practices but adopting a questioning, skeptical stance toward these practices and even reinventing them to suit one's own purposes. Thus, queer inquiry encompasses not only comprehension but also critical and creative interventions.

This raises two important points that are worth noting here. First, though some teachers in my study struggled to find ways of depicting gays and lesbians or the gay community in class materials, there were few, if any, attempts to share these behind-the-scenes struggles with their students. If, as poststructuralists argue, "no one has unmediated and equal access to 'the real,'" then an aim of pedagogy is "to underscore the fact that 'the real' must be constructed continuously in order to be recognized as such" (Britzman, Santiago-Valles, Jimenez-Muñoz, & Lamash, 1993, p. 192). It may be helpful, then, to draw attention to the decisions, constraints, and consequences that are associated with constructing representations *by making representation processes themselves the pedagogic focus in class.* To reiterate an example from Chapter 6, after Tony's class viewed the situation comedy 'Ellen' they could have discussed the lead character as a media representation of a lesbian, instead of as a 'real' lesbian.

Finally, though many teachers who incorporated gay/lesbian themes would carefully deliberate, and even agonize, over decisions about thematic content and activity structures, they rarely involved their students in these decision-making processes. By and large, the students were an underused resource. With this in mind, queer discourse inquiry could make use of 'problem posing,' through which students analyze potentially problematic situations and create solutions—the teacher's role is to facilitate dialogue (see Auerbach & Burgess, 1985). Also useful could be ethnographic tasks through which learners observe and study cultural practices (see Barro, Jordan, & Roberts, 1998), in this case, pertaining to sexual identity and diversity.

In sum, undertaking queer classroom inquiry can foster language learning by engaging students in exploring the language/culture/identity nexus.

Strategy III: Unpacking Heteronormative Discourses for Learning Purposes

A major concern for teachers in this study was how to respond when students said things that teachers felt were homophobic. This situation proved particularly challenging for teachers who, whether gay or straight themselves, had to struggle with their own emotional reactions to homophobia, as we saw in Chapter 4. This struggle was compounded for some gay and lesbian teachers who feared negative consequences professionally if their own sexual identity were to become known to their students, while some straight teachers expressed a lack of confidence in their own knowledge of gay/lesbian subject matter, as we saw in Chapter 5. The challenge of responding to students' anti-gay attitudes was exacerbated by having to accomplish this within a tight time frame since queer issues and perspectives are rarely part of planned language curricula.

Once again, concerns expressed by learners were strikingly similar. In discussing lesbian/gay themes in class, some students were concerned that lesbian and gay people in the class could feel offended by what was being said about gays, while others hoped to avoid sounding homophobic themselves as that could hurt or offend someone unintentionally. Some were weighing up how familiar other students and the teacher were likely to be with gay/lesbian issues as well as how comfortable they themselves felt in talking about these issues in class. Some worried about how to respond when a classmate felt uncomfortable with lesbian/gay content or was silent on the subject. Another concern was how to respond when a teacher makes homophobic comments.

Overall, there was a tendency for teachers to seek to avoid or prevent homophobic speech, as discussed in Chapter 4. However, in any classroom, but perhaps especially a language classroom, moments of confusion or even consternation are to be expected. These can be recast as opportunities to unpack expectations or interpretations that seem to be at odds with each other. Probably more common than pronouncements of hatred are more subtle homophobic 'moments.' Teachers might attempt to discourage students from pursuing a point that they believed could become homophobic, as Gina and Roxanne each did in indirect ways (see Chapters 7 and 8). In such cases, the reasons for the teacher's disapproval may or may not be clear to students, so it may be worthwhile to tease out the 'problem' and discuss it more explicitly.

Given the teacher and student concerns outlined above, in addressing homophobia (or, for that matter, heterosexism or heteronormativity) in the classroom, it might be productive for teachers to focus on questions of discourse rather than the personal belief system of individual students. This might mean posing questions such as the following: Exactly why is the spoken or written text being interpreted by some as homophobic, and what would need to change for the text to not be seen as homophobic? Competing sociocultural norms may also need to be made explicit. For example, in what situations or settings, or with what sorts of interlocutors, might this (spoken or written) text be interpreted as homophobic (or amusing), and what are the likely consequences for the speaker/writer of this text? (See Lemke, 1995; Misson, 1996.) It may be productive to consider what led to a disjuncture in understandings of the sociolinguistic rules of interaction in that particular classroom and what the consequences of such a disjuncture in other settings might be. Attending to discursive features such as intonation (see Morgan, 1997) or modalization might be another way to examine the possible interpretations and consequences of a homophobic statement. In other words, homophobic comments or exchanges can be considered openings rather than closings.

Of course, teachers need to consider not just what students say but how their own teaching practices might perpetuate heteronormative thinking. Since pedagogies cannot be politically or ethically neutral, the question is not whether values should be part of teaching, but which values, and whose values, will prevail (see Auerbach & Burgess, 1985, and many others). In education contexts, Britzman (1997) argues, "heterosexuality must become uncoupled from discourses of naturalness or from discourses of morality. Heterosexuality must become viewed as one possibility among many" (Britzman, 1997, p. 194). To this end, a useful concept is that of benign sexual variation:

> It is difficult to develop a pluralistic sexual ethics without a concept of benign sexual variation. Variation is a fundamental property of all life, from the simplest biological organisms to the most complex human social formations. Yet sexuality is supposed to conform to a single standard.
>
> (Rubin, 1984/1993, p. 15)

One teacher in my study was astonished when colleagues at a teaching conference exclaimed that gay and lesbian people "need to be killed" (4.31). One has to wonder about how well teachers who publicly proclaim such hostile views can address the learning needs of students who, like Alak, are living with a family member who fled anti-gay persecution (8.15), or, like Miyuki, are getting to know their new host sibling, who is gay (6.11), or, like Pablo, moved to a new country seeking a more welcoming environment in which to live as a gay person (8.33). A teacher-educator in this study made a point that is relevant here: In supervising a novice teacher who felt disconcerted that her students were writing about lesbian/gay themes, Claire's advice to the teacher was to step back and recognize that her perspective was just that—a particular perspective—and certainly not the only one (4.28).

Given the diverse experiences, identities, and viewpoints that characterize groups of ESL learners, I would strongly argue that heterosexuality should not be represented in class as if it were the only sexual identity that exists or that is 'natural,' 'normal,' or 'moral.' This means that it is important not to set up tasks that ask students to evaluate or judge lesbian/gay people—that is, whether 'they' are moral, normal, or natural (or should be 'allowed' to live). Setting up such debates constricts multiple perspectives to only two sides and can provoke antagonism. For example, instead of eliciting reasons why some people hate gays and lesbians, as Tony did (see Chapter 6), it may have been better, for example, to ask the class to brainstorm possible consequences for gay and lesbian people that result from the fact that some people hate them.

Furthermore, as discussed in Chapter 3, there is a need to consider not only what is said in the classroom but also what is not said. Excluding from class curricula and discussions any mention of sexual plurality constitutes an insidious form of heteronormativity—and puts students and teachers alike in the difficult (and, from a *language* learning view, counterproductive) position of having to censor much of their day-to-day experiences.

In language classes, then, heteronormative discourses and silencing practices can be critically examined for the purposes of illuminating language and communication issues.

Strategy IV: Valuing Multisexual Student and Teacher Cohorts

Teachers in this study reported mixed desires and concerns about how to represent themselves in class and how much to disclose about their lives outside of the classroom. As we saw in Chapters 5–8, some teachers (especially, but not exclusively, gay-identified teachers) found that dealing with gay/lesbian content made them feel more self-conscious about negotiating their own sexual identity in class, while for other teachers coming out as gay was actually a powerful teaching tool that enhanced their rapport with students and/or stimulated critical thinking. Also challenging for some teachers was working out how to respond to a student's direct question or insinuation that a student or a teacher was gay or lesbian and how to respond when a student came out in class, especially when classmates reacted with fear and hostility (see Chapter 2). Other teachers reported that few gay/lesbian students felt safe enough to come out in class, though some would come out privately to the teacher.

The students reported similar experiences (see Chapters 2 and 6–8). Some were trying to work out whether their teacher was gay/lesbian and wanted to ask them but were not sure whether this would be acceptable. They wondered which classmates were gay/lesbian and whether they themselves were being perceived to be gay/lesbian. Also, one student wondered which classmates were likely to have already worked out that he was in fact gay and whether or not it would cause problems for him if they had.

In short, self-representation quandaries were common to teachers and students—and were not confined to those who self-identified as gay. On the other hand, there was a dramatic difference between the experiences of those who came out in the classroom as straight without giving it a second thought, like the teacher Tina observed who cheerfully mentioned her fiancé to her class (5.13), versus those who endured a high degree of anguish because they did not feel it was safe to come out as a lesbian, like Helen, who was devastated when nearly her entire class expressed the damning view that all gay people were headed for 'hell' (4.7).

Britzman (1997) points out that, in education, the prevailing view that discussions of sexuality belong only in the bedroom is actually a very damaging myth. It stops many straight teachers "from educating themselves in intelligent and sensitive ways, about sexuality as a contradictory and socially complex social construction" (p. 192). In addition, the privatization myth is used to justify the relegation of many lesbian and gay teachers to "'the closet' as if such an imagined space could be a harmless and interesting choice" (p. 192).

Any given class (or any given teaching staff) is likely to involve students (or teachers) who identify across a range of sexual identities, are questioning their own sexual identity, do not relate to the concept of sexual 'identity', and are having, have had, or will have at least one romantic or sexual relationship with someone of their own gender. However, my study suggests that most learners who identify as other than straight are unlikely to make their sexual identity clear to their classmates or teachers. In addition, many straight learners are likely to interact with gay, lesbian, and bisexual friends, family members, coworkers, and neighbors, but these social relations may never become evident in class. Therefore, it is important to design tasks and pose questions that are addressed to, and can be answered by, students of any sexual identity and students who interact with people of every sexual identity. The important point is to avoid framing 'students in this room' and 'lesbian and gay people' as two distinct groups—in other words, to avoid an 'us' and 'them' approach.

Moreover, learners are entitled to self-determine how to present themselves in class and how much they do or do not wish to disclose about themselves and the broader social and community networks of which they are a part. Teachers (and material developers) should craft tasks and questions in ways that allow for—but do not require—a confessional mode. At the same time, ongoing efforts should be made to make classroom and campus environments ones in which being out is supported, though never required. This is important not only to create an ethos of respect but also to stimulate learning: "a classroom with too narrow a spectrum of diversity is cognitively impoverished, whatever else we may want to say about its ethics" (Gee, 1997, p. 297). These same points would apply to teaching staff too.

In language education generally it is important to find out more about the experiences of lesbian/gay students and teachers as these experiences have been largely neglected in published research. But in doing so, the focus should not be on psychologizing sexual minorities but on addressing the social and institutional conditions that constrain or disallow the production of identities (Talburt, 2000b). In fact, rather than constructing gay students (or teachers) as disadvantaged victims, it is helpful to keep in mind that sexual minorities—who must learn to "cloak meanings" (Britzman, 1997, p. 193)—have often had to develop a particularly nuanced awareness of issues of language, literacy, identity, and representation, as noted in Chapter 2. In other words, non-heterosexual people living within the heterosexual hegemony have had to become quite adept at sexual literacy:

> Being literate, for most LGBT/queer folks, is being able to read a given situation and articulate either a safe self-representation or a challenging self-representation that critically re-reads that given situation; they can choose to hide for safety, assert their queerness or challenge heterosexist assumptions, or negotiate a path between the two. Such negotiations usually manifest themselves as a meta-critical consciousness, often experienced as a running meta-narrative, about how dynamics in particular spaces control, contain, prompt, or provoke various self-representations.
>
> (Alexander & Banks, 2004, p. 287)

Throughout the book (especially in Chapters 5, 6, and 8), we have seen examples of these running meta-narratives, in teachers and students. Alexander and Banks (2004) surmise that most straight students are probably less sexually literate than most gay students, which is part of the authors' argument for teaching sexual literacy.

Another important point here is that, following poststructuralism, difference is not an "external factor to be taken into account in the construction of curriculum" but is "constructed and enacted through the practices of curriculum"—in other words, difference is not simply something that students bring to class (Rizvi & Walsh, 1998, p. 9). In this view, student diversity involves more than just interpersonal relations—it should, in fact, be central to academic content and pedagogies: "What is required is a complex multi-voiced approach to educational experiences, which does not assume fixed categories of cultural difference but encourages instead their exploration" (p. 10).

This returns us to the question of what is being taught and whether language curricula are addressing multivoiced thematic content when it comes to sexual identity. For me, one of the most significant findings of my investigation was how very much it meant to a gay student when the existence of lesbian/gay people was acknowledged in his ESL class (even though the ensuing discussion represented just 15 minutes of a 100-hour class!). For Roxanne's student Pablo, having a same-sex scenario as class material made it "OK to think they were lesbian" and to say so to his classmates, which mattered a great deal to him (8.38). This event was so significant to Pablo because being able to express, in a classroom context, even a little bit of his knowledge of gay matters was possible only after moving countries ("If I would be in Mexico I would be worried to say it, but here I can say it anywhere" [8.39]).

In Canagarajah's (2006) 'state of the art' account of English language education, he notes the profound and rapid changes that the field is undergoing as a result of "*postmodern globalization*" (p. 24). The contemporary world seems to be characterized by the movement and flow of languages, cultures, ideas, and people.

> People are no longer prepared to think of their identities in essentialist terms (as belonging exclusively to one language or culture), their languages and cultures as pure (separated from everything foreign), or their communities as homogenous (closed to contact with others).
>
> (Canagarajah, 2006, p. 25)

He goes on to draw out some pedagogic implications, two of which are especially pertinent to the discussion here. First, rather than teaching students how to communicate *within* a particular community, we should prepare them to "shuttle *between* communities," and second, "rather than teaching *rules* in a normative way, we should teach *strategies*—creative ways to negotiate the norms operating in different contexts" (Canagarajah, 2006, pp. 26–27).

With these aims in mind, it becomes imperative to acknowledge that student cohorts and teaching staff are characterized by sexual diversity and to update monosexual curricula, programs, and policies accordingly. Recognizing the existence of queer students and staff in the classroom (and queer loved ones and others beyond it) will help to bring queer concerns and points of view into the pedagogic frame. Queer knowledges and insights—about shuttling between communities, for instance, or creatively negotiating a complex mix of norms—need to become part of the general knowledge base of language education as they represent a valuable resource for all of us in developing the sorts of expertise that are required of life in a postmodern, globalized world.

Strategy V: Asking Queer Questions of Language-Teaching Resources and Research

As we saw in Chapters 3 and 6, many of the teachers in my study decried the lack of published learning materials with sexually diverse subject matter and characters. Most teachers had to develop their own level-appropriate materials, often using media and fiction, but wanted more options from commercial teaching resources. Interestingly, as shown in Chapter 7, some of the students understood that lesbian/gay themes arose in their classes because these themes had featured in the class resources; students showed no awareness that their teachers had in fact selected those particular resources *because* they included lesbian/gay themes. This suggests that selecting resources that include even a brief mention of lesbian, transgender, bisexual, or gay thematic content or perspectives (as opposed to just writing one's own materials) can be a way for teachers to incorporate gay themes in ways that students are likely to consider authoritative and legitimate.

Jones (1994; as cited in Snelbecker, 1994) reported that most of his ESL teaching colleagues in the United States were reluctant to broach gay or lesbian topics in their classes because they felt they lacked the necessary training and materials to do this well and also because they did not think these topics were likely to be relevant to their students. Both of these reasons can be traced, at least in part, to the general dearth of language-education research on sexual diversity issues. I think it is understandable that, without ready access to a knowledge base of empirical and theoretical research (as well as teaching materials), many would feel unprepared to address the sexual dimensions of identity in an intercultural classroom context and would not necessarily realize that their classes included students who were interacting with gay people at work or on the streets, were living with gay people, or were themselves gay.

The nearly 50 teachers who volunteered to participate in my investigation, allowing me to interview them and/or observe their teaching, did so because they were happy to contribute to—and eager to learn from—research on 'sexual identities in ESL.' Many of the teachers mentioned that they were very glad they had participated in this study because it offered a unique opportunity for them to reflect on this aspect of their teaching—and, for those in the focus groups, to hear their colleagues' reflections. In fact, I found, much as Burck (2005) did in her study of multilingual living, that before taking part in my study, hardly any of my research participants (teachers or students) had had the opportunity in a professional forum to articulate their perspectives on the topic under investigation. This meant that in the focus groups and interviews they were actively constructing their accounts, thoughts, and feelings for the first time. Over and over again, I found that teachers and students were eager to talk about the issues—and not just because they wanted to help me with my research, but because these issues were significant in their own lives, for their own reasons.

The issues raised by my research participants in turn have generated much lively discussion when audiences comprising language teachers, language learners, and interested others see (and take part in) performances of an ethnographic play that I wrote, entitled *Queer as a Second Language*. The play uses some of the research transcripts presented in this book (and others that were not included in the book) and has been performed at conferences and on campuses in Australia, Japan, and the United States (e.g., Nelson, 2002). Audience members often comment that seeing the play provides a rare and valuable opportunity for collegial discussion of sexual identity issues in the language classroom.

De Castell and Bryson (1998), writing of education research, pose an interesting question: "What would we make of a school-based research study in which all of our informants were heterosexual? This should be an easy question to answer, given that practically all educational research finds exactly this" (p. 245). The authors explain that, in the numerous research studies they had read over the years, the only mentions made of gay, lesbian, bisexual, or transgender students were in those studies that specifically focused on these groups. In all the other studies:

It seemed to matter greatly whether students were ... low or high achievers ... lived in the city or the country, had a part-time job or not, and a host of other considerations. But it did not seem to matter to the researchers whose work we've read whether the students in question were gay or straight, which is odd, considering how enormously such a thing appears to matter to gay, lesbian, and transgendered youth themselves.

(de Castell & Bryson, 1998, p. 247)

The authors go on to argue that it is highly problematic if education researchers are "either unable or unwilling to see or report the presence of gay and lesbian subjects in their research population" (p. 247).

Similar questions could be asked about language education research—where *are* the lesbian, transgender, queer, gay, and bisexual learners (and, for that matter, teachers)? Why are they so often missing from the pages of our research publications? What does it mean that so many second- and foreign-language researchers seem unable or unwilling to even acknowledge, much less discuss, the presence of queer people in their investigations? Moreover, as the evidence presented in this book highlights, it is not just queer people who are missing from most language education research—it is also people with queer neighbors, mothers-in-law, bosses, and host-brothers. Perhaps the most significant question is: What effects are these acts of erasure and exclusion having on the teaching and learning of language?

Language teachers need to be asking some queer questions of our professional publications—both student resources and research studies. To briefly illustrate what this might look like, I draw on Moita-Lopes (2006) and Curran (2006), who have proposed some questions to use in the classroom in deconstructing written or spoken texts with a view to "highlighting how everyday, often unquestioned, discourses may support the heteronormative status quo" (Curran, 2006, p. 92). In evaluating both student materials and research publications, it is worth asking things like: Does the text portray a monosexual version of the world? Or are diverse sexual identities represented? What values or assumptions are evident vis-à-vis sexual identity? Does the text address a sexually diverse readership?

Perhaps if enough of us are asking these sorts of questions—of what we read and also of what we write—we can begin to create research publications and teaching resources that do not portray strangely monosexual versions of the world.

To write this book I have listened closely to a great number of queer conversations—in language classes and about language classes—and I have quoted from these extensively so that readers can form their own interpretations. Through critical analysis drawing on the participants' perspectives and on a wide range of research, I have mapped out key teaching issues and promising strategies for engaging with sexual plurality as a pedagogic resource.

In closing, I hope this book will stimulate adventurous thinking, innovative learning, and a sense of camaraderie, as teachers and students—whether straight, queer, bisexual, lesbian, transgender, gay, *tongzhi*, *hijra*, *joto*, questioning, or 'none of the above'—open up our classrooms to the diverse voices and vantage points that enrich human communication the world over.

Appendix A
Teachers Quoted

Pseudonym	Position	Source of Quote	Chapter
Alicia	Teacher	Interview	2–5
Carmen	Teacher	TESOL	5
Claire	Teacher-educator and administrator	Interview	2–5
Clay	Teacher-educator	ESL-1, ESL-2	1, 3, 4
David	Teacher	TESOL	5
Eric	Teacher-educator and administrator	TESOL	4
Gina	Teacher	Interview, class observation	7
Gwen	Student teacher	ESL-1, interview	4
Helen	Teacher	ESL-2, interview	4
Ira	Teacher and teacher-educator	TESOL, interview	5
Janice	Teacher and administrator	IEP	2, 3, 5
Jill	Teacher	TESOL	4
Jo	Teacher	IEP	3, 5
Joan	Teacher	ESL-1	3
Jody	Teacher	TESOL	5
Kath	Teacher	TESOL	5
Liz	Teacher	TESOL	4
Maggie	Teacher and administrator	ESL-1	2
Mark	Teacher and student advisor	ESL-1, ESL-2	3–5
Mike	Teacher	IEP	2, 3, 5
Nancy	Teacher	TESOL	5
Paige	Teacher and administrator	Interview	2–5
Paula	Teacher	TESOL	5
Rachel	Teacher-educator and material writer	ESL-1, ESL-2, interview	2, 4
Rhonda	Teacher	TESOL	4
Roxanne	Teacher	Interview, class observation	8

(*Continued*)

(*Continued*)

Pseudonym	Position	Source of Quote	Chapter
Scott	Teacher	TESOL	4, 5
Sophie	Teacher	Interview	3
Tess	Teacher and teacher-educator	TESOL, interview	3–5
Tina	Student teacher	ESL-1, ESL-2, interview	2–5
Tom	Teacher-educator and administrator	Interview	3, 5
Tony	Teacher	Interview, class observation	6
Ursula	Teacher and student advisor	ESL-2	3–5

Appendix B
Transcribing Key

Student	In class transcripts, this refers to a speaker whom I was unable to identify
1, 2	In class transcripts, serial numbers indicate the sequence of turn taking
[?]	A question mark in brackets indicates unintelligible speech
[yeah?]	Text (followed by a question mark) in brackets indicates possible though uncertain transcription
[Gina]	Text (with no question mark) in brackets indicates a shorter or clearer account of what was said (e.g., substituting a pronoun with a clear referent)
(laughter)	Text in parentheses includes comments about the transcript such as non-verbal actions
...	Ellipsis indicates a portion of the transcript is not shown
[...]	Ellipsis in brackets indicates a portion of the transcript that included a turn or turns by other speakers is not shown
What I was- I was saying	Hyphen indicates a false start or syntactic shift
I think it's	No punctuation at the end of a line indicates the utterance was cut off or overlapped by the next speaker
I will say Oooh you are gay!	Capitals mid-sentence indicate reported speech
Kind of a THUMP	Using all capitals indicates emphasis through pitch or amplitude
Gettin	Unconventional spelling generally follows the pronunciation (unless this would render the text incomprehensible)

Appendix C
Students Quoted or Mentioned

Chapter 6—Tony's Class			
Pseudonym	*Gender*	*Country of Origin*	*Age*
Hae-Woo	Man	Korea	early 20s
Jun-Kyu	Man	Korea	late 20s
Lynn	Woman	Taiwan	late 20s
Miyuki	Woman	Japan	early 20s
Norie	Woman	Japan	early 20s
Reiko	Woman	Japan	early 20s
Sharon	Woman	Taiwan	late 20s
Vivian	Woman	Taiwan	late 20s
Chapter 7—Gina's Class			
Pseudonym	*Gender*	*Country of Origin*	*Age*
Ben	Man	Singapore	23
Eva	Woman	Norway	20s
Lucy	Woman	Vietnam	20
Peter	Man	Laos	21
Ping	Woman	China	32
Rita	Woman	El Salvador	20
Sara	Woman	Vietnam	33
Vince	Man	Vietnam	20s

(*Continued*)

Chapter 8—Roxanne's Class			
Pseudonym	*Gender*	*Country of Origin*	*Age*
Alak	Man	Thailand	late 20s
Ebou	Man	Gambia	30
Fabiola	Woman	Brazil	30s
Hassan	Man	Ethiopia	30s
Irma	Woman	Mexico	40s
Mary	Woman	Hong Kong	64
Mi-Young	Woman	Korea	30
Neuriden	Man	Morocco	36
Pablo	Man	Mexico	25
Raúl	Man	Mexico	25
Tran	Man	Vietnam	60

References

Agar, M. (1994). *Language shock: Understanding the culture of conversation.* New York: Quill.

Alexander, J., & Banks, W. P. (2004). Sexualities, technologies, and the teaching of writing: A critical overview. *Computers and Composition, 21,* 273–293.

Allatson, P., & Pratt, M. (June, 2005). Queer agencies and social change in international perspectives: A positioning paper. Queer Agencies and Social Change in International Perspectives, Annual Symposium of the Institute for International Studies, University of Technology, Sydney, Australia.

Allwright, D. (1988). *Observation in the language classroom.* London: Longman.

Allwright, D., & Bailey, K. M. (1991). *Focus on the language classroom.* Cambridge University Press.

Anderson, A., Arnold, A., Bramlett, F., Bode, S., Bond, C. M., Carney, T., et al. (1997). Letter to the editor. *TESOL Matters, 7*(4), 22.

Auerbach, E. R. (1995). The politics of the ESL classroom: Issues of power in pedagogical choices. In J. Tollefson (Ed.). *Power and inequality in language education* (pp. 9–33). Cambridge University Press.

Auerbach, E. R., & Burgess, D. (1985). The hidden curriculum in survival ESL. *TESOL Quarterly, 19*(3), 475–495.

Austin, J. L. (1975). *How to do things with words.* Cambridge, MA: Harvard University Press.

Barrett, R. (1997). The 'homo-genius' speech community. In A. Livia & K. Hall (Eds.), *Queerly phrased: Language, gender, and sexuality* (pp. 181–201). New York: Oxford University Press.

Barro, A., Jordan, S., & Roberts, C. (1998). Cultural practice in everyday life: The language learner as ethnographer. In M. Byram & M. Fleming (Eds.), *Language learning in intercultural perspective: Approaches through drama and ethnography* (pp. 76–97). Cambridge University Press.

Beebe, J. D. (2002). Unfinished business: Identity formation and rejection through language learning. *The Language Teacher (JALT), 22*(6), 17–21.

Belsey, C. (1980). *Critical practice.* New York: Methuen.

Benesch, S. (1999). Thinking critically, thinking dialogically. *TESOL Quarterly, 33*(3), 573–580.

Bennett, P. (1982). Dyke in academe (II). In M. Cruikshank (Ed.), *Lesbian studies: Present and future* (pp. 3–8). New York: Feminist Press.

Berg, A., Kowaleski, J., Le Guin, C., Weinauer, E., & Wolfe, E. A. (1989). Breaking the silence: Sexual preference in the composition classroom. *Feminist Teacher, 4*(2/3), 29–32.

Bernstein, B. (1971). On the classification and framing of educational knowledge. In M. F. D. Young (Ed.), *Knowledge and control* (pp. 47–69). London: Collier-Macmillan.

Bernstein, B. (1996). *Pedagogy, symbolic control and identity: Theory, research, critique.* London: Taylor & Francis.

Blinick, B. (1994). Out in the curriculum, out in the classroom: Teaching history and organizing for change. In L. Garber (Ed.), *Tilting the tower: Lesbians/teaching/queer subjects* (pp. 142–149). New York: Routledge.

Blumenfeld, W. J. (1992). *Homophobia: How we all pay the price.* Boston: Beacon Press.

Boostrom, R. (1998). 'Safe spaces': Reflections on an educational metaphor. *Journal of Curriculum Studies, 30*(4), 397–408.

Bourdieu, P. (1991). *Language and symbolic power.* (G. Raymond & M. Adamson, Trans.). Cambridge: Polity Press.

Brandt, G. L. (1986). *The realization of anti-racist teaching.* London: Falmer Press.

Breen, M. P. (1985). The social context for language learning—A neglected situation? *Studies in Second Language Acquisition, 7*(1), 135–158.

Brems, M., & Strauss, E. (1995). Homophobia in the classroom: Examining a teacher's role (Workshop). TESOL Convention, Long Beach.

Brinton, D. M., Snow, M. A., & Wesche, M. B. (1989). *Content-based second language instruction.* Philadelphia: Newbury House.

Britzman, D. P. (1995). Is there a queer pedagogy? Or, stop reading straight. *Educational Theory, 45*(2), 151–165.

Britzman, D. P. (1997). What is this thing called love? New discourses for understanding gay and lesbian youth. In S. de Castell & M. Bryson (Eds.), *Radical in<ter>ventions: Identity, politics, and differ-ence/s in educational praxis* (pp. 183–207). Albany, NY: State University of New York Press.

Britzman, D. P. (2000). Precocious education. In S. Talburt & S. R. Steinberg (Eds.), *Thinking queer: Sexuality, culture, and education* (pp. 33–59). New York: Peter Lang.

Britzman, D. P., Santiago-Valles, K., Jimenez-Muñoz, G., & Lamash, L. (1993). Slips that show and tell: Fashioning multiculture as a problem of representation. In C. McCarthy & W. Crichlow (Eds.), *Race, identity, and representation in education* (pp. 188–200). New York: Routledge.

Brumfit, C. (1985). Creativity and constraint in the language classroom. In R. Quirk & H. G. Widdowson (Eds.), *English in the world: Teaching and learning the language and literatures* (pp. 148–157). Cambridge University Press.

Bryson, M., & de Castell, S. (1997). Queer pedagogy?! Praxis makes im/perfect. In S. de Castell & M. Bryson (Eds.), *Radical in<ter>ventions: Identity, politics, and difference/s in educational praxis* (pp. 269–293). Albany, NY: State University of New York Press.

Burbules, N. C. (1997). A grammar of difference: Some ways of rethinking difference and diversity as educational topics. *Australian Educational Researcher, 24*(1), 97–116.

Burck, C. (2005). *Multilingual living: Explorations of language and subjectivity.* Hampshire, England: Palgrave Macmillan.

Butler, J. (1990). *Gender trouble.* New York: Routledge.

Butler, J. (1991). Imitation and gender insubordination. In D. Fuss (Ed.), *Inside/Out: Lesbian theories, gay theories* (pp. 13–31). New York: Routledge.

Butler, J. (1993). *Bodies that matter: On the discursive limits of 'sex.'* New York: Routledge.

Cameron, D. (1995). *Verbal hygiene.* London: Routledge.

Canagarajah, A. S. (1993). Critical ethnography of a Sri Lankan classroom: Ambiguities in student opposition to reproduction through ESOL. *TESOL Quarterly, 27*(4), 601–626.

Canagarajah, A. S. (2006). TESOL at forty: What are the issues? *TESOL Quarterly, 40*(1), 9–34.

Candlin, C. N. (1981). Form, function and strategy in communicative curriculum design. In C. N. Candlin (Ed. & Trans.), *The communicative teaching of English: Principles and an exercise typology* (pp. 24–44). London: Longman.

Candlin, C. N. (1984). Syllabus design as a critical process. In C. Brumfit (Ed.), *General English syllabus design* (pp. 29–46). ELT Documents 118. Oxford: Pergamon Press in association with the British Council.

Candlin, C. N. (1987). Explaining moments of conflict in discourse. In R. Steele & T. Treadgold (Eds.), *Language topics: Essays in honour of Michael Halliday* (pp. 413–429). Amsterdam: Benjamins.

Candlin, C. N. (1989). Language, culture and curriculum. In C. N. Candlin & T. F. McNamara (Eds.), *Language, learning and community* (pp. 1–24). Sydney: National Centre for English Language Teaching and Research, Macquarie University.

Carlson, D. (2001). Gay, queer, and cyborg: The performance of identity in a transglobal age. *Discourse: Studies in the Cultural Politics of Education, 22*(3), 297–309.

Carscadden, L., Nelson, C., & Ward, J. (1992). We are your colleagues: Lesbians and gays in ESL (Colloquium). TESOL Convention, Vancouver.

Cazden, C. B. (1988). *Classroom discourse: The language of teaching and learning.* Portsmouth, NH: Heinemann.

Chamberlain, J. (Winter, 2004). What to do about vulgar English? *Essential Teacher,* 50–52.

Chan, C. S. (1996). Combating heterosexism in educational institutions: Structural change and strategies. In E. D. Rothblum & L. A. Bond (Eds.), *Preventing heterosexism and homophobia* (pp. 20–35). Thousand Oaks, CA: Sage.

Clarke, M. A., Davis, A., Rhodes, L. K., & Baker, E. (1998). Principles of collaboration in school–university partnerships. *TESOL Quarterly, 32*(3), 592–600.

Clarke, M. A., Dobson, B. K., & Silberstein, S. (1996). *Choice readings.* Ann Arbor: Michigan University Press.

Clemente, Á., & Higgins, M. J. (2005). Whose English is it anyway? Culture, language and identity: Ethnographic portraits from Oaxaca, Mexico. *Working Papers on Culture, Education and Human Development, 1*(3), 1–32. Universidad Autónoma de Madrid. Retrieved February 22, 2006, from http://www.uam.es/ptcedh

Cruz-Malavé, A., & Manalansan IV, M. F. (2002a). Dissident sexualities/alternative globalisms. In A. Cruz-Malavé & M. F. Manalansan IV (Eds.), *Queer globalizations: Citizenship and the afterlife of colonialism* (pp. 1–10). New York: New York University Press.

Cruz-Malavé, A., & Manalansan IV, M. F. (Eds.). (2002b). *Queer globalizations: Citizenship and the afterlife of colonialism.* New York: New York University Press.

Cummings, M. C., & Nelson, C. (1993). Our time has come: TESOL forms lesbian/gay/bisexual task force, Part I. *TESOL Matters, 3*(4), 5.

Curran, G. (2006). Responding to students' normative questions about gays: Putting queer theory into practice in an Australian ESL class. *Journal of Language, Identity, and Education, 5*(1), 85–96.

Dalley, P., & Campbell, M. D. (2006). Constructing and contesting discourses of heteronormativity: An ethnographic study of youth in a Francophone high school in Canada. *Journal of Language, Identity, and Education, 5*(1), 11–29.

de Castell, S., & Bryson, M. (1998). From the ridiculous to the sublime: On finding oneself in educational research. In W. F. Pinar (Ed.), *Queer theory in education* (pp. 245–250). Mahwah, NJ: Lawrence Erlbaum.

Destandau, N., Nelson, C., & Snelbecker, K. (March, 1995). Coming out in the classroom: Equal educational opportunities (Colloquium). TESOL Convention, Long Beach.

De Vincenti, G., Giovanangeli, A., & Ward, R. (2007). The queer stopover: How queer travels in the language classroom. *Electronic Journal of Foreign Language Teaching, 4*(Suppl. 1), 58–72.

Duff, P.A., & Uchida, Y. (1997). The negotiation of teachers' sociocultural identities and practices in postsecondary EFL classrooms. *TESOL Quarterly, 31*(3), 451–484.

Edelhoff, C. (1981). Theme-oriented English teaching: Text-varieties, media, skills and project-work. In C. N. Candlin (Ed. & Trans.), *The communicative teaching of English: Principles and an exercise typology* (pp. 49–62). Harlow, Essex: Longman.

Edwards, A. D., & Westgate, D. P. G. (1994). *Investigating classroom talk* (2nd ed.). London: Falmer Press.

Edwards, D., & Mercer, N. (1987). *Common knowledge: The development of understanding in the classroom.* London: Methuen.

Ellwood, C. (2006). On coming out and coming undone: Sexualities and reflexivities in language education research. *Journal of Language, Identity, and Education, 5*(1), 67–84.

Epstein, D. (Ed.). (1994). *Challenging lesbian and gay inequalities in education.* Buckingham: Open University Press.

Epstein, D., & Johnson, R. (1994). On the straight and narrow: The heterosexual presumption, homophobias, and schools. In D. Epstein (Ed.), *Challenging lesbian and gay inequalities in education* (pp. 197–230). Buckingham: Open University Press.

Erni, J. N. (2003). Run queer Asia run. In G. A. Yep, K. E. Lovaas, & J. P. Elia (Eds.), *Queer theory and communication: From disciplining queers to queering the discipline(s)* (pp. 381–384). New York: Haworth Press.

Evans, K. (2002). *Negotiating the self: Identity, sexuality, and emotion in learning to teach.* New York: Routledge Falmer.

Fairclough, N. (1992). *Discourse and social change.* Cambridge: Polity Press.

Flax, J. (1989). Postmodernism and gender relations in feminist theory. In M. R. Malson, J. F. O'Barr, S. Westphal-Wihl, & M. Wyer (Eds.), *Feminist theory in practice and process* (pp. 51–73). Chicago: University of Chicago Press.

Folse, K. S. (1996). *Discussion starters: Speaking fluency activities for advanced ESL/EFL students*. Ann Arbor, MI: University of Michigan Press.

Ford, F. (1997). Letter to the editor. *TESOL Matters, 7*(5), 6.

Foucault, M. (1972). *The archeology of knowledge and the discourse on language.* New York: Pantheon.

Foucault, M. (1980). *Power/Knowledge: Selected interviews and other writings, 1927–1977.* (C. Gordon, L. Marshall, J. Mepham, & K. Soper, Trans.). New York: Pantheon.

Foucault, M. (1981). The order of discourse. In R. Young (Ed.), *Untying the text* (pp. 48–78). Boston: Routledge & Kegan Paul.

Foucault, M. (1982). Afterword: The subject and power. In H. Dreyfus & P. Rabinow, *Michel Foucault: Beyond structuralism and hermeneutics* (pp. 208–226). Hertfordshire: Harvester Press.

Foucault, M. (1988). Power, moral values, and the intellectual [Interview with Michel Foucault conducted by Michael Bess, 3 November 1980]. *History of the present,* (4), 13.

Foucault, M. (1990). *The history of sexuality, Volume 1.* New York: Random House.

Freeman, D. (1996). Redefining the relationship between research and what teachers know. In K. M. Bailey & D. Nunan (Eds.), *Voices from the language classroom* (pp. 88–122). Cambridge: Cambridge University Press.

Freeman, D. (1998). *Doing teacher research: From inquiry to understanding.* Pacific Grove: Heinle & Heinle.

Fung, R. (1995). The trouble with 'Asians.' In M. Dorenkamp & R. Henke (Eds.), *Negotiating lesbian and gay subjects* (pp. 123–130). New York: Routledge.

Fuss, D. (1989). *Essentially speaking: Feminism, nature and difference.* New York: Routledge.

Fuss, D. (1991). Inside/out. In D. Fuss (Ed.), *Inside/Out: Lesbian theories, gay theories* (pp. 1–10). New York: Routledge.

Gee, J. P. (1990). *Social linguistics and literacies: Ideology in discourses.* Bristol, PA: Falmer Press.

Gee, J. P. (1997). Meanings in discourses: Coordinating and being coordinated. In S. Muspratt, A. Luke, & P. Freebody, *Constructing critical literacies: Teaching and learning textual practice* (pp. 273–302). St Leonards, Australia: Allen & Unwin.

Giroux, H. (1993a). Literacy and the politics of difference. In C. Lankshear & P. L. McLaren (Eds.), *Critical literacy* (pp. 367–377). Albany: State University of New York.

Giroux, H. (1993b). *Living dangerously: Multiculturalism and the politics of difference.* New York: Peter Lang.

Goffman, E. (1963). *Stigma: Notes on the management of spoiled identity.* Englewood Cliffs, NJ: Prentice Hall.

Goffman, E. (1971). *Relations in public: Microstudies of the public order.* New York: Basic Books.

Golombek, P. R. (1998). A study of language teachers' personal practical knowledge. *TESOL Quarterly, 32*(3), 447–464.

Gore, J. (1993). *The struggle for pedagogies: Critical and feminist discourses as regimes of truth.* London: Routledge.

Griffin, P. (1992). From hiding to coming out: Empowering lesbian and gay educators. In K. M. Harbeck (Ed.), *Coming out of the classroom closet: Gay and lesbian students, teachers and curricula* (pp. 167–196). New York: Haworth Press.

Gumperz, J. J., & Cook-Gumperz, J. (1982). Introduction: Language and the communication of social identity. In J. J. Gumperz (Ed.), *Language and social identity* (pp. 1–21). Cambridge University Press.

Hall, S. (1990). Cultural identity and diaspora. In J. Rutherford (Ed.), *Identity: Community, culture, difference* (pp. 222–237). London: Lawrence & Wishart.

Hall, S. (1993). Deviance, politics, and the media. In H. Abelove, M. A. Barale, & D. M. Halperin (Eds.), *The lesbian and gay studies reader* (pp. 62–90). New York: Routledge.

Hammersley, M. (1990). *Reading ethnographic research: A critical guide.* London: Longman.

Hammersley, M. (1993). On practitioner ethnography. In M. Hammersley (Ed.), *Controversies in classroom research* (2nd ed.) (pp. 246–264). Buckingham: Open University Press.

Hanson, J. (1998). A unit on romance, marriage, and sexual orientation. *Outside In, the Newsletter of the Lesbian/Gay/Bisexual and Friends Caucus (of TESOL), 3*(2), 5–6.

Harbeck, K. M. (Ed.). (1992). *Coming out of the classroom closet: Gay and lesbian students, teachers and curricula.* New York: Haworth Press.

Harding, S. (1989). The instability of the analytical categories of feminist theory. In M. R. Malson, J. F. O'Barr, S. Westphal-Wihl, & M. Wyer (Eds.), *Feminist theory in practice and process* (pp. 15–34). University of Chicago Press.

Harris, S. (1990). *Lesbian and gay issues in the English classroom: The importance of being honest.* Philadelphia: Open University Press.

Hart, E. L. (1988). Literacy and the lesbian/gay learner. In S. H. Parmeter & I. Reti (Eds.), *The lesbian in front of the classroom: Writings by lesbian teachers* (pp. 30–43). Santa Cruz: HerBooks.

Hawley, J. C. (Ed.). (2001). *Postcolonial, queer: Theoretical intersections.* Albany, NY: State University of New York.

Hinson, S. (1996). A practice focused approach to addressing heterosexist violence in Australian schools. In L. Laskey & C. Beavis (Eds.), *Schooling and sexualities: Teaching for a positive sexuality* (pp. 241–258). Victoria, Australia: Deakin Centre for Education and Change, Deakin University.

Hirst, A. (1981). Gay's the word but not in EFL. *EFL Gazette, 28* (reprinted in *TESOL Newsletter,* June 1982).

Holland, S. P. (1994). Humanity is not a luxury: Some thoughts on a recent passing. In L. Garber (Ed.), *Tilting the tower: Lesbians/teaching/queer subjects* (pp. 168–176). New York: Routledge.

Holliday, A. (1999). Small cultures. *Applied Linguistics, 20*(2), 237–264.

hooks, b. (1994). *Teaching to transgress: Education as the practice of freedom.* New York: Routledge.

Hsu, W. (2006). Easing into research literacy through a genre and courseware approach. *Electronic Journal of Foreign Language Teaching, 3*(1), 70–89. Retrieved November 14, 2006, from http://e-flt.nus.edu.sg/v3n12006/hsu.htm

Jackson, P. W. (1968). *Life in classrooms.* New York: Hold, Rinehart, and Winston.

Jagose, A. (1996). *Queer theory.* Melbourne University Press.

Jaworski, A. (Ed.). (1997). *Silence: Interdisciplinary perspectives.* Berlin: Mouton de Gruyter.

Jewell, J. B. W. (1998). A transgendered ESL learner in relation to her class textbooks, heterosexist hegemony and change. *Melbourne Papers in Applied Linguistics, 10,* 1–21.

Johnson, R. (1995). ESL teacher education and intercultural communication: Discomfort as a learning tool. *TESL Canada Journal/Revue TESL du Canada, 12*(2), 59–66.

Jones, C., & Jack, D. (1994, March 10). Inclusion: Gay and lesbian issues and literature in ESL classes (Workshop). TESOL Convention, Baltimore.

Jones, R. H. (1996). *Responses to AIDS awareness discourse: A cross-cultural frame analysis.* Research monograph no. 10. City University of Hong Kong Department of English.

Kappra, R. (1998/1999). Addressing heterosexism in the IEP classroom. *TESOL Matters, 8*(6), 19.

Kato, N. (1999). Working with gay, lesbian and bisexual international students in the United States. *International Educator* [NAFSA: Association of International Educators] *8*(1) Retrieved February 20, 2000, from http://www.nafsa.org.

Khayatt, M. D. (1992). *Lesbian teachers: An invisible presence.* Albany: State University of New York Press.

King, B. W. (2008). "Being gay guy, that is the advantage": Queer Korean language learning and identity construction. *Journal of Language, Identity, and Education, 7* (3/4), 230–252.

King, K. (2002). "There are no lesbians here": Lesbianisms, feminisms, and global gay formations. In A. Cruz-Malavé & M. F. Manalansan IV (Eds.), *Queer globalizations: Citizenship and the afterlife of colonialism* (pp. 33–45). New York: New York University Press.

Kitzinger, C. (1996). Speaking of oppression: Psychology, politics and the language of power. In E. D. Rothblum & L. A. Bond (Eds.), *Preventing heterosexism and homophobia* (pp. 3–19). Thousand Oaks, CA: Sage.

Kramsch, C. (1993). *Context and culture in language teaching.* Oxford: Oxford University Press.

Kumaravadivelu, B. (1994). The postmethod condition: (E)merging strategies for second/foreign language teaching. *TESOL Quarterly, 28*(1), 27–48.

Kumaravadivelu, B. (2003). *Beyond methods: Macrostrategies for language teaching.* New Haven: Yale University Press.

Kumashiro, K. K. (2002). *Troubling education: Queer activism and antioppressive pedagogy.* New York: Routledge Falmer.

Ladenson, E. (Autumn, 1998). Gay Paree; or thank heaven for little girls. *Modern Language Studies, 28*(3/4), 187–192.

Laskey, L., & Beavis, C. (Eds.). (1996). *Schooling and sexualities: Teaching for a positive sexuality.* Victoria, Australia: Deakin Centre for Education and Change, Deakin University.

Lather, P. (1991). *Getting smart: Feminist research and pedagogy with/in the postmodern.* London: Routledge.

Lave, J., & Wenger, E. (1991). *Situated learning.* Cambridge University Press.

Layder, D. (1993). *New strategies in social research.* Oxford: Polity Press.

Lee, A. (1996). *Gender, literacy, curriculum: Re-writing school geography.* London: Taylor & Francis.

Legutke, M., & Thomas, H. (1991). *Process and experience in the language classroom.* London: Longman.

Lemke, J. L. (1985). *Using language in the classroom.* Geelong, Australia: Deakin University Press.

Lemke, J. L. (1995). *Textual politics: Discourse and social dynamics.* London: Taylor & Francis.

Le Page, R. B., & Tabouret-Keller, A. (1985). *Acts of identity.* Cambridge University Press.

Leung, C., Harris, R., & Rampton, B. (1997). The idealised native speaker, reified ethnicities, and classroom realities. *TESOL Quarterly, 31*(3), 543–560.

Lindstromberg, S. (1997). Letter to the editor. *TESOL Matters, 7*(3), 21.

Livia, A., & Hall, K. (Eds.). (1997a). *Queerly phrased: Language, gender, and sexuality.* New York: Oxford University Press.

Livia, A., & Hall, K. (1997b). "It's a girl!" Bringing performativity back to linguistics. In A. Livia & K. Hall (Eds.), *Queerly phrased: Language, gender, and sexuality* (pp. 3–18). New York: Oxford University Press.

Luhmann, S. (1998). Queering/Querying pedagogy? Or, pedagogy is a pretty queer thing. In W. F. Pinar (Ed.), *Queer theory in education* (pp. 141–155). Mahwah, NJ: Lawrence Erlbaum.

Lusted, D. (1986). Why pedagogy? *Screen, 27*(5), 2–14.

Mac an Ghaill, M. (1994). (In)visibility: Sexuality, race and masculinity in the school context. In D. Epstein (Ed.), *Challenging lesbian and gay inequalities in education* (pp. 152–176). Buckingham: Open University Press.

Maher, F. A., & Tetreault, M. K. T. (1994). *The feminist classroom.* New York: Basic Books.

Malinowitz, H. (1992). Extending our concept of multiculturalism: Lesbian and gay reality and the writing class. In J. Collins (Ed.), *Vital signs 3: Restructuring the English classroom.* Portsmouth, NH: Heinemann.

Malinowitz, H. (1995). *Textual orientations: Lesbian and gay students and the making of discourse communities.* Portsmouth, NH: Heinemann.

Martindale, K. (1997). Que<e>rying pedagogy: Teaching un/popular cultures. In S. de Castell & M. Bryson (Eds.), *Radical in<ter>ventions: Identity, politics, and difference/s in educational praxis* (pp. 59–83). Albany, NY: State University of New York Press.

McGroarty, M. (1998). Constructive and constructivist challenges for applied linguistics. *Language Learning, 48*(4), 591–622.

McLaren, P. L., & Lankshear, C. (1993). Critical literacy and the postmodern turn. In C. Lankshear & P. McLaren (Eds.), *Critical literacy: Politics, praxis, and the postmodern* (pp. 379–419). Albany, NY: State University of New York Press.

McLeod, J., & Yates, L. (1997). Can we find out about girls and boys today—or must we settle for just talking about ourselves? Dilemmas of a feminist, qualitative, longitudinal research project. *Australian Educational Researcher, 24*(3), 23–55.

Mercer, N. (1995). *The guided construction of knowledge: Talk amongst teachers and learners.* Clevedon: Multilingual Matters.

Misson, R. (1996). What's in it for me? Teaching against homophobic discourse. In L. Laskey & C. Beavis (Eds.), *Schooling and sexualities: Teaching for a positive sexuality* (pp. 117–129). Victoria, Australia: Deakin Centre for Education and Change, Deakin University.

Mittler, M. L., & Blumenthal, A. (1994). On being a change agent: Teacher as text, homophobia as context. In L. Garber (Ed.), *Tilting the tower: Lesbians/teaching/queer subjects* (pp. 3–10). New York: Routledge.

Moita-Lopes, L. P. (2006). Queering literacy teaching: Analyzing gay-themed discourses in a fifth-grade class in Brazil. *Journal of Language, Identity, and Education, 5*(1), 31–50.

Morgan, B. (1997). Identity and intonation: Linking dynamic processes in an ESL classroom. *TESOL Quarterly, 31*(3), 431–450.

Morgan, B. (2004). Teacher identity as pedagogy: Towards a field-internal conceptualization in bilingual and second language education. *Bilingual Education and Bilingualism, 7*(2&3), 172–188.

Murphy, M. L. (1997). The elusive bisexual: Social categorization and lexico-semantic change. In A. Livia & K. Hall (Eds.), *Queerly phrased: Language, gender, and sexuality* (pp. 35–57). New York: Oxford University Press.

Neff, J. (1992). Confronting heterosexism in the classroom (Workshop). IATEFL Conference, Lille, France.

Nelson, C. (1993). Heterosexism in ESL: Examining our attitudes. *TESOL Quarterly, 27*(1), 143–150.

Nelson, C. (1999). Sexual identities in ESL: Queer theory and classroom inquiry. *TESOL Quarterly, 33*(3), 371–391.

Nelson, C. (2002). *Queer as a second language*: Classroom theatre for everyone (Spotlight Session, a featured presentation) TESOL Convention, Salt Lake City.

Nelson, C. D. (2004a). Beyond straight grammar: Using lesbian/gay themes to explore cultural meanings. In B. Norton & A. Pavlenko (Eds.). *Gender and English language learners* (pp. 15–28). Alexandra, VI: Teachers of English to Speakers of Other Languages.

Nelson, C. D. (2004b). A queer chaos of meanings: Coming out conundrums in globalised classrooms. *Journal of Gay and Lesbian Issues in Education, 2*(1), 27–46.

Nelson, C. D. (2005). Transnational/queer: Narratives from the contact zone. *Journal of Curriculum Theorizing, 21*(2), 109–117.

Nelson, C. D. (2006). Queer inquiry in language education. *Journal of Language, Identity, and Education, 5*(1), 1–9.

Nguyen, H. T., & Kellogg, G. (2005). Emergent identities in on-line discussions for second language learning. *The Canadian Modern Language Review/La Revue canadienne des langues vivantes, 62*(1), 111–136.

Norton, B. (1997). Language, identity, and the ownership of English. *TESOL Quarterly, 31*(3), 409–429.

Norton, B. (2000). *Identity and language learning: Social processes and educational practice.* Harlow, England: Longman.

Norton Peirce, B. (1995). Social identity, investment, and language learning. *TESOL Quarterly, 29*(1), 9–31.

Nunan, D. (1992). *Research methods in language learning.* Cambridge: Cambridge University Press.

Ochs, E. (1979). Transcription as theory. In E. Ochs & B. B. Schieffelen (Eds.), *Developmental pragmatics* (pp. 43–72). New York: Academic Press.

O'Loughlin, K. (2001). (En)gendering the TESOL classroom. *Prospect: An Australian Journal of TESOL, 16*(2), 33–44.

Ó'Móchain, R. (2006). Discussing gender and sexuality in a context-appropriate way: Queer narratives in an EFL college classroom in Japan. *Journal of Language, Identity, and Education, 5*(1), 51–66.

Ó'Móchain, R., Mitchell, M., & Nelson, C. D. (2003). Dialogues around 'Heterosexism in ESL: Examining our attitudes' and 'Sexual identities in ESL: Queer theory and classroom inquiry,' by Cynthia Nelson (1993, 1999). In J. Sharkey & K. E. Johnson (Eds.), *The TESOL Quarterly dialogues: Rethinking issues of language, culture, and power* (pp. 123–140). Alexandria, VI: Teachers of English to Speakers of Other Languages.

Pallotta-Chiarolli, M., Van de Ven, P., Prestage, G., & Kippax, S. (1999). '*Too busy studying and no time for sex?' Homosexually active male international students and sexual health.* Monograph 4. Sydney: National Centre in HIV Social Research, University of New South Wales.

Parmeter, S. H. (1988). Four good reasons why every lesbian teacher should be free to come out in the classroom. In S. H. Parmeter & I. Reti (Eds.), *The lesbian in front of the classroom* (pp. 44–58). Santa Cruz, CA: HerBooks.

Pavlenko, A. (2004). Gender and sexuality in foreign and second language education: Critical and feminist approaches. In B. Norton & K. Toohey (Eds.), *Critical pedagogies and language learning* (pp. 53–71). Cambridge University Press.

Pellegrini, A. (1992). S[h]ifting the terms of hetero/sexism: Gender, power, homophobias. In W. J. Blumenfeld (Ed.), *Homophobia: How we all pay the price* (pp. 39–56). Boston: Beacon Press.

Pennycook, A. (1990). Towards a critical applied linguistics for the 1990s. *Issues in Applied Linguistics, 1*(1), 8–28.

Pennycook, A. (1994). Incommensurable discourses? *Applied Linguistics, 15*(2), 115–138.

Pennycook, A. (1995). English in the world/the world in English. In J. W. Tollefson (Ed.), *Power and inequality in language education* (pp. 34–58). Cambridge University Press.

Pennycook, A. (2001). *Critical applied linguistics: A critical introduction.* Mahwah, NJ: Lawrence Erlbaum.

Phelan, S. (1994). *Getting specific: Postmodern lesbian politics.* Minneapolis, MN: University of Minnesota Press.

Phillips, D. (1996). Agency and identity in the gay and lesbian studies classroom: A perspective from Australia. In D. R. Walling (Ed.), *Open lives, safe schools: Addressing gay and lesbian issues in education* (pp. 103–120). Bloomington, IN: Phi Delta Kappa Educational Foundation.

Phillipson, R. (1992). *Linguistic imperialism.* Oxford: Oxford University Press.

Piepho, H. E. (1981). Some psychological bases for learning strategies and exercises in the communicative teaching of English. In C. N. Candlin (Ed. & Trans.), *The communicative teaching of English: Principles and an exercise typology* (pp. 45–48). London: Longman.

Poynton, C. (1997). Language, difference and identity: Three perspectives. *Literacy and Numeracy Studies, 7*(1), 7–24.

Pratt, M. L. (1999). Arts of the contact zone. In D. Bartholomae & A. Petrosky (Eds.), *Ways of reading: An anthology for writers* (5th ed., pp. 581–596). Boston: Bedford/St Martins.

Redman, P. (1994). Shifting ground: Rethinking sexuality education. In D. Epstein (Ed.), *Challenging lesbian and gay inequalities in education* (pp. 131–151). Buckingham: Open University Press.

Reid, J. (1987). *Basic writing.* Englewood Cliffs, NJ: Prentice Hall.

Richards, J. C. (1990). *The language teaching matrix.* Cambridge University Press.

Rizvi, F., & Walsh, L. (1998). Difference, globalisation and the internationalisation of curriculum. *Australian Universities' Review, 41*(2), 7–11.

Roberts, C. (1997). Transcribing talk: Issues of representation. *TESOL Quarterly, 31*(1), 167–172.

Roberts, C., & Sarangi, S. (1995). 'But are they one of us?' Managing and evaluating identities in work-related contexts. *Multilingua, 14*(4), 363–390.

Rooks, G. (1988). *The non-stop discussion workbook* (2nd ed.). Boston: Heinle & Heinle.

Roseberry, D. (1999). Different perspectives on the campus environment. *LESBIGAY SIGnals* (Newsletter of the 'Lesbigay special interest group' of NAFSA, the Association of International Educators), *5*(2), 1, 4.

Rubin, G. (1984/1993). Thinking sex: Notes for a radical theory of the politics of sexuality. In H. Abelove, M. A. Barale, & D. M. Halperin (Eds.), *The lesbian and gay studies reader* (pp. 3–44). New York: Routledge.

Saint Pierre, R. (1994). On being out in the classroom: Dilemma or duty? In K. Jennings (Ed.), *One teacher in 10: Gay and lesbian educators tell their stories* (pp. 164–167). Boston: Alyson Publications.

Santiago, S. (2002). The wily homosexual (first—and necessarily hasty—notes). In A. Cruz-Malavé & M. F. Manalansan IV (Eds.), *Queer globalizations: Citizenship and the afterlife of colonialism* (pp. 13–19). New York: New York University Press.

Sarangi, S. (1995). Culture. In J. Verschueren, J. Östman, & J. Blommaert (Eds.), *Handbook of pragmatics* (pp. 1–30). Amsterdam: Benjamins.

Saville-Troike, M. (1982). *The ethnography of communication: An introduction.* Oxford: Basil Blackwell.

Schegloff, E. A. (1997). Whose text? Whose context? *Discourse & Society, 8*(2), 165–187.

Schenke, A. (1991). The 'will to reciprocity' and the work of memory: Fictioning speaking out of silence in ESL and feminist pedagogy. *Resources for Feminist Research/Documentation sur la recherche feministe, 20*(3/4), 47–55.

Schenke, A. (1996). Not just a 'social issue': Teaching feminist in ESL. *TESOL Quarterly, 30*(1), 155–159.

Scollon, R., & Scollon, S. W. (1995). *Intercultural communication.* Oxford: Blackwell.

Sears, J. T. (1987). Peering into the well of loneliness: The responsibility of educators to gay and lesbian youth. In A. Molnar (Ed.), *Social issues and education: Challenge and responsibility* (pp. 79–100). Alexandria, VA: Association for Supervision and Curriculum Development.

Sears, J. T. (Ed.). (1992). *Sexuality and the curriculum*. New York: Teachers College Press.

Sears, J. T. (Ed.). (2005). *Youth, education, and sexualities: An international encyclopedia* [two volumes]. Westport, CT: Greenwood Press.

Sedgwick, E. K. (1990). *Epistemology of the closet*. London: Penguin.

Seidman, S. (1993). Identity and politics in a 'postmodern' gay culture: Some historical and conceptual notes. In M. Warner (Ed.), *Fear of a queer planet: Queer politics and social theory* (pp. 105–142). Minneapolis, MN: University of Minnesota Press.

Seidman, S. (1994). *Contested knowledge: Social theory in the postmodern era*. Oxford: Blackwell.

Seidman, S. (1995). Deconstructing queer theory or the under-theorization of the social and the ethical. In L. Nicholson & S. Seidman (Eds.), *Social postmodernism: Beyond identity politics* (pp. 116–141). Cambridge University Press.

Shardakova, M., & Pavlenko, A. (2004). Identity options in Russian textbooks. *Journal of Language, Identity, and Education, 3*(1), 25–46.

Shore, E. (1992). 'Out of the closet and into the classroom': A personal essay on coming out to my students. *GLESOL Newsletter* [Newsletter of Gay and Lesbian Educators to Speakers of Other Languages], *1*(1), 3–4.

Silverman, D. (1993) *Interpreting qualitative data*. London: Sage Publications.

Simon, R. (1992). *Teaching against the grain: Texts for a pedagogy of possibility*. New York: Bergin & Garvey.

Simon-Maeda, A. (2004). The complex construction of professional identities: Female EFL educators in Japan speak out. *TESOL Quarterly, 38*(3), 405–436.

Snelbecker, K. A. (1994). *Speaking out: A survey of lesbian, gay and bisexual teachers of ESOL in the US*. Unpublished Master's thesis. School for International Training, Brattleboro, Vermont.

Snelbecker, K., & Meyer, T. (1996). Dealing with sexual orientation in the classroom. *TESOL Matters, 6*(4), 19.

Spivak, G. C. (1990). Questions of multi-culturalism [Interview with Gayatri Spivak]. In S. Harasym (Ed.), *The post-colonial critic: Interviews, strategies, dialogues* (pp. 59–66). New York: Routledge.

Spraggs, G. (1994). Coming out in the National Union of Teachers. In D. Epstein (Ed.), *Challenging lesbian and gay inequalities in education* (pp. 179–196). Buckingham, England: Open University Press.

Stern, H. H. (1983). *Fundamental concepts of language teaching*. Oxford: Oxford University Press.

Stoller, N. (1994). Creating a nonhomophobic atmosphere on a college campus. In L. Garber (Ed.), *Tilting the tower: Lesbians/teaching/queer subjects* (pp. 198–207). New York: Routledge.

Strongman, R. (2002). Syncretic religion and dissident sexualities. In A. Cruz-Malavé & M. F. Manalansan IV (Eds.), *Queer globalizations: Citizenship and the afterlife of colonialism* (pp. 176–192). New York University Press.

Sumara, D., & Davis, B. (1998). Telling tales of surprise. In W. F. Pinar (Ed.), *Queer theory in education* (pp. 197–219). Mahwah, NJ: Lawrence Erlbaum.

Sumara, D., & Davis, B. (1999). Interrupting heteronormativity: Toward a queer curriculum theory. *Curriculum Inquiry, 29*(2), 191.

Summerhawk, B. (1998). From closet to classroom: Gay issues in ESL/EFL. *The Language Teacher (JALT), 22*(5), 21–23.

Sunderland, J. (2004). *Gendered discourses*. New York: Palgrave Macmillan.

Talburt, S. (2000a). On not coming out: Or, reimagining limits. In W. J. Spurlin (Ed.), *Lesbian and gay studies and the teaching of English: Positions, pedagogies, and cultural politics* (pp. 54–78). Urbana, IL: National Council of Teachers of English.

Talburt, S. (2000b). Identity politics, institutional response, and cultural negotiation: Meanings of a gay and lesbian office on campus. In S. Talburt & S. R. Steinberg (Eds.), *Thinking queer: Sexuality, culture, and education* (pp. 3–13). New York: Peter Lang.

Tan, C. K. (2001). Transcending sexual nationalism and colonialism: Cultural hybridization as process of sexual politics in '90s Taiwan. In J. C. Hawley (Ed.), *Postcolonial, queer: Theoretical intersections*. Albany, NY: State University of New York.

Thewlis, S. H. (1997). *Grammar dimensions, Book 3* (2nd ed.). Pacific Grove: Heinle & Heinle.

Thomas, J. (1983). Cross-cultural pragmatic failure. *Applied Linguistics, 4*(2), 91–112.

Usher, R., & Edwards, R. (1994). *Postmodernism and education: Different voices, different worlds.* London: Routledge.

Valentine, J. (1997). Pots and pans: Identification of queer Japanese in terms of discrimination. In A. Livia & K. Hall (Eds.), *Queerly phrased: Language, gender, and sexuality* (pp. 95–114). New York: Oxford University Press.

van Dijk, T. (1993). *Elite discourse and racism.* Newbury Park, CA: Sage.

Vandrick, S. (1997a). The role of hidden identities in the postsecondary ESL classroom. *TESOL Quarterly, 31*(1), 153–157.

Vandrick, S. (1997b). Heterosexual teachers' part in fighting homophobia. *TESOL Matters, 7*(2), 23.

van Lier, L. (1988). *The classroom and the language learner: Ethnography and second-language classroom research.* Oxford: Oxford University Press.

van Lier, L. (1996). *Interaction in the language curriculum: Awareness, autonomy and authenticity.* London: Longman.

Warner, M. (1993). Introduction. In M. Warner (Ed.), *Fear of a queer planet: Queer politics and social theory* (pp. vii–xliv). Minneapolis, MN: University of Minnesota Press.

Watney, S. (1991). School's out. In D. Fuss (Ed.), *Inside/Out: Lesbian theories/gay theories* (pp. 387–401). New York: Routledge.

Watson-Gegeo, K. A. (1988). Ethnography in ESL: Defining the essentials. *TESOL Quarterly, 22*(4), 575–592.

Weedon, C. (1987). *Feminist practice and poststructuralist theory.* London: Blackwell.

Weeks, J. (1987). Questions of identity. In P. Caplan (Ed.), *The cultural construction of sexuality* (pp. 31–51). London: Routledge.

Weeks, J. (1990). The value of difference. In J. Rutherford (Ed.), *Identity: Community, culture, difference* (pp. 88–100). London: Lawrence & Wishart.

Weeks, J. (1991). Invented moralities. *History Workshop Journal, 32,* 151–166.

Williams, C. (1997). Feminism and queer theory: Allies or antagonists? *Australian Feminist Studies, 12*(26), 293–298.

Willing, K. (1992). *Talking it through: Clarification and problem solving in professional work.* Sydney: National Centre for English Language Teaching and Research, Macquarie University.

Index